RUNNING A HOTEL
ON THE
ROOF OF THE WORLD

Summersdale Publishers Ltd
46 West Street
Chichester
West Sussex
PO19 1RP
United Kingdom

A CIP catalogue record for this book is available
from the British Library.

Printed and bound in Great Britain.

ISBN 1 873475 93 4

Reprinted 1998.

RUNNING A HOTEL
ON THE
ROOF OF THE WORLD

Five Years in Tibet

Alec Le Sueur

SUMMERSDALE

To Conny and the Lhasa Loonies

Contents

1

You Mean You *Want* to Work in Lhasa?!

Flight SZ 504 with 83 passengers on board descended through the grey drizzle shrouding Hong Kong's Kai Tak airport. It was the morning of 31 August 1988. The usual close-up view of the thousands of television aerials, atop the dirty skyscrapers of Kowloon, was obscured by a dense fog. The control tower radioed its last message to flight SZ 504 at 9:14 in the morning:

'All clear for landing.'

Kai Tak's runway, a narrow strip of reclaimed land extending across the polluted waters of Hong Kong harbour, was buried deep in the drizzle. Pilot Zhou Feng Li and the five crew who crowded the cabin of the Chinese flight were unconcerned. Kai Tak airport had an excellent safety record. The last accident had been in 1967. Nothing could go wrong.

Flight SZ 504 was destined to change Kai Tak airport's safety statistics as it skidded across the runway, plunging into the murky harbour and breaking apart on impact with the water. Rescue teams were at the scene almost immediately but tragically seven people died: one passenger, and the six crew who had been standing nonchalantly in the cabin without wearing seat-belts.

I sat in the departure lounge of Kai Tak airport on that same day, waiting to board my first ever flight on CAAC, China's national airline, on my first trip into China and Tibet.

While they combed the runway for parts of the fuselage of the old CAAC Trident I had a seven hour delay in which to contemplate my decision to work in this country: a place I had never been to, an airline with rather obvious disadvantages and a two year contract in one of the remotest parts of the world.

Just one month earlier I had travelled from Europe to Hong Kong with my short resumé typed out as lengthily as possible and my best English suit packed. I was looking for a job in the luxury hotels of the Orient – reputedly where the finest hotels in the world are found. If I had done my homework properly I would have known that you do not visit Hong Kong in a thick, heavy woollen suit in the height of summer, but it was my first time in the tropics and I had much to learn. Dripping with perspiration from the sweltering, humid heat of Hong Kong, with my sodden suit clinging to my body as if it was made of neoprene, I entered the Holiday Inn offices for the last interview of my trip.

As interviews go it was a disaster from the beginning. I was only there because the helpful gentleman I had seen at The Peninsula had recommended that I see his friend at Holiday Inn, but my heart was not set on it. There is a tremendous snobbery built in with hotel work. For some reason it is assumed that if you work in a five star hotel you are automatically part of an elite upper class of hoteliers who mingle at ease with the rich and famous. As the reason behind my trip to Asia was to continue my career in luxury hotels I was infected with this snobbery and had little interest in working for Holiday Inn.

The high powered air-conditioning in the office swept through my dripping suit and I shivered uncontrollably as I chilled to the bone. The lady conducting the interview was kind enough not to make any comment on this, for which I was very thankful, but from both sides the interview was going nowhere. We chatted for a while. All I wanted to do was to leave this refrigerator room as soon as possible. Even the sticky heat outside would be preferable to freezing in my own perspiration.

I made to leave. 'Thank you for coming. Don't call us, we'll call you,' said from both sides with polite hoteliers' sincerity and with smiles all round. As I was leaving the room I casually mentioned that I would love to go to Lhasa, as I had seen a brochure for the Lhasa Hotel outside her office. From that moment my fate was sealed.

'You mean you *want* to work in Lhasa?!' was the incredulous response to my passing remark. The door was closed behind me and before I had turned around my interviewer was on the phone to the company's Vice President.

I had to face him that day, as the next morning I would be returning to my job in Paris. Still wondering what I had let myself in for, I entered his office; an elegant apartment decorated with immense scrolls of Chinese calligraphy. Some of the scrolls had merely a few characters messily swiped over the rice paper with a large brush. It looked to me like the scribbling of a child let loose with a pot of black poster paint. My host, appreciating my observation of the calligraphy pointed out the red chops on each scroll that showed we were looking at works of art from great Chinese masters. From the Chinese writing he read the names out to me and I nodded in admiration of these masterpieces, wondering how much one got paid for producing these things and whether my little nieces could be millionaires before the age of ten.

The Vice President swivelled pensively on his chair . . . a sumptuous black leather swivel chair, from which he made decisions every day concerning the multi-million dollar Chinese empire of Holiday Inn. This was the person who would decide the future direction of my career. Broad shoulders, a large square face with a mop of grey hair and thin wire-framed spectacles added to his sombre and learned appearance. He nodded for me to sit down and then proceeded to scrutinise me in detail. The intensity of his look and the wry smile on his face were unnerving and not quite knowing where to look, my

9

eyes darted from his face, to the scrolls on the wall, to the spectacular view of Hong Kong from his window.

Crimson and silver taxis edged along the congested streets far below us in a world which was miles away. It is strange to see the world from above. Somehow it is a private place which humans were never meant to see, like the kitchens of a restaurant or the bathrooms of royalty.

Far below, perspiring heads glimmered in the sunlight. Litter and fallen laundry covered every ledge and portico beneath the high-rise. Daylight betrayed the rusting brackets of the neon street signs which crept even this high up the skyscrapers. Unsightly air-conditioning units jutted out of the exterior walls, spewing annoying little drops of water onto the hapless pedestrians far below.

This last thought on the air-conditioning brought my mind back to the present. I was decidedly uncomfortable. My suit had still not dried out, and the Vice President's grey eyes, enlarged by the thick glass of his bifocals, continued to stare at me, penetrating my inner thoughts. After several minutes of silence he tilted back in his chair and spoke with a deep, slow, authoritative voice:

'So, young man, you are going to be the Sales and Marketing Manager. You are going to spend six months a year in Tibet with the yaks and six months a year screwing your brains out in Hong Kong. How does that sound to you?'

Startled by his own question he jumped suddenly from his chair and nervously asked me not to repeat what he had just said. Trying to regain his composure he sank uneasily back into his swivel chair and gave me some advice on survival in China. He had worked there for many years and was reputed to know the system better than anyone.

'Be careful,' he said, 'it is not like the Western world.' He paused. 'When you see a local girl just remember this one proverb: You can't try the shirt on before you buy it.'

Not really certain what he was on about I nodded in agreement.

'They will be watching you,' he continued. 'Remember, even when you break wind they will know it. Be careful.'

With these last words fixed in my mind and still wondering why I should be buying shirts with local girls, I returned to Paris to hand in my notice.

'Where are you going Alec? The George V? The Ritz? Back to London?'

'No, I am joining Holiday Inn.'

'Holiday Inn?!' he exclaimed. 'Why? Which one?'

'Lhasa.'

'Lhasa?' he repeated, looking quizzically at me.

'Yes. Lhasa. Tibet.' I answered.

He could barely bring himself to whisper: 'Au Tibet?! Au Tibet?! Au Tibet?!'

The drizzle and fog at Kai Tak airport had cleared and I watched with a morbid fascination as the airport engineers hoisted the nose of the plane out of the water. I am not a nervous flier but I must admit to being more than a little apprehensive as later that day we took off on CAAC's flight SZ 4401 – over the remains of SZ 504.

I told myself that even CAAC couldn't down two of its own planes in the same day and I closed my eyes to let my mind wonder what the future had in store for me.

Tibet. What had I done? Why was I leaving my comfortable job in a luxurious Paris hotel? Instead of walking the Champs Elysée to work where would I be now? Why wasn't I returning to the family home in the Channel Islands, where I could be now, with all the love of wonderful, caring parents?

Despite my homesick thoughts I knew that I was doing the right thing. I was 25 years old, single, and looking for a challenge. Paris had become dull and faded. It was time for something, somewhere, new.

Tibet. Images of a land of magic; towering castles, inhospitable mountain peaks, ancient palaces in swirling mists. Yes, this is what I wanted to find. I had not even set eyes on the place but my heart was burning with desire to be there. Some foreigners are drawn to Tibet for religious or political reasons but I was not in search of discovering myself or freeing a country. I was simply out for adventure.

There were no direct flights to Lhasa. All aircraft had to land and spend the night in Chengdu: the smelliest city of Sichuan where the sun never shines.

Chengdu is the *ccccccrrrrrrrrrggggggggkkkkhhhhpt* capital of China. This is not a word to be found in the *Oxford English Dictionary*, so is not much use for Scrabble, but it does very accurately describe the first sound encountered upon arrival in Chengdu. It is one of the national pastimes of China, and you too can try it when you get there. It issues from as far back down your throat as possible, preferably from somewhere down between your toes, then you pull on the back of your vocal cords, involve your nasal passage somehow, bring it all up and give a good wholesome (and as loud as possible) shot on to the carpet. If there is no carpet available, which there often isn't at Chengdu airport, you may try to get it into one of the brimming spittoons which have been placed for your convenience in the waiting rooms.

Having fun? Well wait until we get to some of the other games they play such as the no-tissue-needed-one-handed-double-nostril-fulsome snort-onto-the-pavement job. When I pointed out that this wasn't a very pleasant way to blow your nose, I had my first lesson in Chinese etiquette. I was told that our Western method of blowing your nose into a tissue and then putting this paper and its additional contents into your pocket is quite disgusting. They do have a point there. In fact a very good point. How did our Western culture ever develop such a habit? Luckily that is the only tissue waste we put in our pockets. It could have been worse. Much worse.

The adventure had started. This certainly wasn't Paris.

Mr Li, who had picked me up at the airport, told me of all the great sights in Chengdu and asked me why I didn't spend a week there on my way to Lhasa. And anyway, what did I want to go to Lhasa for? It was such a terrible place.

Mr Li, from Hebei province in China, was our man in Chengdu. He spoke fluent English and French, had a university degree in mathematics and had a knack of being able to get things done in the most difficult of circumstances. He was hopelessly over-qualified for his job but considered himself extremely fortunate to be in the employment of Holiday Inn Lhasa without being required to work there. His only concern was that his papers were still registered in Tibet and he lived in fear that one day he might be called up. 'I don't want to go there,' he kept repeating, lifting his eyes to the heavens. If there was anything I could do to help him have his papers released he would be most grateful.

Despite Li's enthusiasm for Chengdu, the only point of interest that I could see was the car-wash on the way in from the airport. This was a relatively new concept in China. About two thirds of the way into the city from the airport all cars had to pull off the road into the five lane car wash. Each lane was manned by six people who carelessly sprayed the car with fierce jets of water and scratched it a bit with spiky brushes. Chengdu taxis are not the most robust vehicles in the world and at best you get soaked, at worst the car splutters to halt with a flooded engine a hundred yards further down the road. Our taxi needed a push to get it going again and although I didn't understand the taxi driver's exact words I certainly understood the gist of what he was saying about the new service. The cost for this obligatory car wash was one dollar. It was explained to me by the cheerful Mr Li that this was a new policy to keep the city of Chengdu clean. This seemed fair enough until Li told me that this was the only car wash in Chengdu, and cars can enter the city as filthy as can be from any other direction.

Checking-in at the Jin Jiang hotel I met two Canadians completely covered in luminous waterproofs.

'Going to Tibet?' one enquired.

'Good luck!' added the other.

Greg and Dave were a two man mountaineering team en route for Everest but instead of being at base camp where they had expected to be now, they were drowning their sorrows in the lobby bar of the Jin Jiang hotel. In return for a rather large fortune paid to the Chinese Mountaineering Association they had found their path to Everest blocked by insurmountable piles of red tape. Greg kept showing me the very costly permit which gave them permission to climb Everest. However, the Mountaineering Association had overlooked the fact that they also needed a permit to enter Tibet.

Their argument that as the mountain was in Tibet, they could not possibly climb it unless they were allowed to enter Tibet, had not convinced the man at the airport. As he was the one wearing the uniform, it was his word that counted.

We commiserated together over dinner. I thought it would cheer them up if we tried the legendary Sichuan cuisine, renowned for its spices and fire. We were joined by Mr Li who assured us that he knew the best place in town: one of the restaurants along the large open sewer which he had mistakenly identified as Chengdu's main river. I knew that Sichuan food was piquant but the chef's idea of hot was clearly different from mine. Li devoured his bowl with enthusiasm. I watched the sweat poor off Greg and Dave after their first spoonful of soup, letting off steam in answer to their day's frustration. My reaction was no better and soon we were reduced to nibbling raw cabbage – the only ingredient not to have touched the caustic sauce.

With my mouth still on fire I accompanied Li for the customary evening stroll from the Jin Jiang hotel up to the Chairman Mao statue. Mao stood in the twilight with his arm in Communist salute. Lining the road in front of him were hundreds of street vendors flogging paintings to eager tourists. Capitalism hard at work below the great Communist hero.

One night in Chengdu is always too much and so it was with some relief that I was woken by the phone ringing at four o'clock the next morning. 'Your taxi,' said Mr Li over the phone in a surprisingly cheerful voice for such an early hour, 'it's taking you to the airport.'

Some people panic about flying CAAC, about seeing military on the streets, martial law, tanks . . . but I have always maintained that the scariest person in China is the Chinese taxi driver.

They spend their nights chewing garlic plants and practising malodorous grunts.

Never, *never*, sit in the back of the car. Firstly this annoys the taxi driver intensely (and you want to keep him as relaxed as possible). Secondly, he will spend long periods of time driving at 80 miles an hour down small roads, with his head completely turned to the back of the car so that he can grunt something incomprehensible to you and breathe garlic in your direction.

So, instead, make a quick move for the front seat. If you are fumbling around in the dark for the seat-belt, don't bother. There isn't one. It is with some trepidation that you must then prepare yourself for the drivers' death race to the airport.

With one hand on the horn and the other at three o'clock on the steering wheel, so that he could swerve violently to the left or right with the minimum of effort and control, our car broadsided out of the Jin Jiang hotel car park, scattering early morning road sweepers in its wake.

Grey clad cyclists on lightless black bicycles appeared from nowhere out of the grey background mist. We swerved to the left to avoid a certain collision, to find ourselves head on with an approaching car; we swerved to the right to find a man with half a pig on the back of his bicycle staring aghast at us just a few feet in front of the windscreen; an oncoming truck swerved to the right, we swerved to the left onto the hard shoulder, the man with the half pig vanished behind us in the mist, a motor bike without lights appeared coming straight at us on the wrong side of the road . . . and so it continued until we reached the safety of the airport. The usual time for the airport run is 35 minutes but if you have one of the death-race team you can make it in as little as 16.

Once at the airport you are faced with the crush of hundreds, sometimes thousands, of passengers cramped together in a small room, all shouting at the tops of their voices, waving yesterday's boarding passes and ticket stubs at whoever they can. As there is practically permanent fog over Chengdu, flights can be delayed for days – with the consequence that if your flight actually does leave, you often find that it is packed with the passengers of the previous few days and you are left standing there to try again tomorrow.

The only calm that can be seen at the airport is in the airport staff who happily sit in their uniforms behind their desks, reading newspapers and drinking from their jam-jars of tea apparently oblivious to the screaming and chaos all around them.

It is here that you learn your first few words of Chinese. No such thing as *manana* exists in the vocabulary of these people. Here it is simple *may-oh* which means *no*. It is a wonderful word which occurs with increasing regularity with the more questions you ask. It means that there are none of what you are asking for, there never have been any, there never will be any and why did you bother to ask?

Which brings us to the second word encountered: *putchidao*. This means *don't know*. So after you have received the first negative answer *may-oh* and you politely enquire where you may find a better answer to your question you will then be told *putchidao*.

It is very important not to lose your temper at this stage. I have often laughed at other foreign passengers hopping up and down from one foot to another, slamming the counter with their fists, doing facial impressions of beetroots as they contort themselves in rage. Of course it is a completely worthless exercise as the result is still a calm *may-oh* from the airline staff.

I have to admit that I once sunk to these levels and even now it embarrasses me to think that I forgot the system and joined the ranks of the ignorant foreigners who push their blood pressures to the limits.

I was coming back in after a long break. *Ccccccrrrrrrrrrggggggg-kkkkhhhhpt* all around me at the airport, people pushing and shoving with their days old boarding passes in the usual airport battlefield. After 45 minutes in the melée I managed to squeeze my way to the check-in counter and lift my bags onto the scale.

'May-oh.'

I could not proceed as my luggage was overweight. An expressionless uniformed staff waved me away to the excess baggage counter.

'May-oh.'

I could not pay for my excess baggage as the person who had the key to the drawer where the receipts were kept had not turned up to work.

'Putchidao.'

No one knew when he would arrive and they went back to yawning, slurping from their jam jars and reading newspapers. Back to the check-in counter.

'May-oh.'

I could not proceed as I had not paid. I returned to the excess baggage counter and, disturbing someone from his read, managed to persuade him to take my money and write the amount down on my ticket.

Back to the check-in counter. The officer took my ticket but 'may-oh', I did not have an official receipt so could not proceed further.

Back to the excess baggage counter. The man with the key to the receipt drawer had arrived! But, 'may-oh' he could not help me because I did not have my ticket.

Back to the check-in counter.

'May-oh.'

I could not have my ticket back until I showed him the receipt for excess baggage. My plane was due to leave in 15 minutes and at this moment I completely lost control. The anger of a patient man . . .

The swaying, noisy mob parted around me. For a brief moment they were silent, all heads turning to look at this strange, screaming foreigner. But they had seen this many times before and lost interest after a few seconds, returning to their aimless pushing and shoving. The officials remained as inscrutable as ever and did not even look up from the counters where they stayed securely with their jars of tea.

It is at times such as these that you wonder if it was not easier to travel in the days of the ancient explorers, who crossed the Himalayas with great caravans of mules, camels, yaks, with men carrying months of supplies and equipment over treacherous mountain passes with dwindling supplies of fuel and food.

When China expatriates get together, one of the main topics of conversation is CAAC. Everyone has his favourite CAAC story. The other topic of conversation is 'Did you hear about the guy caught in the lift of the Palace Hotel in Beijing?'

For several years in China this was the common knowledge of every expatriate hotelier, from Tianjin to Tibet. An expat staff of one hotel had been caught 'trying on a shirt' with a local girl in the lift of the best hotel in Beijing. This alone was scandal enough, but the most juicy part of the story is how the unfortunate couple was discovered. I had always imagined that the lift door opened at a certain moment, but not at all. Apparently the whole affair was watched on the in-house TV monitor by the entire hotel security staff. According to reliable sources there was a high price put on the video but the tape mysteriously disappeared. Of course the fate of the couple was that he was sent out on the next plane, and of her, nobody had any news.

After the ice had been broken by the lift story and the many other variations on the same theme, the tales inevitably turn to CAAC experiences. Everyone has their favourite coming in to land story, the bits falling off story, the near miss story, the deck chairs down the aisle for the over booking story and so it goes on until the Tsing Tao beers have run out.

Frequent travellers to China have renamed CAAC as 'Chinese Airways Always Cancel' or somewhat cruelly there is also the version: 'Chinese Airways Always Crash'.

I prefer calling it by the official title 'CAAC' (pronounced 'cac') which in the French language has a meaning which exactly describes the service.

I have now flown the frightening skies with CAAC so often that I could be a leading member of their frequent flier programme. If they had one. But on that first day I had little idea of what to expect.

'Connections,' whispered Mr Li, were the key to getting through the crowd at the check-in counter. The Chinese refer to this as *guanxi* and it is impossible to arrange anything in China without it. I watched Li dart in and out of the human mass and sweet talk the uniformed CAAC guardian into giving out a boarding pass. He added my suitcase to the Samsonites of a Japanese group so that I had no overweight baggage to pay for.

I was surprised when Li refused money for the help which he had given me. 'Please ask about my papers,' he called out as he dived back into the crowd. I wanted to thank him but he had been engulfed by the mob and had disappeared from sight.

After the crush of the check-in and the departure of the helpful Mr Li, my spirits were lifted by seeing a sign over one of the empty desks which read: 'CHINA SOUTHWEST AIRLINES, NON-NORMAL FLIGHT SERVICE.'

With this intriguing thought in mind I set off to the security check.

As I approached the walk-through metal detector, it suddenly dawned on me that I had forgotten to take my large penknife out of my pocket. It was too late to go back and find my check-in luggage so with a sinking feeling of resignation I emptied the metal objects out of my pockets into the basket at the security counter. The girl in charge was practising her English. 'Money,' she said as she passed my coins over to the other side, 'Walkman. Knife.'

With a pleasant smile she passed everything across the counter.

There were no announcements in English in the departure hall and it is not uncommon for tourists to sit there happily up to several hours after their planes have departed. I had been warned of this strategy, so closely shadowed a Chinaman with the same coloured boarding pass as I had been given, and hoped that this was the Lhasa flight. I couldn't lose him as he was carrying a large bag of garlic shoots which he was taking as hand luggage on to the plane.

After a lengthy delay in the dense smoke of the waiting room an incomprehensible announcement in Chinese blared out over the loud speaker. They do not have volume controls on their audio equipment, only distortion control and this one was on maximum distort. Fortunately, my friend with the garlic shoots and about 150 other people seemed to understand it, as they immediately leapt to their feet and started to crush six abreast down the narrow stairway and into the waiting buses on the runway.

The plane was an even greater shock than the airport: an aged Boeing 707 which looked older than I was. The first thing one notices upon entering the aircraft is an overpowering smell of rotting cabbage and a group of slovenly looking youths dressed in dishevelled uniforms. These are the crew, who have a small tea drinking area which one must walk through to reach the passenger seats.

When you have recovered from the waft of moulding vegetables, you pass through the 'first class' area to the economy seats. In front of you are the 150 people who had run to get the best places. Although seats are numbered it is not taken very seriously and there are often several boarding passes issued with the same seat number. Most of the rush concerns grabbing the overhead lockers.

There seems to be no official policy on the amount of hand luggage which may be taken aboard a CAAC plane. Thus, the only limiting factor is a physical one: how much can one person carry? Small Chinese ladies defy credibility by heaving huge suitcases up and down the aisle. Families of smiling Tibetans struggle relentlessly up the steps with over-stuffed sacks on their hunched backs. Nothing can dampen their spirits as they push their way along the aisle, ready for the next game: squashing the bags into the overhead lockers. You have to be a bit careful as bits of fuselage stuffing and bare wires protrude from the backs of the lockers, which do tend to get in the way. Stewardesses shout and order people about, but nobody listens to them, as they are all too busy trying to cram 20 kilo bags into 10 kilo spaces. Inevitably, several of the lockers will be left open with bags hanging out over unsuspecting passengers. The rest of the luggage is piled up on any empty seats. I once sat next to a basket containing half a frozen pig, which started to defrost shortly after take-off and drip onto the carpet. No one, except myself, seemed at all concerned.

The ceiling tiles hang down slightly and as the plane accelerates along the runway it is always fun to guess how many oxygen masks are going to fall out, amusing the passengers in their seats. Sometimes you only have half a seat belt to hang on to nervously as you watch the poor stewardess who is trying her best to get through the safety demonstration before being bowled off her feet as the plane hits take-off velocity.

To calm the nerves it is always advisable to ask for a copy of the in-flight magazine. To give CAAC their credit this is the best in-flight entertainment available on any of the world's airlines. When I read my first copy I laughed so much I had tears running down my cheeks and the stewardess had to come over to ask me to stop. It is an impressive looking glossy magazine. The gloss is so good that it could have been printed in Hong Kong, but the English can only have come from a person in China who had never used the English language. The result is the best publication in the history of aviation.

There is a wonderful article with the title: 'Youth, Glistening in the Blue Sky' which is dedicated to CAAC stewardesses:

> The stewardess of Southwest Airlines must go through four steps, such as hardship, tiredment, dirt, feeling. Beside the quality of general stewardess.

Reading further about the four steps does not exactly inspire confidence in CAAC, and the nervous passenger, clinging to his half seat-belt as the plane taxis along the runway, is not advised to read the passage concerning hardship:

> Hardship, is obviously observed on flight Chengdu – Lhasa line, plane often bring trouble to passengers with bump caused by airflow, because of dangerous topographyand changeful climate. The stewardess must look into passengers, they have such trouble as same as passengers. Stewardess, Ge Ling has had a scar on her head, because of a sudden bump.

But not only do the stewardesses run the risk of injury, they must also keep the passengers satisfied:

> Tiredment, that the stewardess is often effected by. Flying thousand kilometers, they service passengers more than fifteen times in passenger cabin with only thirty meters long, they fly four times per day as usual.

And when the stewardesses are exhausted after servicing all those passengers, they still have to face the most difficult task of all:

> Disregarding dirt, is a distinguishing feature of stewardess of Southwest Airlines. a passenger had incontinence of faeces, stewardess, Zhu Jiang Yin and Tan-GouPing, helped this passenger without hesitation. The passenger was so moved full of tears.

So, no problem if you should have any 'incontinence of faeces' troubles – you will be in the good hands of the 'Youth, glistening in the blue sky'.

A later edition of the in-flight magazine also confirmed one of my other suspicions about CAAC. I had long maintained that just before take-off, a man went around the outside of the aircraft checking everything with a screwdriver to see that it was all still screwed on. No one believed me, but there in the magazine was proof: a full colour picture of the screwdriver man and his friend, with the caption: 'Conscientious and meticulous'.

On my first journey I closely followed the work of the screwdriver man, wondering if the heavy engines really were screwed on tight enough. They shook a lot down the runway but were soon shrouded in the thick mist as the 707 struggled skywards.

Twenty minutes after take off the aircraft emerged through the clouds which fill the Sichuan basin. Dawn broke over the cumulus and a rosy pink hue cast across the cloud ocean. China was way below, and there, ahead, above, lay the Tibetan plateau.

Fifty million years ago, or thereabouts, continental plates crashed together here, throwing up the Himalayas. Tibet lay on the edge of the Asian continent, while the Indian continent sailed full steam ahead on collision course, forcing Tibet's sunbathing beaches several miles into the sky. The average height of the Tibetan plateau is over 16,500 feet (5,000 m) and there are more than 50 peaks higher than 23,000 feet (7,000 m). There are mole hills higher than Mont Blanc. Well, there would be if any moles lived in Tibet.

From the aircraft the dawn view of the approach to Tibet is a moving experience. The abrupt geographical line between China and Tibet tells you something about where you are going. You are gripped with a sensation that this flight is not like any other (as if you had not already realised) but this is a flight to somewhere special, somewhere magical, high above and beyond the clouds.

The plateau is deeply cut by twisted gorges between high mountain ranges. Even in this day and age the area is unsafe: outlaws and outcasts eke a meagre existence by the sides of the road cut through by PLA (People's Liberation Army) troops and prisoners in the 1950s. Due to the inhospitable terrain, the road was constructed with great loss of life. Sadly, today it is rarely used, as landslides tear long sections down each monsoon season. The Chinese military keep command of the route and it is rumoured that there are important military posts on the way, tunnelled into the hill-sides.

Before the road was built, brigands and bandits inhabited every valley and watched over the remote passes. The French explorer Louis Liotard lost his life in an ambush over one of these mountain ranges. In 1940, his compatriot Andre Guibaut wrote of the furthest Chinese outpost on the edge of the plateau: 'Robbers abound in this frontier town . . . It is quite common at dawn to find people lying stabbed and entirely stripped of their clothes'.

Perhaps CAAC isn't so bad after all.

Thin fingers of deforestation now stretch up the green slopes as trees are felled for the lumber markets of China. This beloved land of the early twentieth century plant hunters, who came in search of the seeds that created many of today's European gardens, is rapidly being carted away to the east, down the shaky PLA highway.

As the 707 toils on above the plateau, the deep ravines become shallow, and soft undulating hills stretch up to rounded snow caps. New roads fan out to reach the furthest tree covered slopes until the landscape changes to rugged snow peaks with bare black rock faces. Glaciers flood the valleys and dazzling turquoise lakes lie in the oval hollows between mountains. How people can survive down there defies the imagination but every so often there is a small cluster of Tibetan houses.

It is normally at this time, with your thoughts far away in the snow peaks that you drift off to sleep, just in time to be woken up by the stewardess bringing along your present. One of the perks of flying CAAC is that you always get a little present. I now have a great collection of them, ranging from: tie pins, belts, bags, table cloths, fans, plastic wallets, key chains, pollen extract, to my favourite – the CAAC postcard collection. One side of these cards have pictures of pretty CAAC scenes: planes flying into the sunset, stewardesses glistening in the blue sky etc. The reverse sides of the cards are taken up with helpful travel tips which are guaranteed to wake you up.

WHAT FACILITIES AND SERVICE CAN BE PROVIDED IN THE CIVIL PLANE?

The washing-room on board are located the front (middle) and back part of the passenger compartment. Please don't forget to but the door when you use them.

On the left hand and right hand sides, there are two emergency exits. Please use only them at emergency situation.

During the flight, our crews will serve you with free cold and hot drinks, sweets, newspapers, magazines, etc. as well as delicious food only at meal time.

Ther cabin is seated by heighten pressure, so please do not knock and carve the window glass in account of your safety. During take off, land or bump of air plane, please fasten your safety belt.

WHY PASSENGERS MUST FASTEN THEIR SAFETY BELTS ON BOARD OF CIVIL PLANES?

Before civil planes take off and land, the hostess always ask passengers fasten their safety belts, Why?

Civil planes, although flying in the air, must depend on the ways to take off and land. During this course the aircrew maybe restricted by some factors, then it's hard to avoid accidents, for example, obstecles on the runway and failure of planes. etc. For these reasons, the aircrew has to take emergency measures, and stop the flight. And then if you don't fasten your safety belts, you'll be injured by strong inertia and resistance of the planes, even though special accidents don't occur.

In order to reduce the air resistance, planes fly ordinaryly above the atmospheric layer. When planes fly through fogs and clouds, serious jolt will occur because of strong air current. At that time, if you don't fasten your safety belts, you'll be injured. Due to igovance of safety many passenger have taken blood lesson before.

So please fasten your seat belt properly for your life safe, when planes take off, land and bump.

While passengers are working out how to use their presents and what to do if there should be one of those 'hard to avoid failure of planes' etc, the stewardesses come around with what the CAAC postcard described as: 'delicious food only at meal time'.

Either the person who wrote this had a terrific sense of humour or there is something seriously wrong with his or her taste buds. I suspect the latter.

The meal always comes in a cardboard box which has an imaginative route map on the back with maps of planes going all over China in every direction – even to places where there are no airports. The box contains a greenish egg, a variety of dry pastries with unidentifiable contents and a plastic bag of vacuum-packed pickled vegetables labelled 'CSWA fly food'.

The health warning that CAAC prints in the in-flight magazine, advising passengers not to overeat is unnecessary.

DO NOT EAT TOO MUCH BY AIRPLANE

If you fly with civil airplane, please do not eat too much. On board, there will be a little blood-supply for stomach, then the secretion of gastric juice will be decreased, and stomach peristalsis will be slowed down, which will be unfavourable for the digestion.

In the other hand, much air will get into your stomach, if you eat too much on board. And due to the lower pressure in the air, passengers eating too much will be liable to sickness, vomiting, abdominal distension and pain, etc. It is better that passengers take food one hour before the flight, and only underfed. And do not take food that will produce much air.

Anyone overeating on this food would qualify for CAAC's other travel advisory:

These years, some sick and wounded passengers were criticallt ill or died on board of airplanes or in

the waiting room of airport. Therefore sick and
wounded passengers must think that the airport.
Therefore, sick and wounded passengers must
think that the airplane will be suitable for you.

I must say that there have been tremendous improvements since
my first flights on CAAC. The cardboard box now has a seal
and a date stamped on it – so that you can check it is on its first
flight with CAAC. This prevents problems occurring, such as
what happened to a group of tourists who arrived in Lhasa
after a short visit to Gansu province. On their way to the city
of Lanzhou, a two hour flight from Chengdu, they had received
the typical cardboard boxes. Most left the box untouched, one
person just had a bite out of his stale bun and tossed it back
into the box. Three days later on their return to Chengdu they
were presented with cardboard boxes of 'delicious food only
at meal time'. Suddenly one of them called out: 'Hey!
Someone's had a bite out of my bun!'

Happily the days of the aged Boeing 707's for CAAC's
flights to Lhasa are now numbered, as they have finally decided
to take them out of the sky before they drop out. For many
years Chinese authorities insisted that only planes with three
or more engines could fly to Lhasa due to difficulties in landing
other types of aircraft at an altitude of 12,000 feet. These
apparently conscientious safety regulations were very
convenient for CAAC. It just so happened that by a complete
coincidence, CAAC was the only airline in the region operating
aircraft with three or more engines – their good old Boeing
707's.

In order to convince the Chinese that a plane with less than
three engines could land successfully at Lhasa airport, Boeing
Corporation flew in a 757 – with the American Ambassador to
China aboard. The Chinese requested that the anxious
Ambassador, wearing his Victory Desert Storm sweatshirt, be
put through a series of one engine landing and take-off tests
before placing their multi-million dollar order for the 757's.

The Boeing pilots performed superbly and the aged 707's are now being replaced. It has taken some of the fun out of flying CAAC but even if the machines are new, the service has the same charm. The immaculate interior of the new aircraft is rapidly changing in appearance and familiar odours peculiar to CAAC planes are already hanging in the aisles.

On my first flight into Lhasa I had managed to sleep for most of the two hour journey. I was tired after the trip to the Far East from Europe, the one night stopover in Hong Kong, Chengdu and then the early morning departure. Even the stewardesses were asleep now.

For no apparent reason, I woke suddenly from the depths of a dream – where I had seen nothing around me but barren rocks and Chinese soldiers. Regaining my conscious thoughts, I strained my eyes at the window to estimate our position. Way beneath, veins of ocean blue river traced across the white sand of the Tsangpo river bed. Mountain ranges rippled away in waves towards the peaks of the Himalayas. To the south, somewhere beyond the tiny speck of Yumbulagang temple was the mountain kingdom of Bhutan. My head was spinning with questions. Could that mountain be Everest? Or perhaps that one over there? They do tend to look alike when seen from above. Where is Nepal? Where are the boundaries between China and India where their soldiers peer at each other from frozen dugouts?

As my mind pondered on these questions, gazing at the tangled mass of mountains that stretched away into the distance, the aircraft lurched forwards into its descent. The passenger next to me stirred from his sleep. His mouth stretched into a gaping yawn and the pieces of eggshell, which had fallen into the creases of his blue Mao jacket during his meal, now tumbled out onto the floor. They would soon be trodden in to the carpet by the trampling hordes on their way down the aisle. Hundreds of years ago the Mongolian hordes had wreaked havoc on the advanced civilisations of Asia, and soon they would be doing the same to the Boeing 707 carpet.

Tufts of black hair stood up at unnatural angles from the top of his head, where they had been pressed during the two hours that he had slept. His yawn lasted an eternity. His mouth opened so wide that it took up practically the entire sphere of his otherwise featureless face, giving me an unprecedented view of Chinese dental work. Judging by the display of pickled vegetables in various states of decomposition that were caught between his molars, it was apparent that dental floss is either not widely used or simply unavailable in China. I wondered if I had packed any in my 20 kilogramme luggage allowance.

Coming out of his yawn, he squinted to focus on me and seeing that he was sitting next to a foreigner he beamed into a Cheshire cat Chinese smile.

'Hello,' I said.

'Lhasa!' he replied, pointing out of the window.

I could see that communication was going to be a problem but at least the Chinese seemed to be a friendly people. After reading countless Western newspaper articles about China and Tibet I had been conditioned into mistrusting the Chinese. It was quite a pleasant surprise to find that as long as they were not standing behind a desk in a uniform or working in any capacity, the Chinese were generally extremely likeable people.

'Lhasa!' beamed the Chinaman again, pointing eagerly to the floor of the plane. I peered out of the window. Still nothing.

2

Touchdown in Tibet

The relentless, almost imperceptible descent over the Tsangpo valley is slightly unnerving for the first time. I could feel that the plane was descending but below there were no signs of any city or airport or runway. The plane did not circle or turn in any way but just continued to sink lower and ever lower in the morning sky. The mountain tops, viewed with delight from far away, now appeared ominously close outside the windows. Some were even above the plane.

The inquisitive mind can stretch the minutes of the descent into anxious hours. 'Was the pilot really the uniformed youth we saw slurping from his jam jar of tea at the top of the steps? Has he been in a plane before? Did the man with the screwdriver do his job? Why can't we see anything of the airport?'

Hearts pounded as the aircraft rapidly approached the river bed and dunes. There were still no signs of modernity below; just the ever nearing earth. As if in answer to the many prayers being said aboard the plane, a flash of grey runway appeared at the windows at the moment of impact and the jet liner rolled securely along one of the longest runways in Asia. Four kilometres of precision laid Chinese concrete.

The relief of a safe touch-down is normally missed by the foreign passengers who watch in disbelief at the sight of many jolly Tibetans happily standing in the aisle at this tense moment, stretching, yawning and then unpacking their belongings from the overhead lockers. The stewardesses notice nothing unusual.

I once sat on the plane to Lhasa with an American visitor who screamed, 'SIT DOWN! EVERYBODY SIT DOWN!' at the top of her voice. All heads turned to this frantic lady who was gesticulating wildly at the Tibetans to get back in their seats. Rather sheepishly, those standing in the aisle, looked at one another, then back to the wild woman and decided that there would be less trouble if they just perched on the arms of their seats and waited until the plane had landed before going back to the overhead lockers.

After touchdown the stewardesses pushed their way along the aisle to return firearms and weapons to their respective owners. Chinese soldiers received revolvers and three tall Tibetans, each with a long red tassel braided into their hair, received daggers. Being somewhat larger than the Swiss army knife which I had been allowed to keep with me, these objects had been stored in CAAC brown paper envelopes for the duration of the journey. The envelopes were hopelessly small for the weapons they contained and the daggers repeatedly fell out of their sheaths, slicing through the air and digging into the Boeing carpet.

As the recipients of the daggers grinned with delight at having their weapons returned I realised that I was seeing *Khampas* for the first time. I had read much about these fearsome people: the warriors of eastern Kham province.

It was the Khampas who were called upon to fight against the British invasion of Tibet in 1904 and who were the main force of the uprising against the Chinese in 1959. More recently, it was the Khampas who the CIA supported in a guerrilla warfare mounted against the Chinese from neighbouring Nepal. The Nepalese government eventually had to clean out the Khampas. Some say that it was under pressure from the Beijing government, but there is a popular story that the Nepalese became weary up of having the Khampa bandits terrorising Nepalese villages with American-bought machine guns.

Whatever the truth, these three Khampas looked fearsome enough. The crush of bodies pressing together in the aisle parted as the Khampas motioned that they wished to stand there too. The plane had still not come to a stop but everyone, except the bewildered tourists, was trying as hard as possible to stake a place in the aisle – ready for the dash to the exit.

As the door opened the Tibetans and Chinese strained their way to the front, flattening everything in their path. Heavy parcels of stinking garlic grass were dropped from overhead lockers onto the seats below. The few passengers who remained seated laughed it off with a shrug and a gaping mouth stuffed with the debris of the lunch box which they were still trying to finish. Any leftovers from the lunch boxes (and of course the wonderful CAAC giveaways), were crammed into the already rupturing hand luggage during the run down the aisle. Confusion arose at the entrance, as despite efforts to prove this to the contrary, only one person and their bags can get out of the door at a time.

Once on the runway, they scurried off towards the airport building dragging their bundles behind them. The Khampas stood apart from the rest, taller than the other Tibetans and towering above the Chinese. They did not walk, but swaggered, with their daggers glinting in the sunlight. The flock of hesitant tourists followed them, muttering that there was no bus, and asking each other what to do, as there was no indication of where to go next apart from the cloud of dust left by the Tibetans and Chinese disappearing into the distance.

The airport buildings were far away, the noise of the plane had died down and I was left in peace to survey the scene around me. The sky directly above was an impossibly bright blue that I had only seen before on faked postcards. Woolly clouds hung in the air just over the mountain tops, while the first rays of the sun struck the valley bottom sending a light mist rolling over the foot hills. Mountains lined the north and south of the valley rising gently to rounded green peaks.

At first I was slightly disappointed that there was no snow to be seen. I had expected the landing strip to be hacked out of ice between glaciers, but here everything looked soft and green. I didn't realise at the time that I was seeing Tibet at the climax of its short summer and that, just two months later, I would be craving a glimpse of something green – other than the fluorescent Holiday Inn sign.

As I walked across the runway the clouds to the west of the valley parted to reveal what I had asked for: two magnificent snow covered summits. The more southerly one was a vertical tube of rock with snowcapped icing resembling a wedding cake. Stretching to the north from the base of the wedding cake was a great wedge of a mountain. A perfect 45 degree slope leading to a snowy crest, which stopped abruptly and dropped into a vertical cliff face. Intrigued with the notion that it should be possible to walk to the top of the mountain without actually doing any climbing I set about the more immediate task of finding my car and driver.

'They probably meet you at airport.' Li had told me in Chengdu.

Something was wrong. I had only walked 20 paces across the runway when I had to stop to take in lung-fulls of air. I was gasping like a fish on the river bank. The first sensation of breathing Tibetan air was that of great relief after the rotting cabbage of the aircraft and the dreadful pollution in Chengdu but the healthy feeling is short lived. At the airport's altitude of 11,500 feet the air contains nearly 30 percent less oxygen than at sea level and I could feel it. After a few moments to regain my breath I followed the Khampas in the direction of the airport building.

Stepping over a ditch which ran along the side of the runway a young man approached me waving a white cloth. 'Holiday Inn?' he smiled. I nodded and returned the smile.

'Ah, I am Tashi,' he said, busy unravelling the cloth which turned out to be a beautiful silk scarf. Still smiling, he placed the scarf over my head, bowed slightly and uttered the words *tashi delai*.

'Good to meet you Tashi Delai. I am Alec Le Sueur.'

'No, no, I am not Tashi Delai. I am Tashi. Tashi Delai.'

'So who is Tashi Delai?' I asked. He looked puzzled.

'Nobody is Tashi Delai.'

This conversation was getting us nowhere.

'*Tashi delai* is Tibetan greeting,' he explained. 'My name is Tashi. Only Tashi. Not *tashi delai* – that is Tibetan greeting.'

'Ah, I see,' I said. Not seeing at all. I tried another '*Tashi delai*.'

'Yes, *tashi delai*!'

We laughed all the way along the muddy track, repeating *tashi delai* to each other ad nauseam. Whoever Tashi was I could see that we were going to be friends.

On the grass beyond the ditch we entered the general arrivals field. It was the meeting place where the numbered tourists would be matched up with their corresponding guides. None of the guides knew the names of the people they would be meeting, so they held up signs showing their group's number. Each sign had been written hurriedly at the airport on a scrap of whatever paper was available – usually on the back of a cigarette carton. Unfortunately, the tourists arriving were never aware that they had been reduced to a number by the authorities and so matching the correct guide with their group always took some time.

From the selection of rusting buses and Beijing jeeps which filled the car park, I was glad to see that Tashi was taking me to a fairly new Toyota Landcruiser. The outline of a yak had been stencilled crudely onto the side of the car, with the faded lettering 'Lasa Hotel'. Tashi read them out aloud and laughed. *Lasa Hotel* had been the old name of the hotel, before Holiday Inn had taken it over.

The driver of the car, a Mr Dorje, greeted me with as many smiles as Tashi and just as many *tashi delai's*. Dorje made no attempt at English, after all why should he, and immediately set into a mime: an aircraft coming in to land, straining with heavy bags, gripping a steering wheel and then pointing to something which was far away. I was having trouble with the last bit but with some added help from Tashi, who said the word 'hotel' as Dorje was pointing into the distance, I understood that my bags would follow later.

I asked Tashi how long it would take to reach the hotel. This was a mistake. The smile disappeared from Tashi's face, his eyebrows came down over his eyes and his forehead wrinkled into a deep frown. Struggling in thought for some time, he eventually shrugged 'sorry' and smiled again. Conversation during the car journey was going to be limited. I would just have to learn Tibetan when we reached Lhasa.

The city lies beyond the hills to the north, almost due north, of the airport but the road must follow the course of the Tsangpo river and then its tributary the Kyi Chu in a lengthy and dwindling detour away from the rising sun. According to the Chinese, the reason why Lhasa's airport was built by the tiny village of Gonggar, some 60 miles from Lhasa, is due to the topography of the region. I have a theory that some PLA General just pointed to the wrong valley when he gave orders for construction work to start.

Dorje swung out onto the main road; a narrow, undulating stretch of tarmac which I was to learn is the best quality road in Tibet. Green lakes of barley, the staple crop of Tibet, shimmered in the breeze. The corn was on the verge of ripening and it would soon be time for harvest. On the other side of the road were the uncultivated foothills, grazed only by sheep. High above in the mountains we could just make out the black shapes of yaks.

I have often been asked by tourists what yaks are. Putting it simply: yaks are hairy, high altitude cows, although I must admit that this is not a foolproof definition. I once told this description of yaks to a particularly annoying couple whom I had the great misfortune to pick up at the airport. I was supposed to be meeting Goldie Hawn but good old CAAC had changed the flights without telling anyone and instead I had to give a ride to a couple who should have been banned from travelling further than their front doorstep.

As I drove in to Lhasa with them a flock of sheep ran across the road. 'Oh look, are those yaks?' the lady called out with excitement. I had to disappoint her by informing her that in Tibet those were called sheep and in fact yaks were somewhat larger animals with long pointy horns and black shaggy coats. Perhaps I had explained it badly.

Tashi was doing the explanations for me on my first trip in from the airport. 'Gonggar Dzong' he pointed out. *Dzong* means fortress, but there was nothing where Tashi had pointed. A few rocks were strewn about on a hill but that was all. More precisely it was where Gonggar Dzong had been, before it was blown away in fighting when the Dalai Lama fled into exile in 1959.

The Chinese propaganda machine has made a concerted effort to show that despite what certain *splittist* Tibetans may think, Tibet has always been an integral part of China. From the very first moment that you enter Tibet, it is clear that there is a great divide between these peoples: different culture, different religion, different language, different race. But the one area of common ground which does support the Chinese claim and tie Tibet irrefutably to China soon becomes clear: there can be no doubt that Tibetan drivers have direct genetic links with the taxi drivers of Chengdu.

Dorje had an interesting driving technique which involved keeping the car off the ground for as much time as possible. 'Terrible!' Tashi called out whenever we were airborne, grinning from ear to ear and bracing himself for the inevitable impact when the Landcruiser would hit the tarmac again. It was hardly surprising that our car had virtually no suspension.

Dorje had an advantage which would have made his Chengdu taxi comrades green with envy: visibility. In the pure, rarefied air of Tibet the view is not hindered by smog or pollution. Mountains which are tens of miles away appear crisp against the horizon. Apart from a few army trucks, the roads are free of traffic and the only limiting factor on Dorje's driving was how hard could he keep his foot pressed down on the accelerator pedal, weighed up against the likelihood that at any moment one of the rattles could lead to the total disintegration of the vehicle.

Just visible through the vibrating windows were rectangular coracles setting out across the river. Tashi saw me trying to look at them, 'Yak-skin boats,' he shouted over the roar of the Landcruiser engine. It seems that every part of the yak has a use. To make water-tight boats the skins are stretched over a wooden frame, sewn together with wool made from yak hair and the joins are then sealed with yak butter.

Every so often we would speed through a village lined with waving Tibetan children. Their villages looked wonderful and so inviting but Dorje was not showing any signs of slowing down. Small clusters of single and double storey buildings with walled-in courtyards jostled together in the foothills to gain maximum exposure to the sun. The houses looked solid, built to withstand the harsh environment. Walls were made of stone up to waist height and finished off with mud bricks to the roof.

Windows, set deep into the whitewashed walls were surrounded by peculiar black frames: the base of every Tibetan window frame is several inches wider than the top. This is echoed in the general construction of the buildings, as the walls also tend to lean inwards.

Tin cans lined the window ledges, with the bright orange of marigolds in full bloom livening up the stark black and white of the houses. Branches of trees adorned with colourful prayer flags stood high into the wind from the top of the flat roofs. The auspicious blue, white, red, green and yellow colours of the fabrics stood out against the rich blue of the Tibetan sky. Each prayer flag carries a picture of *lungta*, the jewelled dragon-horse who carries the owners' prayers up to the divinities every time the flag flaps in the wind.

The larger villages had a healthy copse of trees, usually willows or poplars which looked quite out of place in the generally treeless landscape. Wood is a precious commodity in the highland areas of Tibet and is never wasted. The few shrubs which grow wild on the hill-sides are harvested for use as brushwood and each courtyard wall is piled high with kindling gathered from the mountains.

The lack of solid fuel in the shape of wood is of little consequence to the Tibetans who have an ingenious wood substitute: yak dung. The dung is collected during the day by young children who are out on the hills tending to flocks of sheep or yaks. What better way to pass the time when out on the hills than by collecting every piece of dung which can be found? It certainly sounds more attractive than being locked up in a school room.

When the children return in the evenings with their panniers of dung, it is usually the mother of the household, or an elder sister, who has the task of mixing the raw material with a little water and, if available, some barley straw. This concoction is then made into attractive chocolate chip cookie shapes and slapped against the whitewashed walls to bake in the sun. Once dry, the cookies are stacked in rows on top of the walls, to be used as fuel throughout the year. They burn with a fierce flame, but unfortunately leave a recognisable odour, which is virtually impossible to extract from clothing worn in the vicinity of the fire.

Somehow, Tashi had managed to fall asleep. His head lolled from side to side on the headrest of the front seat and jolted upwards when we hit air speed. Dorje kept his hands tight on the steering wheel, his eyes fixed on the contours of the road ahead. I kept holding on to the hand rail above the door, gripping tight to keep myself from flying across the back seat when we swerved to overtake army trucks.

A few miles after crossing the Chinese bridge to the north side of the Tsangpo, Dorje hit the brakes and we screeched to a halt. He was pointing to a building about 60 feet away which stood by itself between us and the river. There was nothing else to be seen. A closer look revealed that the building had a facade of gaudy orange and blue tiles. Amongst the tiles was a picture of a man's head and a picture of a lady's head. With a mime from Dorje which needed no words, he told me that this was the only toilet between the airport and Lhasa, if I needed to go.

This is the great modernisation of Tibet by the Chinese: tiled toilets in the middle of the countryside. Tashi remained asleep. Dorje didn't bother to walk as far as the public conveniences, and after a very brief inspection of what the Chinese thought was an improvement to the Tibetan way of life, I followed Dorje's example. I wondered what the American tourists behind us would make of the modernisation of Tibet.

The only other stop on the way to Lhasa was for an obligatory picture taking session at a 40 feet high carving of Sakyamuni Buddha. Every tourist stops here and wastes a picture on the Buddha, who is invariably in deep shade, by the time cars from the airport reach him.

'Potala,' a voice said from the front of the car.

Tashi had woken up as we entered the suburban sprawl in the Lhasa valley, just in time to point out the small triangle standing above the buildings at the far end of the valley. Even from this distance I could make out the whitewashed base and the gold of the roofs of the Potala Palace – the former winter residence of the Dalai Lamas. This first picture of the Potala is now obscured by another piece of Chinese progress: a concrete army barracks, which entirely blocks the view from the western approach to Lhasa. Most of the land to the immediate west of the city is owned by the military. The road from the airport leads through a sea of green uniforms and the very worst of Chinese architecture.

Amongst the ugly concrete, one building stood out: an oblong block of insipid green corrugated iron. How anyone could ever have imagined that this building was anything less than hideous is hard to believe.

'Hotel,' said Tashi.

I panicked, thinking he meant the corrugated iron monstrosity, but regained my breath when I saw that he was pointing up the road. Dorje swung into a left turn and passed in front of the Norbulingka summer palace. This was more like it – would the hotel be part of the palace? We drove on past some dilapidated blocks of flats which had sides of meat hanging from the windows.

'Staff,' said Tashi pointing at them.

Before I could ask him to explain, the familiar green of the Holiday Inn neon sign came into view.

Behind a row of flags stood three creamy grey blocks of concrete. It reminded me of Second World War German bunker defences. I told myself this concrete was beautiful. It had to be beautiful. I was going to be promoting it.

I was met at the door by a Chinese man in a suit who ran down the steps laughing. He shook my hand profusely and presented me with another silk scarf. Harry was his name, the Front Office Manager. Chinese from Singapore. 'Not from here,' he added quickly.

The sight of the lobby was a great relief after the shock of the concrete bunker design of the exterior. A vast expanse of rich marble swept across the floor to the cool marble reception desk. Wooden beams with a hint of Tibetan design took the eye up to an immense tapestry of the Himalayas. A mezzanine area – the lobby bar and home to the Holiday Inn Lhasa string quartet – looked out across the tapestry and marble.

Tashi and Dorje had vanished. The Chinese receptionists smiled as Harry ushered me past them to the small coffee shop. All new expatriate staff are taken here for an obligatory drink before being shown to their quarters. A high liquid intake in the first few days is considered to reduce the risk of altitude sickness, so tea was ordered while Harry went to call the General Manager.

The coffee shop was of a rather basic design. The furniture consisted of metal framed tables and chairs which would have been better suited to a cheap village banqueting hall than an international hotel. The green tiles on the floor matched the insipid corrugated iron colour from down the road. What saved the coffee shop was a magnificent awning of blue dragons which stretched from above the cashier's seat at one end to the tea machine at the far corner. This had been commissioned from the Lhasa tent factory in the same manner that wealthy Tibetan families ordered decorative tents for the picnic season.

A waitress spotted me from her leaning post by the tea machine. She put herself into slow speed and pointed herself in my direction. I was hoping that she would bring the tea which had been ordered but she came empty-handed. When she arrived she stood in front of me and said: 'meal voucher.' I tried to ask her what she meant but all she could do was to repeat 'meal voucher'.

Fortunately, Harry returned in time to save me from the meal voucher robot and he went to fetch some tea.

A chef arrived from the kitchen dressed in whites from head to toe.

'The Executive Chef,' Harry whispered to me, letting me know that this was not just any chef but the number one in the kitchen. Short and plump with closely cropped hair and an angry expression, there was really no one else whom the person steaming towards us could have been.

Executive Chefs have reached the pinnacle of their careers. They have worked hard through all the stages: from *Commis de Cuisine* to a *Chef de Partie*, through *Executive Sous Chef* to the crown in the kitchen – *Executive Chef*. It is a difficult route, requiring a combination of artistic culinary skills, great knowledge on ingredients and equipment, tough physical work, and above all a driving ambition to beat contemporaries to the top. From the apex of his pyramid, as Executive Chef, he can go no further and from then on he will spend his time running the Food and Beverage Manager out of the kitchen, insisting that he be called 'Chef' and consolidating his position as king of his domain.

My first encounter with an Executive Chef was in a five star hotel in London. I had just started work in the kitchens and was busy topping and tailing green beans when the Executive Chef came up to me and asked me how I was doing. 'Fine, thank you Mr Dupont,' I replied.

This brought on a most unpleasant and unexpected response which was screamed at me at the top of his voice: 'You say "Fine thank you *Chef*" to me!'

My only explanation for this is that chefs must have peculiarly small brains and as they are already crammed full with culinary terms, there is no further space for them to remember their own names. When one Chef meets another Chef, they find it extraordinarily amusing that they have found someone else with the same name and spend a number of minutes going 'Hello Chef' to each other and chuckling at their original and witty joke.

'Good morning Chef,' I ventured to the man in whites who had arrived at our table.

'It's a bloody mess in zer. Zey brought yaks on ze hoof again. Ver's the Food and Beverage Manager?' is all he could come out with before charging off again.

The waitresses in the corner stopped chatting and stood up straight from their leaning post. The cashier cut her yawn short and picked up her pen.

No matter which hotel in the world you are working in – it is always the same when the General Manager approaches. Without knowing it, he has an aura with a radius of approximately 60 feet, within which every member of staff is seen to be working intently. Once the General Manager has passed, all pretence of work is given up and the staff return to their normal daily habits.

'Has he been drinking?' a voice bellowed out from behind me. The General Manager had arrived and was making his presence known.

'You must be young Le Sueur. That name won't work here, better stick to Alec. Now, you must drink. At least three litres today. Three tomorrow, three the next. Rest today. Drink. See you Monday.'

'More tea!' he scowled at the waitresses as he passed them on his way into the kitchen.

It had been a short briefing. On the face of it, it certainly wasn't a bad first meeting with my boss. It was only Friday morning and I had been ordered to rest until Monday. Little did I know that this was to be the longest time off in Tibet that I would have. No one had told me yet that work in China meant six and often seven days a week for twelve hours a day.

Harry showed me up to my room. South block, second floor, number 3205. We walked along carpeted corridors, stepping over the bumps where luggage trolleys had pushed the carpet into high creases. The corridor looked over the garden outside the coffee shop which was dominated by a large concrete pond containing a rock sculpture. Natural pieces of rock had been crudely cemented together in a simulated rock formation. It had no purpose that I could see, but at least a pair of white wagtails were nesting in a gap in the cement.

The overwhelming first impression upon entering my room was that of *brown*. The sofa and curtains were streaked beige, the carpet chestnut, the wallpaper khaki cream, the ghastly five-pronged chandelier a sort of lobster bisque brown and the cupboards an artificial wood brown. Why naturally, brown wood should have been painted over with a brown paint, to make it look like wood, defeated me. The only thing that was not a shade of brown were the curious green stains on the carpet.

The view from my room was across an area of waste land, which had been used as a building site when the hotel was constructed, and then over a high wall to the dilapidated blocks of flats which I had seen from the car. They were the worst kind of slums: carcasses of animals hung from the window ledges and wild dogs barked ferociously from the stairwells. Beyond the flats were the inviting summits of the hills on the south bank of the Kyi Chu.

Harry had told me that I was lucky to have a south-facing room.

'You will see why in winter,' he chuckled. 'Anyway, it's better than being in the staff quarters across there,' he said, pointing out of the window to the slums.

At lunch time I met the rest of the expatriate managers. There were ten of us altogether. Mostly men, mostly chain smokers. Each had his own particular reason to be there. For some it was money, others were on the run from something or someone but, the most unfortunate had made their way to Lhasa under the impression that they were entering exotic Asia. Despite the warnings, these people had expected palm trees and night life and had got a shock when they discovered that Lhasa was set amidst barren mountains in the middle of nowhere, more than two and a half miles above sea level. The usual tour of duty was two years but in these extreme conditions it was rare that anyone lasted the full contract. Holiday Inn Lhasa was known in the hotel trade as the hardest hardship posting of all.

I asked Harry why we didn't eat in the Everest Room restaurant with the other guests. He shuddered, 'That's the group buffet,' he explained, 'obviously you haven't seen it yet. We always eat in the coffee shop.'

The General Manager was already sitting at the head of a long table laid out for ten people. Every expat had his favourite place around the table and jealously guarded it against newcomers.

Vacant spaces were only created when an expat left, then the seat would be offered to the others in order of their seniority. It happened that my predecessor had occupied the seat next to the General Manager and, as no one wanted to move into this position when it became vacant, it was pointed out as mine. On my other side was Mr Liu, the Financial Controller from Hong Kong. He was not a great conversationalist, preferring to keep his eyes fixed on his plate during the entire meal, closely examining every fork full before putting it into his mouth.

The other expats were eager to talk. The ritual was to tell the newcomer that however bad the hotel looked, it was far better now than ever before. I had arrived as the end of the first batch of Holiday Inn Lhasa expats were leaving. These were the hardy pioneers who had survived the first two years of operation.

The hotel had been built by the Chinese in 1985 as part of the great modernisation of Tibet. It had been one of the 40 construction works donated by other provinces of China to commemorate the twenty fifth anniversary of autonomy for the region. Most of the donations were completely inappropriate and remain today as great eyesores on the skyline. Across from the hotel is the monstrous 'Cultural Theatre' which is occasionally used to hold party conferences or entertain the troops. Down the road is another gift; the empty concrete bus terminal building with its clock tower permanently set at ten to two.

The hotel was a gift of Gansu province, one of the poorest provinces in China and in need of a great deal of aid itself. The Chinese were continually trying great leaps in various directions and it was hoped that the leap forward to tourism would provide a much needed boost for the Tibetan economy. The imaginative name of 'Lhasa Hotel' was thought up by the Communist marketing strategists. In Shigatse the new hotel was called the 'Shigatse Hotel', in Gyantse the 'Gyantse Hotel' and so the naming continued in each of the Tibetan towns which were opened to tourism. The major flaw in their great leap was that once they had built their hotels, they had no clue how to run them.

The Chinese struggled for six months with the Lhasa Hotel before courageously admitting defeat and looking for help from outside. The first team from Holiday Inn arrived to find the hotel in chaos. Each of the department heads had his own disaster story to tell for what they had found.

The Housekeeper described arriving at a hotel which seemed to be set in a field of snow. As the bus drew closer he saw that the white of the snow was actually hundreds of sheets placed out on the grass. Lhasa Hotel had the most advanced laundry unit in western China but no one knew how to use it. All the sheets had been washed by hand in the river and dried by the sun in the hotel grounds.

Derek, the Chief Engineer, told of his first inspection of the hotel when he found that flood waters from the kitchens had submerged the boiler room and were just an inch away from blowing the boiler sky high.

The Food and Beverage Manager, a sombre Austrian called Gunter, told of his discovery that the coffee shop floor tiles were green. They had been covered in an overflow from the corridor toilets and their original colour was hidden under a layer of a substance which should not usually be found in food areas.

Harry, the Front Office Manager, described what had happened to the 468 guest rooms. Over 350 of them were used by the staff and their friends. A cook gave a receptionist a steak. The receptionist gave the cook a room key. A very simple arrangement. One of the problems was that the rooms featured en suite bathrooms with flush toilets. The only previous flush toilet in Tibet was the English one installed in the summer palace of the Dalai Lama and consequently the local staff had no knowledge of how they functioned. The rooms were used until they were considered too dirty for further use and a second room would be taken. The number of rooms left for paying guests was diminishing every day.

The allocation of keys to guests had also been based on very different ideas to Holiday Inn management. There were only two drawers for the 468 keys: one for occupied rooms, one for unoccupied rooms. When a guest asked for his key the receptionist had to search through the entire drawer to find it. If the key was in the correct drawer, this process might only take 20 minutes or so, but if the key had inadvertently been slipped into the wrong drawer then the process of reclaiming a key could take hours. The longest queues at the reception formed when the groups returned to the hotel at lunch time, as this was the time when the receptionists would have their lunch break.

Checking out was a similar story of inefficiency. A guest would arrive at the cashiers' desk and ask for his bill. 'Room not occupied' the cashier would reply and despite any protests of honesty, the guest would be waved away to his bus to take him to the airport. If you are offering to pay for something, how many times do you keep offering if the person to whom you are meant to pay keeps insisting that you are wrong?

As a result of this madness, the great scheme to attract the tourist dollar was backfiring and the Lhasa Hotel was becoming a bottomless pit of subsidy for the government. The tourists were not entirely satisfied either. In fear of his own safety, the General Manager would pass to his hotel room around the back of the hotel so that he did not have to walk through the lobby and encounter screaming guests.

Chef told me of the battle that ensued every morning when guests appeared in the Everest Room for breakfast. Buses to the airport would leave as early as 5:30am and guests would enter the restaurant at five o'clock. This was considered too early by the staff who would only report on duty by mid morning. Guests would line up in the kitchen to cook their own breakfasts. This may sound like fun but few of the early visitors to Tibet were paying less than $10,000 for their trip of a life-time. It had said nothing in the tour brochures about fighting for their breakfasts.

All those around the lunch table assured me that the hotel had completely changed now. What they had been describing was two years ago and now everything ran smoothly. They nodded in agreement and then laughed. Even Mr Liu managed a smile as he scrutinised his next fork load.

'We haven't told him about the vacuum cleaners,' said the General Manager between drags on his cigarette. He leant back in his chair in preparation for his favourite story. It had become the classic story of the Holiday Inn Lhasa and could only be passed down to newcomers by the General Manager himself. It is a tradition which still exists today.

'We bought thirty of them. Very expensive. From Hong Kong, Charlie had to bring them in himself after one of his breaks.' He pointed to Charlie, the Housekeeper, who nodded to acknowledge his moment of fame in the vacuum cleaner story.

'After a month we didn't see them any more. The maids were back to sweeping the corridors with brushes. Chinese brushes which left more bits on the carpet than they picked up. So, one day I asked where they were, the vacuums, and I was taken to a store cupboard with thirty broken vacuum cleaners. These were the finest in the land! There were no better in China!' He thumped the table to emphasise his point.

I was to discover that table thumping was one of his favourite forms of speech, either used when very angry or when enjoying himself tremendously.

'Every one of them had a burnt out motor. And, do you know why?'

I did, because I had read the story in the Hong Kong newspapers, but I was not anxious to have a table thumping display at my expense, so I said that I had no idea why all the motors should have been burnt out.

'Because they never emptied the bags. They thought the dust went up that little magic black cord which plugged into the wall!' Another thump of the table.

His cigarette lay untouched on the ashtray, burning itself into dust, when the run for the dessert table started. The return of Mr Liu with two yellow bananas on his plate had launched a stampede from the management table. The General Manager explained to me, when he too had returned with his prize, that yellow bananas were a rarity in Lhasa. 'Fruit!' he bellowed. 'I hope you had some in Hong Kong.'

Having witnessed a flurry of bananas rushing past, a party of hopeful guests headed for the dessert table in search of fresh fruit.

'Nobody comes to Tibet for bananas,' said Mr Liu, breaking his silence. It was just as well, there was none left.

The General Manager stayed to smoke another cigarette while the other expatriates returned to their offices. He was concerned for the welfare of every new recruit.

'Don't worry if you have a loss of appetite today – that's normal at high altitude. Nothing to worry about. Just keep drinking. Worse is the headache that you can get.' He shook his head. 'The headache. Terrible. Terrible. It can lead to pulmonary oedema or cerebral oedema which is very nasty. Let's hope it doesn't happen to you. Ha! You should have seen Mr Liu when he came up here! I thought he'd never make it.'

His eyes lit up with excitement as he launched into one of his stories: 'And once there was a guest in hospital, I shouldn't tell you this today, but it was incredible, first they had to put a tube in his throat, this big, through a hole they made in his neck and get the water out of his lungs with a . . .'

I let the words pass over my head and struggled through the remains of my Giant Yak Burger. I preferred to think that the headache I could feel coming on was caused by lack of food and not from the shortage of oxygen. I chewed on through the heavy, stringy yak burger, hoping that it would help in some way.

Altitude sickness was the fear of every newcomer to Tibet. The sudden increase of 12,000 feet and the subsequent lowering of the oxygen level in the air had potentially fatal consequences. There is a diuretic pill, sold on prescription in the West, which reduces the effects of the altitude but no one tells you that, until you get to Lhasa, where of course they are not available.

There was no way of predicting who would be struck with altitude sickness, and no cure apart from being flown back down to sea level.

Anxious to see something of Tibet in case I was going to be flying on CAAC sooner than I would have wished for, I asked for a taxi to the *Barkhor* – the ancient bazaar in the heart of Lhasa.

3

The Shock of the System

'Taxis?' the General Manager thumped the table.

'This is Lhasa!'

The only transport service, apart from public buses and tractors, consisted of a set of mafia-style rickshaw drivers who pedalled shaky three-wheelers about town. Each rickshaw was of the sports convertible design, with a cloth hood that could be raised or lowered over the passengers, depending on weather conditions. The driver who pedalled the contraption had no such luxury and braved whatever the elements could throw at him. Two passengers could just squeeze into the carriage over the back wheels and if the price was high enough a driver would even accept three passengers and luggage. It was a cut throat business with high money at stake from first time tourists who did not yet know that all rickshaw prices must be keenly haggled for.

The first rickshaw driver who approached me made an award winning display of disappointment when I gave him the news that I would not be paying his initial asking price. We eventually settled for a fee equivalent to one day's wages for an office worker for the 20 minute pedal across town to the bazaar. He was still upset with me but smiled to his colleagues as we pulled away from the hotel down the wide cycle lane.

It cannot be said that the Chinese in Tibet have not made good provisions for cyclists. Whether this is how the Chinese should be judged is another question but there can be no doubt that cycling facilities have improved since the Chinese established their rule in Tibet. The only drawback is that no one pays the slightest attention to the most basic cycling etiquette.

Lorries and army jeeps are parked across the cycle track, cyclists pedal down the lanes in any direction they feel like and groups of pedestrians saunter along in the centre, preferring the risk of being run over by a rickshaw, to the much greater risk of breaking a leg down one of the open manholes in the pavement. There are also some open manholes along the cycle track but these are usually only along the gutter edge of the track and a skilled rickshaw driver knows when to swerve to avoid them.

More difficult to avoid is the chaos created by the large skips piled high with stinking refuse which are stationed at regular intervals across the tracks. Packs of dogs and a few gaunt cattle always gather around the skips, giving rise to unpredictable moving objects in the path of the rickshaw.

While yaks are taken to the high pastures during the summer months, ordinary cattle are kept in the city and are left to roam the streets and graze on whatever they can find in Lhasa. As the green areas in the city centre are rapidly disappearing, the normal menu for these street cows consists of newspaper and cardboard boxes dumped in skips.

After dodging the cattle and shouting at dogs that approached us, we emerged under a string of prayer flags at the south face of the Potala Palace. What had appeared as a small triangle in the distance when I came in from the airport, now towered above us, dominating the Lhasa valley. High white walls swept skywards to the red ochre palace, topped with golden roofs sparkling in the sun.

The Potala Palace – home of the Dalai Lamas. Here was the image I had dreamt of, yet in reality the palace exceeded the visions of my dreams. Until the Chinese entered Tibet this building had been home to the leader of the country, parliament, treasury, law courts and high security prison. Within these walls

Dalai Lamas have studied, ruled and died, revolutions have been hatched and traitors poisoned. Gold and precious stones of untold beauty have lined the vaults and heinous tortures have been carried out in the dungeons. We pedalled on. The Potala was not open to pilgrims or visitors today.

A few hundred yards further into the city, past the tantalising aroma of roast lamb kebabs, the rickshaw drew up to the edge of a wide open cobbled square. This area had remained as a rabbit warren of Tibetan houses until 1985 when the Chinese liberated the people from the inconvenience of walking through the small streets and demolished the old Tibetan buildings to make an official people's square.

Somewhat ironically, the square which was meant to be for the good of the people, soon turned out to be a favourite spot for rioting and anti-government demonstrations. 27 September 1987, saw the first group of monks chanting for independence in the square. The monks were arrested and on 1 October, Chinese National Day, an angry crowd of Tibetans gathered outside the police station on the square to demand their release. The exact sequence of events that followed is unclear but it is generally accepted that panicking Chinese soldiers fired into the unarmed mob, killing at least six Tibetans. Somewhere in the chaos that followed the police station was burnt down.

The Chinese had many lessons to learn from their first experience of rioting in the 'New Tibet.' Unfortunately one of the lessons they did not learn is that when your police station has been burnt down, you should get a new set of fire extinguishers. They still don't seem to have learnt this basic rule, as every time there is rioting in Lhasa, the police station on the square burns down again. Clearly there is an opportunity for a good sprinkler salesman.

The square itself shows no signs of the troubles that have passed over its cobbled stones. Its dilapidated state is not from riots but from dirt and zero maintenance. An unkempt garden with a muddy concrete-lined pond and broken fountains stands in the centre. To the western end of the pond a sorry looking rose attempts to climb a metal arch painted in Blackpool beach colours. This appears to be a favourite picture spot for both Chinese and Tibetans alike and a brisk trade is carried out by the dozen or so photographers who tout for business.

At the far end of the square, beyond the railings, roses and pool, is the modest entrance to the Jokhang temple – the centre of the Tibetan Buddhists' world.

I had arrived in Tibet nearly a year after the 1987 riots and despite some more shootings in the Barkhor in March 1988 I had been assured that the troubles were a thing of the past. Even tourism was picking up again, which was just as well as it was now my job to see that business to the hotel increased. Confident that I would be riding the crest of a wave as tours poured back into Tibet, I approached an unmistakably American tourist to ask the way to the bazaar of which I had heard so much.

Barbara, from a Smithsonian Institute tour, had been twice around the bazaar and was now on her way back to the group bus. 'You gotta go clockwise,' she said, pointing to a queue of people walking from right to left in front of the temple. 'Just follow them.'

Barbara was being followed by a determined group of Tibetan Khampa ladies haggling profusely. It was their livelihood and they knew how to haggle to perfection. Bracelets, necklaces, prayer wheels, rings, brooches and useless trinkets were being pulled out of bags and thrust under Barbara's nose. She really had no chance.

'Only one thousand. I like you. Six hundred. You how much? Holy silver. Holy, holy! Five hundred. You how much? Very cheap. One hundred. You how much?! You special price. Seventy five.'

The sound of the prayer flags flapping above in the wind was momentarily drowned by a crescendo of the haggling chorus as Barbara climbed on to the tour bus. She could not be permitted to be out of reach or they would lose the close on their sales.

The Khampas rushed around to the side of the bus and knocked fervently on the window by Barbara's seat. It was a pleasure to watch professional sales people at work. With the engine revving and the driver waving the girls to move away Barbara finally gave in at 'Okay. For you fifty.'

The driver shook his head. All the Tibetans knew it was only worth five, but Barbara would never know and would be happy to show off her bargain from the bazaar over dinner parties back home.

The Khampa girls returned from the scene of their sale giggling at the fun of it all. Another tourist ripped off and happy. Some more money for the family.

Khampa women have a joie de vivre as strong as the pride of their fierce husbands. Beautiful rounded faces with sparkling eyes above rosy cheeks smile out at every foreigner. Strings of turquoise beads are woven into the hair and occasionally crowned by a centre piece of coral or amber. A scowl at a Chinaman, a smile to a foreigner: the Khampa girls love to flirt. Gold-capped teeth flash from their inviting smiles but they know that they are safe – no one would wish to pick trouble with their Khampa husbands.

I followed the direction in which Barbara had pointed and found myself on the edge of the square at the opening to the Jokhang temple. Deep behind the whitewashed walls of the opening passage, red painted pillars, the width of stout men, support a balcony draped in yak hair cloth. Two gilded deer and a *Dharma* wheel shine down from over the balcony on all who pass beneath. But your attention is not held by any of the interesting structural technicalities or adornments of the building, instead it is focused on the people who crowd the forecourt.

The granite paving stones are worn to a polish that no hotel Housekeeper could ever produce. Apart from a lapse during the Cultural Revolution, every day for hundreds of years has seen many thousands of prostrations over these slabs. With hands first clasped together in front of the head, the chest and the waist, each prostrater then lies flat down on the ground with arms outstretched in the direction of the temple.

Merit is what Buddhism is all about. At least that is what I had gathered so far from my meagre research into the subject. I had found most books on Buddhism terribly difficult to digest – all those incomprehensible names and anatomically impossible beings. I could guess that the Eleven-Headed One Thousand-Armed Avalokitesvara would not be a Bodhisattva to take on at table-tennis, but I had yet to consider any of the more complex ideologies of Buddhism.

Without going into tiresome detail and very long names, the simple formula to follow is that the more merit you have gained during this lifetime, the better your chance of being reincarnated as something higher than an earwig in the next. If you are really pious and score high numbers of merit points, you could come back as a human being again and if you earn just those few more points you could come back as a rich nobleman or a high lama, instead of having to be a down-trodden peasant again. It's a bit like collecting Air Miles.

Hitting the jackpot, in terms of merit, would be to score so many points that you could leave the endless cycle of rebirths and achieve *nirvana*. Once you have reached this Buddhist's bingo there are no more worries about who or what you are going to come back to.

With this clear incentive to keep prostrating, some manage to keep going for over a thousand per day. Others stick to the holy number of 108 prostrations which is quite difficult enough. To ease the pain of sliding outstretched across the granite, special gloves fashioned in the shape of small clogs are often worn. Aprons can be used to protect clothing from wearing out and women prostrating will often tie their long dresses close around their ankles if they are going in for a lengthy session.

Around the temple entrance is also where the first time visitor to Tibet has his initial encounter with an unfamiliar odour: yak butter. Or the more fragrant variety: rancid yak butter. It is brought into the temple by devout pilgrims who carry blocks of the yellow grease in yak bladder bags. They scoop the butter out by the spoonful into each of the stone and silver vessels of yak butter which burn in the holy chambers of the temple. Yak butter is not an easy odour to forget. It clings to every person in the Barkhor, to every item sold on the stalls, to every piece of clothing. Even when you think that you have left Tibet far behind, the smell of yak butter will still be lingering in your suitcases, waiting to hit you when you open them to pack for next year's holiday.

Fortunately, two holy incense burners are within a few yards of the temple entrance, and a step towards them brings the very pleasing fragrance of a blend of burning juniper and a finely scented *artemisia*. Piles of dried herbs and small bundles of wood collected from high in the hills around Lhasa are offered for sale to those who did not bring their own supplies for the burners.

Starting from the entrance to the Jokhang temple the market street continues clockwise in a half mile perimeter circuit right around the temple and back to the entrance again. By no small coincidence the market street is also a holy walk. Every temple, monastery, holy mountain, holy lake and holy entity is surrounded by a holy walk known as a *kora*, and by walking this *kora* in a clockwise direction you gain merit. All these merit points keep adding to your running total of merit to give you a better chance for a good reincarnation next time around. The beauty of the Barkhor bazaar is that you can gain merit and do your shopping at the same time.

A ramshackle collection of metal stalls lines each side of the street selling a mixture of imports, antiques, fakes and forgeries. Trinkets from Kathmandu and nylon clothes from China share stands with Tibetan rugs and traditional jewellery. Bulky silver rings studded with beads of red coral or turquoise, heavy-set earrings of gold, old Indian coins made into brooches and any amount of religious paraphernalia are all on offer for sale.

The word 'antique' is used for anything which dates from pre-1959, when the Dalai Lama went into exile. Customs laws are strict in China and they declare that anything that is 'antique' or a 'cultural relic' cannot be removed from the country.

'Holy Turquoise!' called out a Khampa girl, thrusting a piece of blue plastic in my face and then running off down the street giggling to her friends. I followed, caught up in the clockwise stream of bodies that flows continually around the Barkhor. Only the most ignorant tourist and a few belligerent Chinese attempt to walk against the flow.

Just past the Jokhang entrance on the main Barkhor street I was attacked by a small child. A boy of no more than five years of age grabbed my right leg and clung on as hard as he could while launching into his sales pitch in perfect English: 'I have no money. I have no parents. I have no money. I have no parents. I have no money. Please give me money. I have no parents. I have no money. Please give me money . . .'

The 'Rapper,' as we called him, was the most persistent of all the Barkhor beggars. His ruthlessly pitiful approach was used to great effect. He could only be shaken off with either a considerable amount of force or a large contribution to his funds which he would then take back to his parents who eagerly awaited him at the front of the temple.

One of the favourite claims by the Chinese is that they eradicated begging when they liberated Tibet in 1951 and that they turned the beggars into 'the new proletariat of the New Tibet'.

I pictured the Rapper clinging on the leg of a die-hard Communist and wondered who would win: the lecture on the no-begging policy of New Tibet, or a contribution to the Rapper's welfare funds?

For the Tibetans, there has never been anything unwholesome about begging. There are claims that before the

Chinese entered Tibet there were some 20,000 beggars making their living across the country. In the constant search throughout life to gain merit, giving money to beggars scores high points and giving money to beggars in the Barkhor scores some of the highest merit points of all. For some pilgrims the walk to Lhasa, their spiritual capital, was the accomplishment of a lifetime which had taken their entire life savings to achieve. They would beg in the Barkhor to raise enough money to see them through the trip home.

Colonel Waddell who accompanied the British invasion of Tibet in 1904 and who may well have had the Rapper's great, great grandfather around his leg, described the Barkhor beggars as 'repulsively dirty.' It is a description which could be used very accurately today and after removing the Rapper and his sticky lolly pop from my trouser leg I set off down the side streets for some relief from the bombardment of sensations at the Barkhor.

In the narrow streets behind the Barkhor I would find my favourite part of Lhasa – where time has stood still for hundreds of years. Streets twist and turn, sometimes 30 feet wide, sometimes six feet wide, veering off at right angles between old whitewashed stone buildings three to four stories high with black trapezoid windows. Here you only see Tibetan faces – the Chinese do not venture alone down these little alley ways.

One street corner always has a ram tethered to a door post. He has a very short rope and can only stand or sit on the large granite doorstep. There is never any food visible yet he is permanently chewing something, sitting on his doorstep gazing at the world going by. Sheep are often saved from the slaughterhouse by Tibetans who take them on as pets. It is thought that this saving of a soul from death is a very merit worthy action and therefore adds to the running total of merit of the new sheep owner. It is quite common to see Tibetans walking around the Barkhor with a sheep on a lead, or taking a couple of sheep on a long pilgrimage.

At least I used to hope that this ram was one of the saved ones. It did dawn on me one day that perhaps it was a different ram there every time and that they were just being fattened up for slaughter.

In a dimly lit doorway across from the ram, an old Tibetan lady in full Tibetan dress slices a turnip on a chopping board across her lap. Another spins wool into thread. Small girls lean out of first floor windows calling, 'Hello, *tashi delai*, hello!' to passers by. Everyone has time to greet you, whether by a smile, a nod, a *tashi delai* or occasionally by the really traditional greeting of sticking a tongue out at you. This is the Tibet of the past that so many wish was still here today.

Trying to find my way back to the Barkhor market, I found myself trapped between two narrow streets filled with excrement and the decaying carcasses of dogs. The pungent stench of rotting flesh and maggot-infested pools sent me scrambling for the fresh air of the open square. Even rancid yak butter was perfume compared with this. Half way down the narrow alley, at a point where the path consisted of stepping stones through the sewage, two men came out of a doorway, their eyes wide with excitement and their breath heavy with a strong alcohol. They stopped in front of me, blocking the only dry path through the nauseous street. Both had the distinctive profiles of *Khampas*. They stood tall and proud with red braid wrapped across their matted black hair. One was bare-chested with his *chuba*, the Tibetan cloak, tied around his waist. They stared at me in silence for some time, looking me up and down. Their surly expressions did not change and they held firm their position blocking the only dry exit. There was no one else around. There were no old ladies in the doorways, no little children smiling and waving from the windows. Alone in excrement alley face to face with two alcohol-steaming Khampas. I was a long way up the creek without a paddle.

'Do drigey rey?' the bare-chested one broke the silence.

I had no idea what he was saying.

'Do drigey rey?' he shouted.

I smiled at him but to no avail. He pulled a sword from its sheath, stooped over me and held it up to my chest. Why had I been so mean to the Rapper? Is this what happens if you don't earn merit? Where was a Chinese soldier when you needed one?

The other Khampa looked over his shoulder and moved in closer to me. 'Katse rey?' he called out with a nod of his head. The bare-chested one waved the sword closer to my face. Sunlight flashed in my eyes as he tilted the steel blade towards me. I could even see every detail of the intricate engravings running along the centre of the blade between the two razor edges.

He withdrew the sword, pointed to the space beside us and made a series of cuts in the air to demonstrate a nifty disembowelling motion. He shook it in front of my face again.

'Katse rey? *Katse rey*!?' he shouted.

The bare-chested one frowned in thought, recalling the only English words which he had heard learnt from his wife.

'You how much?' he called to me.

It was with an enormous sense of relief that I suddenly realised they were not threatening to decapitate me if I crossed their path, but were merely trying to sell me the sword. Their scowls turned into broad gold-capped grins as I took the sword and examined it closely. The swirling engravings of the steel blade ended abruptly inside a gaping dragon's mouth of silver which formed the base of the handle. The body of the dragon curled around on itself to provide the bulk of the grip. It was newly made, perhaps one of the imports from Kathmandu, and certainly practical for the man about town. But disembowelling daggers were not high on my shopping list and I had no intention of buying it, I just wanted to get out of the place with dry feet and in one piece.

I shook my head and passed the sword back to him. Recalling Tashi's words of greeting at the airport, I ventured the only Tibetan words that I knew: 'Tashi Delai.' This earned me a great slap on the back that pushed me dangerously close to the edge of the excrement area. My two new Khampa friends strode off down the lane howling with laughter.

There are only so many smells and sensations that the body can take on the first day of reaching an altitude of 12,000 feet so after I had found my way back to the Barkhor I haggled for another rickshaw to return to the hotel.

Two luminous figures ran out of the lobby at me as I walked across the forecourt. Greg and Dave had made it to Lhasa. Their permit had arrived from Beijing and the man in Chengdu had waved them through with a smile, happy to see the back of these two troublesome foreigners.

Once in Tibet, they were anxious to set out immediately and had decided not to take the customary rest to acclimatise. 'We can rest when we come back,' joked Dave as he charged off to the head quarters of the Tibet Mountaineering Association to check on the final arrangements.

It is said that a successful climb on Everest is as much to do with luck as mountaineering skills, and while no one was questioning Greg and Daves' capabilities, their luck was certainly running very thin.

Dave returned an hour later with the news that the Chinese Mountaineering Association had forgotten to inform their Tibetan counterparts, the Tibet Mountaineering Association (TMA), of the delay with the permit. Quite understandably, the TMA had assumed that the climb was cancelled and had already been out partying with the fully paid up deposit and proceeds from sale of the equipment, that Greg and Dave had sent in advance.

The porters had all been sent back to their villages. Tang Chong, the manager of TMA had decided that there was only one thing for it, the TMA would hold a banquet for Greg and Dave (naturally to be charged to the Canadians' expenses at a later date), in order to honour their arrival in Lhasa and cover up any bad feelings that may have been caused. Tang Chong had promised that the expedition would start off in a 'few days,' when he had recovered the equipment and found new porters.

'It is always like this when you deal with those people,' said a friendly Tibetan voice in perfect English. The words had come from the smartest Tibetan I had met so far who was now walking towards us across the lobby. A stocky man in his early fifties with a winning smile, a good suit and well groomed hair that all seemed to be growing upwards.

He looked at Greg and Dave. His smile disappeared as he spoke to them, 'Go away and deal with it yourselves, it is not our problem.'

Well, perhaps not quite as friendly as I had first thought. Greg and Dave, exhausted from their day of frustration didn't bother to answer. They trudged off to their rooms to make phone calls.

Harry rushed across the lobby to introduce me to the Tibetan.

'Alec, here is Mr Jig Me,' he whispered urgently in my ear as Jig Me glared behind us at the Reception desk, 'you know, the DGM. *Head of Party A*.'

'I know who *you* are,' said Mr Jig Me, turning to face me, 'welcome to our hotel. Tashi Delai.'

He walked over to a Receptionist and shouted at her in Tibetan. The lobby cleared of all the local staff who did not have a good reason to be there.

As Jig Me disappeared down the corridor Harry explained the bizarre system of management that exists in all the foreign hotels of Communist countries. 'There is a *Party A* and a *Party B*. We are *Party B*; the foreigners. They are *Party A*; the locals. They watch us all the time. They know who we are, where we are, what we are doing, who we are with and even what we are doing with who we are with.'

The words of warning of the Vice President in Hong Kong echoed through my mind.

Although I had been cautioned of the Big Brother aspect of Party A, no one had told me about the Party system of management. It is not commonly encountered in management text books and nothing in my training or past experience had prepared me for Communist management – Party style.

Party B managers are not permitted to make decisions without the consent of Party A managers, and Party A managers may not take any decisions without permission from Party B. Each Party is dependent on the other and tied down by mind-boggling bureaucracy and endless rounds of meetings.

Party A control their side of hotel through a series of assistants, officially called 'deputies,' who are assigned to each of the expatriate managers. Every week the deputies report to the head of what is known in local Communist terms as the *unit*. The head of the Lhasa hotel unit being Mr Jig Me: Commander in Chief of Party A and Deputy General Manager of the hotel.

The deputies are known by the expatriates as 'shadows,' because they have the annoying habit of following your every move and being right behind you when you least expect them. They have two main purposes. Firstly, they have the task of learning all they can from the expatriate, so that eventually they can take over. The deputy earns roughly 3000 percent less than the foreigner he shadows – which is reason enough to do away with all the foreigners as soon as possible.

Secondly, the deputy has the far more important responsibility of ensuring that his foreigner is not involved in any activity that may bring disrepute to the unit. Political stability and following whatever directive the government has requested, is infinitely more important than good business results. The only way to stay in power is to follow the Party line, agree with what is being said from those higher than you in the Party and make sure that those beneath you agree with what you have just agreed to from those above you. No one is allowed to stand up and shout 'But this is absolutely ridiculous!' That would take them out of the Party and hence out of power.

Meanwhile, Party B, (that's us – the foreigners, in case you are as confused as I was when it was explained to me) try to get on with running the hotel efficiently, giving customer satisfaction and making money for the company. The General Manager liked to call the relationship between Party A and Party B a 'marriage'.

It was certainly a stormy love affair and tensions frequently flew high. There was a famous incident in Beijing where a General Manager of a foreign managed hotel was beaten up by his deputy while the hotel security guards cheered on. General Managers often resigned or were moved by their company head office because they could not work with their deputy.

Fortunately, the marriage between Party A and Party B in Lhasa was not as tempestuous as those in Beijing and although there were quarrels, tiffs and trial separations, there was also the occasional honeymoon.

Jig Me was well suited in his position of Deputy General Manager and head of Party A. In common with several of the most influential Tibetans in Lhasa he was from noble stock and had been sent as a five year old child to commence his education outside Tibet at St Joseph's School in Darjeeling. This was before the days of air or vehicle routes over the Himalayas, so the torturous voyage along narrow mountain tracks took him well over a month. He travelled in convoy with other young children of noble families, strapped to their horses as they were led on the 300 mile journey across the highest mountain range in the world. He spent five years in India and returned to be with his family in Tibet just before the Chinese took over in 1951.

With the Chinese eager to show the benefits of Communism to the Tibetan population, Jig Me was sent to Beijing for further schooling. He survived the Cultural Revolution as it raged throughout the country and, despite Tibet being foremost in his heart, he emerged afterwards as one of the successful Communist Party members who would be used for positions of power in the New Tibet. After a succession of minor jobs in the town of Gyantse, Jig Me became the Deputy General Manager of the major foreign enterprise in Lhasa; in charge of

800 local staff and cooperating with ten foreigners who would live on the premises and be his total responsibility. Along with power came social status and opportunities for financial reward but also one of the most difficult positions in Lhasa.

But the intricacies of local politics could wait. Jig Me had rushed into the coffee shop kitchen to support his Party A member over the argument that had erupted again over live yaks. Chef was screaming at the Food & Beverage Manager who in turn shouted at his Deputy. A few guests remained in the dining area, still chewing their way through Giant Yak Burgers.

They gazed up at me as I tiptoed past the coffee shop entrance. Only a thin partition wall separated the dining area from the kitchen and every word of the kitchen fracas could be heard by the embarrassed guests, who hastily chewed on to the end of their burgers. Jig Me's voice soared above the rest as he shouted to defend his Party A man and to point the finger of blame at Party B incompetence. His man from Party A spoke little English, but knew that Jig Me would be defending him, so shouted 'Yes!' where he thought appropriate and nodded continually whilst Jig Me was speaking. Chef bellowed out a lengthy and colourful description of where the Food & Beverage Manager could try to fit the live yaks if bovine creatures ever came into his kitchen on the hoof again. It is at moments such as this that you realise just how much imagination Chefs have. The kitchen door flew open as the Food & Beverage Manager stormed out and the waitresses who had been trying hard to suppress their giggles now stood firmly to attention. The guests looked down to their burgers and decided that they had eaten enough.

'Never work with a German Chef!' the Food & Beverage Manager called out to no one in particular. He turned to the kitchen door; 'They are only good for *bratwurst* and *sauerkraut!*'

The guests were already leaving the restaurant and he ran after them so that he could hold the door open and wish them all a pleasant evening.

'Ah, hello Alec,' he called out after me, 'I am going to pack. You won't see me any more. Good-bye.'

I continued along the corridor to the peace and quiet of my room.

My suitcases had arrived from the airport while I was out at the Barkhor and I spent the rest of the evening unpacking them in amazement. The effect of the altitude on some of the items in my 20 kilogrammes of luggage was startling. It appeared that someone had attached a bicycle pump to my toothpaste tube and inflated it to double size. My tube of shaving foam had changed shape from flat to nearly spherical.

I made the mistake of flipping the top open. The force of air pressure inside the plastic bottle spat a jet of shaving foam across the room, scoring a direct hit on the suit I had unpacked for Monday morning. I opened the toothpaste and the shampoo bottles in the bathroom, behind the shower curtain, and they too produced spectacular results. I had been warned of many of the effects of high altitude but no one had told me to expect my toothpaste tube to explode.

Worried about what effect the altitude could be having on my body I followed the General Manager's orders and gulped down three large glasses of water before going to bed. I dreamt of Barbara and her American tour group blown up like giant helium balloons floating around the lobby. The tour guide had tied strings to their ankles and was pulling them back down to ground level to squash them through the door and onto the tour bus.

There is something about high altitude that causes vivid dreams. Sleepless nights are also experienced by many guests but this is more likely to be from the pack of wild dogs which keeps up a howling chorus under the hotel windows throughout the night. Sleeplessness also arises from the natural side effect caused by drinking three litres of water a day.

I was very pleased to wake up the next morning with a clear head and to find that I was not floating around the ceiling doubled in size. When I met Dave in the Coffee Shop at lunchtime he was not quite so fortunate. Holding his head in his hands he was looking for a cure for an almighty hangover.

'The TMA banquet,' he winced taking a sip of coffee.

I was not sure if he winced because of the hangover, or because he had tasted the hotel coffee for the first time. It had a most peculiar taste which seemed to have no connection what so ever with coffee. The General Manager had explained to me that we imported it from Shanghai, as we could not afford to import real foreign brands. To make up for the lack of coffee taste it was used in large quantities and boiled for hours, which left it so strong that you felt it was just as likely to dissolve the spoon as the sugar.

Greg arrived at the coffee shop and wisely ordered tea. He spread maps and photographs around the table top and they immediately started enthusing over possible deviations to their planned route. They should have been at Base Camp well over a week ago – if they left it much later the weather on the north face of the mountain would have deteriorated too far to give them any chance of 'hitting the top,' as they called it.

I too had my preparations to make. Not for the bleak rock face of Everest but on Monday morning I would be at work for my first day in what the Hong Kong press had dubbed 'the most unlikely Holiday Inn in the world'.

4

Losing Face

I was woken from a dream-filled sleep on Monday morning by the sound of shouting and doors slamming down the corridor. The clamour was approaching my room.

'Housekeeping!' shrieked a voice from outside the door.

I leapt from my bed as I heard the scraping of a key in the lock and I arrived just in time to find a small Tibetan girl standing in the open doorway demanding my laundry. I asked if she could come back later.

'*May-oh*,' she replied, shaking her head and beaming a Tibetan smile at the same time. I packed up the clothes I had been wearing on the trip in through China and added the suit jacket that had been hit by the exploding shaving foam. The chambermaid kept smiling throughout, nodded and walked off down the corridor with my bundle, stopping in front of the next door to shout 'Housekeeping!' at the top of her voice.

It was still early but I could not get back to sleep. A dog from across the road had strayed onto the strip of wasteland between my window and the staff quarters. The inappropriate planting of dwarf conifers and stunted weeping willows along the edge of the land had done little to beautify the area but the bushes did provide excellent cover for the resident pack of dogs, who now lay in wait, watching the intruder. They considered the wasteland to be an integral part of their home territory and defended it fiercely (and extremely vociferously), against dogs from other packs. Approaching strays were either attacked or mounted or both. Anyone trying to separate the dogs was growled at menacingly, presumably being accused of interfering in their internal affairs.

The intruding dog made the mistake of wandering too far into the residents' territory. The hotel pack gave chase with a war cry of barks and howls that was guaranteed to waken any hotel guest who had not already received a surprise wake up call courtesy of the Housekeeping Department.

I set off for breakfast and found my reserved place at the management dining table in the coffee shop. I was greeted with silence. Mr Liu looked up at me and quickly back to the large Danish Pastry filling his plate. There was a similar pastry at every place around the table except where Gunter, the Food & Beverage Manager, was sitting. The atmosphere was tense.

'I didn't want one anyway. I'm not hungry,' Gunter said defiantly. He looked around the table and snarled at the other expatriates; 'The Chef is an ignorant pig!'

The waitresses giggled. The General Manager reacted firmly, hissing an angry whisper in reply.

'Not in front of *Party A*. Don't make us lose face!'

He made a quiet but forceful smack on the table to show that he meant business. The public fight between Chef and the Food & Beverage Manager could go on no longer.

Wherever members of the animal kingdom live close together in confined areas there are always problems. Holiday Inn Lhasa proved to be no exception to the rule. For the expatriates living in the hotel, business life, social life and in fact all forms of life altogether revolved only around the concrete walls of the compound. The sense of loneliness and isolation is brought home by the reminder that outside the hotel there are only a dozen or so other foreigners resident in Tibet; an area two thirds the size of western Europe. While this creates an interdependent bond between the expatriates, it also leads to the smallest differences being exaggerated out of all proportion.

There are traditional quarrels between hotel departments that are found in every hotel in the world: Housekeeping fight with Front Office, Food & Beverage fight with the Kitchen, but with the extra strain of a hardship posting, the management team also tends to disintegrate along lines of seniority and experience. The new recruits resent the 'old China hands', who never listen to fresh ideas, only dampening their enthusiasm with wet blanket 'that won't work here' replies to any new suggestions.

For their part the expatriates with years of experience in the field resent the naivety of the newcomers, who habitually come out with ridiculous ideas before they understand the constraints of working in unreal and illogical surroundings.

Mr Liu, the Controller from Hong Kong, had worked many years in mainland China and was particularly intolerant of naive new recruits. He had printed out a world map from his computer with a large arrow pointing to a speck in the blank area above the Indian sub-continent. The words 'YOU ARE HERE' were printed in heavy bold type across the top of the page. Whenever he was asked a question by a new expatriate he would produce an A4 copy of the map from his pocket, pass it to his new member of staff and chuckle. It was his idea of a joke. Nobody found it very funny, but as Mr Liu was the Controller, and therefore in charge of the payment of salaries and reimbursement of expense accounts, everyone laughed when he attempted a joke.

The responsibility for minimising the disputes between the departments and between the management staff is one of the least popular duties of the General Manager. But in Lhasa, even more important than actually keeping the foreign management team together, is keeping up the appearance that the team is together. Any disputes amongst the expatriates is considered to be a 'loss of face' for Party B.

'Losing face', and the contrary, 'giving face', were new expressions to me. Mr Liu rose from the breakfast table, leaving his Danish Pastry untouched, and signalled that it was time to move on to the morning meeting.

Harry remained seated, finishing his pastry. 'Without understanding *face*,' he said to me, 'you don't have a chance here.' I stayed to listen.

'Losing face,' he continued, 'happens when you make a mistake, you screw up, you fight with one of your friends. You know, you just do the smallest thing wrong and they come along and make a big deal out it. That's loss of face for you. It puts you in an inferior position. If you lose face, they get stronger and they can do what they want. If we lose face in front of Party A, Jig Me starts trying to run the hotel *his* way and then we can all go home.'

He gulped down the last dregs of his tea and stood up from the table.

'Now, *giving face*, that's the very opposite. You heap praise on someone for what they've done to make them think they're the world's best.' He paused for thought. 'It's all a game,' he continued, 'but you have to understand how to play, if you get the rules wrong then you have to leave.'

'Face' explains why a tour guide wishing to please, will never admit that he doesn't understand what you are asking, or will never say that he doesn't know the answer to your question. To avoid losing face, he will just give a reply that he thinks you will want to hear. This can be very difficult if you are asking a question that needs an accurate answer such as; 'What time should we leave for the airport?' If in any doubt he will just say 'Yes' to every question.

As we left the coffee shop, Harry brushed aside the waitress who came up to me demanding my meal voucher.

'This is Mr Alec. No meal voucher. He works here. *Yin Yi Bu Jingli.*'

Apparently this was my title. 'Yin Yi Bu Jingli.' I quite liked it. 'Mr Alec. Yin Yi Bu Jingli,' I repeated to the waitress. We hurried down the corridor after Mr Liu and the other expats.

'We mustn't be late for the meeting or Party B lose face,' explained Harry, 'Jig Me has all his Party A staff there ten minutes before the meeting – if they are late he fines them!'

We ran up the set of stairs to the meeting room, puffing and panting in the rarefied air. Although I had only suffered from a headache on my first day, breathlessness over the slightest exertion was an effect of the altitude that never went away. Trying to give an impression of respectability upon entering the meeting room is difficult when you are shaking and openly gasping for breath, and I decided to get there earlier in future.

A morning meeting, officially called the 'Operations Meeting,' takes place, in some form or other, in all the foreign managed hotels in China. It is held every working day, from Monday to Saturday, and is the decision making time that sets the mood of the day. The management team and department heads discuss the business results and problems of the previous day, the forecasted results and problems of the day ahead and any special activities that may be taking place.

Seating arrangements at the morning meeting in Lhasa were even stricter than around the management dining table. Party A and Party B sat together in a complicated pecking order that descended down the sides of the long table. The General Manager and Jig Me sat at the head of the table, with the General Manager's secretary, Heather, perched uneasily on the corner, between the General Manager and Mr Liu. Thirty people crowded along the table edge; all of the expatriates, their deputies and other Party officials with dubious functions that none of us understood.

Heather had the delicate task of translating and taking the meeting minutes. English and Mandarin Chinese were the official languages used, although the full range of mother tongues around the table stretched from Tibetan to Cantonese, Hokien and other forms of Chinese, and a selection of European languages; German, Italian, French and Flemish.

Despite her very English name, Heather was decidedly Chinese. She had been given the name 'Heather' by her English teacher at school and had kept it for use with foreigners. An outwardly frail girl, she had an inner core of steel that could withstand the severe discipline of the General Manager. Her lank black hair fell flat down the sides of her face and over her thin shoulders. Shampoo and make-up would undoubtedly have been of great benefit to her, but instead of spending time on her personal appearance, she selflessly devoted herself to her work, putting in far longer hours than the majority of local staff. It was rare to find someone so good. Like the other Han Chinese, she yearned for her own country and like any 18 year old girl in a strange place, a long way from her family, she was homesick and lonely. She lived only for the day when she could return to China.

But Heather had made a mistake; being good at her job meant that she was likely to stay in Lhasa for a long time. This was a fundamental problem in motivating the staff. The Chinese actively held themselves back, so that they could be released as soon as possible and return to their homeland. The Tibetans, after 40 years of Communism, were generally very laid back, without much of an interest in doing anything. Salaries were virtually the same for every level of employee and promotions were more dependent on Party status than on job performance.

The waitresses were typical of staff throughout the hotel. They tried their level best *not* to be promoted to Restaurant Supervisor. For practically no more pay, this new position would mean that suddenly the waitress would lose her friends, be responsible to the management and would inevitably lead to shouts, tears and the embarrassing demotion to dish-washer.

A colossal total of 560 staff were employed by the hotel. It was never very clear exactly what all these people did, and some of the names on the staff register appeared to be on permanent leave. Annual vacations were saved up and then claimed for months on end. The vacations would not include travelling time, which could amount to an extra month either side of the normal holiday. Maternity leave lasted twelve months (without travelling time) and any good staff falling pregnant, although a great cause for celebration, would seriously impair the running of the hotel.

Leave for abortions was also commonplace, as the Chinese government, desperate to avoid the catastrophe of over population, effectively limits the number of children that Han Chinese may have to a single child, by imposing financially crippling tax burdens on families with two or more children. Tibetans, as a minority race, are permitted to have two children, but Tibetan officials in Lhasa and practically all Tibetans in the countryside have no such controls imposed on them.

'Take a seat Alec,' the General Manager said to me, pointing to the only vacant chair around the table. The rest of the expatriate managers sniggered. Gunter, who was sitting four places further down the table from the vacant seat, laughed out loud when he saw where I would be sitting. He gave me a thumbs up sign, and even exchanged glances and a laugh with Chef who sat opposite him along the table.

I sat down cautiously, waiting for some practical joke to unfold. Or perhaps there would be an induction ritual for my first Morning Meeting. Were we all going to put on aprons and exchange funny handshakes?

Sitting on my right was a Tibetan lady, Mrs Qi Mei, whose title nobody really knew. She looked normal enough. Apparently she was something high in the Party but beyond that, none of the expats had been able to tell me what she did. Mrs Qi Mei smiled to me as I sat down. So far so good.

On my left was a Chinaman, Mr Pong, the Deputy Controller. His nickname, I had been told before by Harry, was Alien III and now that I saw him for the first time, I had to admit that he did bear an uncanny resemblance to the futuristic being. He squinted through wire-framed spectacles at me and opened his mouth in a small spherical smile to reveal a mass of contorted teeth in various states of decay.

Then it hit me. The very aptly named Mr Pong had the kind of breath that could stun at over ten feet. I was transported to the depths of excrement alley at the Barkhor. This wasn't just bad – there was something rotten down there. Something had crawled in and died. Gunter howled with laughter as he saw the look of horror on my face. It was the best entertainment he had seen since he had watched Chef chasing yaks through the kitchens.

The General Manager banged the table and started the meeting off with a welcome speech.

'It has been over six months since we have had anyone in the Sales Department, so let's welcome Mr Alec who we are sure can boost our sales and increase business.'

Heather translated into Chinese and everyone nodded.

Jig Me followed with a welcome on behalf of all Party A and wished that, 'we will have a very good cooperation.'

He spoke in perfect English and Heather again translated everything. I could see that these meetings were going to take a long time.

Jig Me pointed out my deputy, a Miss Tsao, who had cleverly secured a seat down at the far end of the table well away from the breath monster next to me. Mr Liu read out the previous day's financial results and Harry gave the forecast for the coming week – which was rather bleak. After the high occupancy and revenue of the summer months, business had now entered the gradual slide down towards the low winter season. We were still over 70 percent occupancy which sounded quite respectable to me, but next week we would fall into the 60's.

As I was contemplating the drop in hotel occupancy and what could be done to reverse the trend, a low gurgling noise started its rumble in the chair next to me.

'*Ccccccrrrrrrrrgggggggggkkkhhhhpt.*'

Mr Pong was clearing his throat in preparation to speak. This warning signal had already woken every expat around the table and sent them leaning as far back on their chairs as possible. Even Gunter, four chairs away, was not safe, and panic stricken, he pushed his portly frame as far down the table as he could.

In painfully long statements of Mandarin, Mr Pong pointed out that there had been a problem in the kitchens with some confusion over the purchase of yaks. Heather translated for us. He said that he was sure that it would not happen again, if the expatriates would not argue and if there was a better cooperation. He suggested that perhaps so many expatriates were unnecessary.

It was exactly the kind of calculated attack that Party A tried when they saw disputes amongst the foreigners. The General Manager pointed out that there were only ten expatriates present, instead of the 19 when the hotel opened and the 27 allowed in the management contract and that any less would severely impair the efficient running of the hotel.

Much to everyone's relief, Mr Pong did not reply, and the Deputy Food & Beverage Manager, a Mr Tu Dian, announced the good news that in the evening there would be a banquet held by the 'Protocol and Friendship City Division of the Friendship with Foreign Countries Association.'

Mrs Qi Mei followed this with an announcement that I would have to go to the People's Number One Hospital for a health check and the meeting was adjourned. As we walked down the stairs I told Mrs Qi Mei that it was very kind of her to arrange the health check, but it was completely unnecessary as I had already had extensive medicals at the request of Holiday Inn, both in Paris and Hong Kong. She smiled and said, 'Yes.'

Miss Tsao, my deputy, was having a word with Jig Me after the meeting, about her papers. She had volunteered to come to Tibet 20 years ago and now wanted to return to her home province, but as her papers said that she was resident in Tibet, she was not permitted to move to any other part of China.

I carried on to my office, on the ground floor of the main block behind the gift shop. It was a small room with two desks, one filing cabinet, three chairs and one sofa. A large orange telephone sat on my desk, together with a flask of hot water. I was expected to provide my own jam jar. The floor was entirely covered with piles of paper. I was greeted enthusiastically by

Tashi who I had not seen since he picked me up from the airport. 'This is Mr Alec,' he announced in English to the three other office staff. 'He is a big potato.'

It transpired that the Chinese have a system of measuring someone's importance in relation to the size of root vegetables. Thus I was the 'big potato' for the Sales and Marketing Department and my staff were introduced to me as 'small potatoes'.

Tashi gave me the news that no matter what I had understood, I had to visit the hospital. He had been given orders to accompany me and to be my translator. I was not sure if this would be a good idea.

The hotel Landcruisers were in use, so we took a rickshaw down the tarmac cycle lane, past the cow-filled skips of refuse to the People's Number One Hospital. Another feature of Chinese modernisation stood before us. Short railings around flower beds of grass and litter, filled the grounds of an austere, cement-rendered building painted in a sickly shade of 'garlic grass'. A group of lamentable beggars surrounded the main door, their filthy hands tugging at the clothing of anyone entering or leaving the building, until they received some small change. Two monks sat against the entrance chanting from a pile of woodblock printed prayers. A cardboard shoe box lay in front of them for donations. Whenever they saw a patient or a relative approaching they would speed up their chants and gesture towards the box.

Passing through the open glass door, it was some comfort to be hit by the smell of antiseptic, or disinfectant, or whatever that all-pervading hospital smell is. I wondered if a concentrated dose of it could be injected into Mr Pong's stomach.

The inside walls were painted in a paler shade of sickly green up to the halfway line, and then whitewashed to the ceiling. The grey tiled floor was littered with surgical debris. Two doctors leant against a wall in the foyer, cigarettes in hand.

We were ushered along a dingy corridor to a dimly lit room which contained a table covered with a dirty sheet and shelves lined with glass jars. There were two chairs and a bicycle. We waited for a nurse to arrive.

Clouds of dust rolled along the corridor, followed by a Tibetan lady who was attempting to sweep the hallway filth into a tin can which had been cut in half and nailed onto the end of a stick. It appeared that she was a nurse of some kind, as when she saw us, she came into the room, wiped her hands on her dusty coat and looked around the jars of surgical appliances to find the one containing needles.

I asked Tashi to inform the lady that I had already had all my tests both in Paris and in Hong Kong so that there was really no need for any more. Tashi said 'Yes' to me and spoke to the nurse in Tibetan. She nodded. Smiling, she approached me with a large needle she had found in one of the jars. She made a poking gesture, smiled and nodded again to me. I told Tashi that it wasn't anything to do with a lack of confidence in their health system – it was just that I had already had all the tests I needed. Tashi again said something in Tibetan to the nurse. She laughed and wiped the needle on her sleeve to demonstrate that it was clean.

I was saved momentarily by the interruption of a dog running into the room. It had picked up something out of the dustpan and was looking for a quiet corner where it could stay undisturbed and chew its find. Our nurse chased it from the room, brandishing my needle at it and shouting at the two cigarette-smoking doctors as the dog ran past, tail between its legs and prize between its teeth.

Foolishly I consented to the blood test, but only when the nurse had found another needle in a sealed packet. For all future examinations I took a supply of my own needles bought in the West.

After a drop of blood was collected from my ear lobe, Tashi and I were taken to the X-ray room. Heavy doors marked 'Danger – Radiation' stood wide open, and to my surprise I found the room filled with patients queuing up in front of the X-ray machine. Flashes of X-rays went off around the room as pregnant women, nomads and small children lined up expectantly in front of this modern technology. It seems that someone had lost the operating handbook – where it clearly stayes that you should stand behind the lead shield. After a single chest X-ray I was taken to a further examination room.

An elderly nomad from northern Tibet was seated by a low table, with a contraption for testing eyesight on his head. He wore a long sheepskin *chuba*, with the fur innermost and the rough cut skin on the outside to face the elements. The trailing edge of the *chuba* was finished with an inch wide hem of brightly coloured braid. He looked up at us as we entered the room and smiled a toothless grin as a greeting. I tried out a *tashi delai* and he beamed with delight, sticking his tongue out in reply.

The nurse shouted at him, removed the machine from his matted hair and put it straight on my forehead. At the same time a doctor stirred in the corner of the room. He had being enjoying his morning snooze on the examination couch and had been woken by the disturbance. He stood up, rubbed his eyes and stretched into a lengthy yawn. The nomad watched with keen interest as the doctor took a filthy probe out of his pocket and stuck it into my ears. The doctor said something to Tashi in Tibetan.

'Sorry Mr Alec, I don't know the words in English.'

Tashi continued to apologise to me, shrugging his shoulders as he excused himself for not being able to translate. He then started an elaborate mime that the nomad enjoyed tremendously. From Tashi's actions, I was concerned that the doctor had found a large lump of something very, very bad in one of my ears, but it turned out after further miming that he was saying I had to give a stool test. Our nomad friend loved every minute of it.

The nurse rushed back into the room brandishing her empty dustpan, hot on the heels of the mangy dog that had crept back into the hospital in search of further treasures. It ran past the nomad and caught the side of a brimming spittoon pan, knocking it clean over. The slippery contents trickled across the tiled floor and over the doorstep into the corridor. Strangely, this did not seem to bother anyone except for myself.

I asked Tashi to tell the doctor that I had already had a stool test, and for once, the doctor seemed satisfied with this answer. I suppose that he was looking forward to making the examination even less than I was to producing the sample in those conditions.

I gave the eyesight contraption back to our nomad friend and treading around the pool on the floor, Tashi and I were able to leave the hospital with no further questions or prods. I made a note never to return if I became ill. Nothing could be less likely to lead to recovery than spending any time in there.

Back at the hotel I had a surprise when I entered my room. There was a joke in the hotel to the effect of: 'What is small, grey and wrinkled?' I thought this would be a run of the mill joke about elderly elephants, but the answer is; 'Your returned laundry.'

On my bed lay a plastic bag of small shirts, flattened beyond recognition and tinged with a colour that was not there before they were sent for cleaning. Buttons also suffered under the Lhasa laundry technique and every week one or two would be reduced to a fine powder. Sometimes they would look deceptively good until you touched them, whereupon they would disintegrate in your fingers. My suit jacket had also undergone considerable changes. The wool was pressed razor thin and now shone like the high gloss finish of a used-car salesman's favourite jacket. I complained to Charlie that he had told me we had the finest laundry equipment west of Beijing.

'Yes, but I did not tell you we have local washing powder and local labour,' was his rather inadequate reply.

I was not impressed by the Peoples' powder that washed greyer than grey, but why should I have been? We were in Tibet. I thought of the nomad's sheep skin *chuba*. It had not had a clean since it had been taken off the sheep. Everything has to be taken in perspective, and doubtless, his life on the plateau involved more significant concerns than the whiteness of his wash.

Gunter, the Food & Beverage Manager, was also having more important issues to come to terms with than his washing. Despite his immaculate preparation, the banquet for the Protocol and Friendship City Division of the Friendship with Foreign Countries Association, had not been a success. The tables were set with the hotel's finest glass and silverware, the waitresses and waiters were all at their stations on time and Chef had prepared a fine display of Western cuisine. It was difficult to eat a whole steak with a pair of chopsticks but this was not a problem for the guests.

They had been invited to honour the retirement of the Association chief and Western food had been ordered especially to highlight the importance of the banquet. Western dishes added prestige and the Chinese were suitably impressed with the alien and inedible food. Bottles of Johnnie Walker Black Label were disappearing in rapid bouts of drinking – all the signs showed that the dinner had started well.

During the course of the evening, Gunter had found a scruffy little man at the buffet table using a pair of chopsticks to dismantle the *pièce montée*. He had piled his plate up with steaks, potatoes, cold meats, cakes and yoghurt in one heap, and he was now trying to take the apple from the suckling pig's mouth. Gunter was furious, and presuming this man to be a driver who had found his way in to the banquet room from the group buffet, marched him out of the restaurant. No amount of protests would stop Gunter. It was his restaurant, this was an important banquet, and no filthy truck driver could mess it up for him.

It was Jig Me who broke the news to the General Manager. Gunter had thrown out the new head of the Friendship with Foreign Countries Association. Jig Me was seething. It was a serious loss of face all round. There was no other option. Gunter had to go. He handed in his resignation, due to 'personal reasons', the following morning and spent the day in his room. Holiday Inn would try to find him a suitable position elsewhere in Asia – but nothing could be guaranteed.

The only good thing to arise from Gunter's dismissal was that there was now an extra space free around the table at the Morning Meeting. Mrs Qi Mei and the three people to my right had all moved down a place, so I could now follow their direction and sit two seats away from the breath monster.

Morale was low. Mr Liu read out the news that 31 television sets were missing from the hotel – Party B was on the attack. We had suffered greatly from the embarrassing dismissal of Gunter and we needed a victory to put us back into control. The Security Department, which was run entirely by local staff, was blamed for a total lack of professionalism. The Security Chief pointed out that in the missing property report of two years previously, there had been 48 television sets recorded as missing, so if there were now only 31 sets missing now, his department had done a very good job. The idea of burglars tiptoeing through the corridors late at night to return stolen television sets was an intriguing one and rather put a stop to our attack.

To change the mood of the meeting, I announced my ideas to increase winter business, which at least cheered up the General Manager. I had found a telephone book with one 1400 addresses of foreign companies in China. I planned to send a letter to each of them, to entice their high earning expatriate managers to visit Lhasa during the winter months. Known officially as 'doing a mail out', this is only the most basic sales activity, and similar sales efforts take place in every marketing-orientated hotel in the world.

A few days of organising lay ahead: the copy writing, printing the brochures, printing labels for the envelopes and under normal circumstances, the 'mail out' should be finished by the end of the week.

Printing the brochures is usually the longest part of a mail out, so Tashi and I started with a visit to the Lhasa printers. It was a fraction cleaner than the hospital, but exuded the same air of efficiency – and curiously – the same smell. We were taken to meet the director in his office but before we could discuss any business, tea had to be served and cigarettes offered to everyone. A minion rinsed out two large blue and white tea cups while the director showed us to our seats between piles of printed booklets. A spoonful of green tea leaves was dropped in each cup and boiling water added from the office thermos flask.

Chinese tea is not an easy drink to handle. The leaves float to the surface, and drinking it requires the skill to take a noisy slurp while simultaneously blowing the leaves away from your mouth. It is a complicated procedure which I was never able to master. If you are not careful you end up with mouthfuls of tea leaves which you can either swallow or spit out into the office spittoon.

He looked at us with some surprise when we asked him if he could print us a simple black and white brochure by the end of the week. It transpired that he was not at all interested in doing any print work for the hotel, as he had not been paid for the last work that he had done. He went to the cupboard and pulled out a stack of laundry lists. There were no straight lines of print but instead the letters followed roller coaster rides across the page. Capital letters were used freely in the middle of words and there was no letter 's'.

He explained that they could not find an 's' when they printed the list, so instead had used an '=' sign. Thus 'socks' on the laundry list had become '=ock='. He thought it looked perfectly good and could not see why Holiday Inn should have been so fussy. To anyone with a sense of humour they would have been ideal, but for a professional company they were certainly lacking.

Tashi remembered the case of the printed laundry lists from the Morning Meetings. He told me it had taken nine months to produce the laundry list and when it finally appeared in such a state, it was returned.

Before leaving we were taken on a tour of the print works. Chinese and Tibetan characters were cut out of metal and stored in row upon row of wooden boxes. It looked very primitive. Along the back wall stood a line of machinery covered in dusty sheets. The director proudly pointed to them.

'From Germany,' Tashi translated. 'Very good. Gift of the Australian government.'

State-of-the-art printing machinery lay covered in sheets while only slightly more modern versions of the Caxton printing press were being used alongside.

'Can we use them?' I asked hopefully.

'May-oh.'

'Why are they here then?'

'Putchidao.'

Nobody knew what they were there for, or how to operate them – but they had a high prestige value. The director could proudly tell his friends that he had foreign equipment in his factory. It wasn't going to help me with the mail out, so I concentrated on the resources in the hotel.

'Mr Alec wants to make propaganda for the hotel,' Tashi told the other office staff. I was shown the highly prized electronic typewriter that was in the possession of the Sales Office. Replacement ribbons could only be purchased in Hong Kong and in any case the letter 'a' had somehow been chipped off the daisy wheel. I seriously considered typing a letter by avoiding the use of the letter 'a' but decided that I would have to use such peculiar phrases that no one would understand what I was asking them to do. 'A's' could always be painted on by hand if I could just photocopy the letter 1,400 times.

Of the three Canon photocopier machines in the hotel, only one was still partially functioning. A piece of tyre rubber had been glued on to the top where the cover had been broken. Light grey paper coated with dark grey toner chugged through the contraption, usually becoming chewed into concertina shapes by the machine's intestines. There was no way this was going to produce 1,400 copies of an attractive letter to be sent out to prospective hotel guests.

Harry lifted up my hopes by telling me that there was an unused offset printer in the hotel that had sat in its packaging for two years. One thousand dollar's worth of brand new machinery sat in the Engineering Department, eagerly awaiting its first use. It was complete and perfectly functional. There was just one small flaw; an essential can of oil was missing and it was such a specific oil that it could only be obtained from a certain manufacturer in Hong Kong, known only to the supplier of the printer. There were no records to say where the printer had been supplied from and none of the local staff could remember anything about it, except that it needed a special oil which had been ordered at the time of the purchase two years previously. As the oil had not arrived since its order in 1986, it seemed unlikely that it would arrive by the end of the week.

Mr Liu, the Controller, was the only hope. He alone had a laptop computer in his office and a small printer. After much negotiation I was permitted to use the computer and printer over night between the hours of 8 pm and 8 am for a limited period of one week only, as after that he had to do the 'month end closing' and would not be letting the precious PC out of sight.

It took four sleepless nights to print out the letter on the tiny printer without an automatic paper feed. Meanwhile I had to devise a way to get the letters to their intended readers. Mr Liu had made it categorically clear that I was not to use the computer to input the addresses, as the memory was nearly full. He ran the entire hotel accounts from this computer with a peanut memory and did not wish to risk overloading it.

The only solution was to use the photocopier. Derek had taken the three machines apart and reassembled them to make one that gave its best performance for years. The dark grey tone stood out just a bit darker than usual and the background greyness smudged across the paper a little less than before.

Pages from the address book were photocopied and my staff spent an entire day cutting out each address with the office pair of scissors. Tashi had been shopping for large pots of glue and the rest of the week was spent pasting the addresses on to the envelopes. When it was finished, Tashi pointed out that the addresses were written in English but the postman at the Lhasa sorting office would only be able to read Chinese. We then sorted the letters according to which province in China they were going, and my Chinese staff wrote out the province name in Chinese characters on the envelopes.

Inserting the letters in the envelopes took another day and then we hit another delay. There was no self-adhesive strip or gum of any kind on the back of the envelopes and we had to paste each one individually. All that was left was to take them to the post office to be franked.

We bundled the letters into farm sacks and took a lift down to the main post office with Dorje the hotel driver. Cows and cyclists jumped out of our way, as we sped down the cycle track in the Landcruiser. Nobody at the post office knew what a franking machine was. Tashi didn't know either, so it was difficult for him to translate. They looked in horror at the sack loads of mail that we had brought, and reluctantly sold us stamps. 35 fen was the required amount for each stamp but of course they only had stamps of ten, three and two fen. Each envelope would require five stamps.

Tashi called in for more glue on the way back to the hotel. I should have taken this as a sign of what was to come, but at the time I didn't realise the significance. He explained when we returned to the office. Chinese stamps do not have glue on the reverse side – every one of them had to be glued on by hand. This took three more days of sticking. Finally, we set off for the post office with our sack fulls of totally glued envelopes.

'May-oh.'

No, the postman would not take so many at one time. He said it was not possible to carry so much and that we could only send out 200 per day – some of these were returned because one of my staff had been sticking the stamps on the back of the envelopes, instead of the front.

I was in the office early the next morning, trying to steam stamps off envelopes, when the two Canadian mountaineers burst in with a bottle of Chinese brandy. Greg and Dave were at last ready to leave. I left the envelopes soaking in water and followed Greg and Dave out to the forecourt where a convoy of Landcruisers and trucks stood ready. A team of Tibetan drivers, eager to start the race, revved the engines to fever pitch, causing gusts of exhaust fumes to blow through the main entrance into the hotel lobby.

I waved as Greg and Dave climbed into their Landcruiser and the convoy pulled out on to the Everest road. Statistically, they only had slightly more chance of making it to the top of Everest as of not coming back at all. It was a sombre thought as I went off to the Morning Meeting.

Jig Me announced that Chinese National Day was approaching and there would be celebrations throughout the land. The Vice Governor would host the traditional 1 October banquet at the Holiday Inn and all foreign staff and other expatriates in Lhasa would be invited. It was truly a day of celebration, commemorating Chairman Mao's glorious founding of the People's Republic of China on 1 October 1949.

Just one small point. Would Mr Alec inform the hotel guests that they would not be allowed to the Barkhor due to security reasons. Guests who had paid thousands of dollars for a trip of a lifetime would have to avoid the spiritual centre of Tibet and the famous bazaar. The ban would only be for five days, I was told, then we wouldn't have to celebrate any more.

Anything could happen on National Day, which by no small coincidence was the anniversary the 1987 Tibetan riots and the date of the customary burning down of the police station. Chinese military filled the streets and the People's Armed Police were placed on full alert.

5

Banquet Blues

During the Morning Meeting of 30 September, Jig Me announced that the National Day banquet which Chef had been preparing for National Day, 1 October, would now be a day early because National Day was a public holiday. Heather translated into Chinese and the Tibetans and Hans smiled; a day off work. Mr Pong rumbled in his chair, giving the expatriates time to push their seats back in anticipation of the tidal wave of halitosis that would engulf all around the table, but the General Manager stopped him short: 'You mean the banquet that we are preparing for tomorrow is now going to be today?'

'Yes,' it was Jig Me who replied, 'today at seven pm.'

Although there was considerable relief that Mr Pong had been kept silent, the confirmation that the National Day banquet was a day early had caught all the expatriates off guard. Chef had given his Sous Chefs the day off, the storerooms were empty and the local Purchasing Manager had not been seen for three days. Nevertheless in ten hours the top VIP's of Lhasa would be arriving for the National Day banquet – the highest social event on the Lhasa calendar. The evening had to be a success. There could be no more embarrassments. The loss of face over the dismissal of Gunter was still fresh in everyone's mind and we badly needed to restore the prestige image of the hotel and boost the morale of the expatriates.

Chef left immediately for the kitchens to check which extra provisions he would need for the evening. Tu Dian, the Tibetan Deputy F&B Manager, followed him.

'May-oh wenti!' Tu Dian called out as he left the room. Translated literally as 'no problem,' *may-oh wenti* was always a worrying remark. With the laid back attitude of the Tibetans, instead of meaning; 'no problem, we can solve this one' *may-oh wenti* usually meant; 'no problem – the evening will be a disaster.'

Chef was determined that there would be no problems with the food that evening. He wanted to show that his side of the F&B Department could run just as well now that Gunter had left. He was particularly keen on giving a good impression for the General Manager, as he was relying on a recommendation for a transfer to a less stressful part of Asia.

I passed Chef's office on my way back from the Morning Meeting, and caught a glimpse of him giving instructions to his staff. It was a surreal scene: 30 Chinese and Tibetans dressed in kitchen whites packed in a tiny office, staring with expressionless faces at a peculiar European flailing his arms about in the air. Although his Chinese vocabulary did not extend far beyond the essential phrases of 'may-oh', 'putchidao' and 'may-oh wenti', he had an exceptionally high level of understanding with his staff. He had been without an interpreter for over a year and had developed a form of kitchen sign-language with which he could communicate perfectly with both Tu Dian and the cooks.

With the index and middle finger of his right hand he made jumping motions across the table, and with his left hand he made a series of mock karate chops over his knuckles. He nibbled his right index finger and made an imitation of steam blowing out of his ears. There was much discussion and nodding amongst the cooks who smiled in recognition of the dish – Sichuan frogs legs with chilli peppers.

The other VIP dish was harder to mime, but as it was always requested at the top banquets it was an easy one to guess. Chef pulled his head back and hunched up his shoulders to hide his neck. He brought up his hands, palms outermost, to the top level of his shoulders and waved his fingers at his cooks. This confirmed what they had expected – turtle would be served at the National Day banquet. Tu Dian rushed off into town with the market list. Dorje, the hotel driver, was waiting for him in one of the Holiday Inn Landcruisers so there was no doubt that it would be the fastest shopping trip possible.

The General Manager spent the afternoon putting the restaurant staff through their paces. The banquet would be in the form of a self-service buffet; the simplest Food & Beverage formula, where it would be difficult to make mistakes.

The idea of waitress service for a banquet of over 200 people had been abandoned. Even in the small coffee shop the *a la carte* service was a disaster. It was hardly the fault of the waitresses; they had never seen any world other than their own isolated land of Tibet and had no idea how a Western restaurant should work.

The most basic rules of restaurant service were totally alien concepts to them. No matter how many times it was explained that the starter should be delivered *before* the main course they invariably made the guests wait half an hour and then brought starter, main course and dessert in every conceivable order except for the correct one. All the permutations and combinations of dishes were tried out: main course first, soup next, dessert last; all at the same time; none at all; only the drinks and not the food; the starter for the adjacent table with a dessert that had never been ordered. The waitresses considered it to be of little importance, as long as the guest received his food he should be happy. Pointing out a mistake to the waitress was inadvisable whilst the meal was still in progress. This would lead to everything being grabbed from the table and rushed back into the kitchen. The same food would come out ten minutes later (and ten minutes cooler) and the waitress would try to remember who had been eating from which plate. It was very complicated.

A straightforward buffet for the National Day banquet was the safest bet for a trouble-free evening. All that the waitresses had to do was to set the tables, serve drinks, and clear the tables afterwards. It seemed simple enough.

I was called into the banquet room late in the afternoon to check on the English lettering for a 40 feet long, five feet wide banner which was being hoisted above the head table. The giant white letters of 'NATIONALDAYRECETPION' beamed out across the room, pinned onto a background of bright red cloth. The only minor problem was that all the letters ran in a continuous line. There was some dismay when I asked for the words to be separated and for the spelling to be corrected. Chinese and Tibetan characters, presumably saying the same message, had already been glued across the top of the banner and there was no space left to split the lettering onto different lines. We eventually settled for the solution of squashing the letters closer together so that there was enough space to distinguish the individual words.

Beneath the banner, the long top table was being set for 20 Lhasa VIP's. Charlie had been persuaded to part with the only white table cloths to be found in Lhasa on condition that he personally supervised the method of securing them to the table – an intricate valance of blue, red and gold brocade edged with red silk, hung around the front of the table. The hotel's two silver candlesticks decorated with spirals of gilded dragons stood in the centre, between the silver place settings for the Vice Governor of Tibet, the Consul General of Nepal and the head of the Foreign Affairs Office. The top table was fit for a king.

By a quarter to seven, the General Manager could take five minutes to relax, confident that after spending the entire afternoon showing the waitresses how to clear tables and serve drinks, they would make a star performance.

Tu Dian had found all the ingredients in the market and Chef and his team had prepared a mouth-watering buffet. At least *mouth-watering* if, like the VIP guests, you take a fancy to lightly poached turtle in its own broth, tiny frogs legs that blow you away and Chinese hacked chicken, chopped into portions guaranteed to contain a greater percentage of minute bone splinters than edible meat. Fortunately the banquet menu contained a few Western favourites; tenderised yak steaks, pork chops and mashed potato and a tasty dish of beef slices with green peppers.

Chef had even been able to find his best watermelon engraver in the staff quarters and had set him to work on a display for the buffet table. Minute sections of the dark green outer skin of the watermelons were carved away with the point of a kitchen knife, forming contrasting patterns with the paler green inside. Delicate pictures of cranes and Chinese ladies now turned the humble melons into temporary works of art.

The General Manager made his last inspection of the banquet room at five to seven. He stopped at the centre piece of the buffet: an enormous watermelon depicting rural scenes from mainland China. His eyes screwed into focus on a moving black cloud that hovered above melon. His gaze followed into the centre of the room and back to the buffet table.

'*Flies*!' he screamed out. 'Where is Housekeeping? Where is Chef? Why do I have flies at the most important banquet of the year?!'

The waitresses disappeared and the cooks behind the buffet table made themselves busy. Derek the Chief Engineer arrived.

'Why are there no fly screens on the windows in this room?' the General Manager bellowed at him. There was no table to thump as he was standing up.

'Well, I, err. You see the fly screens needed repair and my men have been very busy and well, we thought the banquet was tomorrow and err . . .'

'No. Don't answer me. Get me Housekeeping! Get me the spray!'

Charlie came puffing and panting into the banquet room with a box of aerosol cans. Chef rushed his food display back into the kitchen as the General Manager tore the wrapping from the first can.

'If you want something done around here, who has to do it?' he muttered to himself as he fumbled with the cans in the box. Taking one can in each hand, he held his arms aloft and with his forefingers tightly on the spray buttons, marched down the gangways between the tables, showering the contents of the cans into the room.

The hosts for the evening, the Foreign Affairs Office of Tibet, arrived just as the last cans had been emptied. A cloud of insecticide hung across the room and the waitresses held napkins to their faces in an attempt to avoid inhaling the sickly spray.

'A very beautiful room,' the chief of the Foreign Affairs Office remarked to the General Manager through Mrs Chen, the official interpreter, 'and a very pleasant scent you have made in the room for us tonight.'

'Yes, especially for you,' the General Manager bowed graciously in reply.

The Chief of the Foreign Affairs Office thanked him profusely and set about forming a line of FAO personnel by the door to welcome the banquet guests. Arriving military commanders and Party chiefs were shown to their respective places along the head table. This always took some time as if you are invited to sit at the head table, it is usual etiquette to feign; 'Oh no, surely not *me* sitting at the head table!' and to insist on first taking a place at one of the normal round tables where the common masses, or proletariat, would be sitting. Only after several more pleadings from the hosts do you then proceed to the head table, still shaking your head in disbelief at the great honour bestowed upon you, and making loud protests that you are not worthy.

The General Manager was dragged from behind the buffet table where he had been inspecting the cooks' uniforms, and forced by the Foreign Affairs Office to sit at a position of honour towards one end of the head table. It was no feigning when he pleaded not to sit there but despite his protestations that he had to oversee the banquet, the hosts made it very clear that as head of the international hotel in town, he was to take a seat at the VIP table.

For the minor dignitaries and the other foreign residents, seating had been arranged by the Foreign Affairs Office at round tables. Each table was reserved for a particular *work unit*, which is the comradely phrase used by the Chinese to describe any entity which provides employment. Table six, where I was sitting with the expatriates from the hotel work unit, was in the furthest corner of the room, pressed tight into the right-angle formed by the wall and the line of windows behind the head table. A loudspeaker stood as high as my chair, just behind me in the angle of the corner. I should have thought ahead to what this would mean but at the time I was too busy being introduced to our hosts to realise the significance of this unfortunate seating position.

At our table was one of the Deputy Directors of the Foreign Affairs Office, his translator, and several people whose jobs the translator couldn't translate. The translator, a young girl in her early twenties with a Tibetan mother and a Han-Chinese father, had recently returned from the Foreign Affairs School in Beijing, where she had been taught 'diplomatic English'. This is a clever type of language which involves talking constantly to diplomats without telling them anything at all.

The National Day banquet was her first official function and as a Deputy Director of the Foreign Affairs Office was sitting at our table, she was especially anxious to ensure that all the foreigners at table six were having a good time. She smiled nervously at everyone.

'Please enjoy yourselves. Help yourself. Please enjoy yourselves,' she repeated incessantly, with the frequency of worn-out vinyl.

Spilling over one of the chairs at our table was a rotund Tibetan who I had not met before. He wore a Western suit with an assortment of stains down the front, an unbuttoned shirt and a wrongly knotted polyester tie. He looked most uncomfortable. He sat silent, scowling through most of the party but his whole face lit up whenever anyone spoke to him. Our translator introduced him as a 'living Buddha' and head of the Tibetan Buddhist Association. I suppose that being a living Buddha himself, he would be the right person for the job. He did once break a long silence in conversation around the table by proposing a toast to everyone for their hard work. He knocked back a glass of Lasa Beer and apart from a further statement that the hotel should have more Tibetan decoration, he remained more or less silent to the very end. He was by the far the most interesting person at our table and I wished that I spoke Tibetan, so that I could have learnt more from him, rather than just exchanging pleasantries through the stilted words of our jittery 'please enjoy yourselves' translator.

Sitting at table eight were the Germans from the Lhasa Leather Factory. Chancellor Kohl had promised German support for a Tibetan project during his visit to Lhasa in 1987, and this unlikely business enterprise was the result. Three German technicians and their wives battled against the odds to produce high quality leather products from Tibetan yak skins. It was an uphill struggle. Most of their work went into producing shoes and jackets for local use but a small outlet in the hotel provided some foreign exchange from selling yak skin trinkets to eager tourists. They had lived for a while in the hotel, before their own accommodation had been built at the leather factory on the outskirts of the city near the new army barracks.

Closer to the hotel were the expatriates of the two Lhasa-based charity projects or 'NGO's' (Non Governmental Organisations) as they like to be called. Save the Children Fund from Britain and Médecins Sans Frontières from Belgium, maintained highly active offices near the city centre. The numbers of foreigners working there varied according to project needs, but usually consisted of a small community of between five and ten staff from Britain, Holland, Belgium and France. The Swiss Red Cross was the only other NGO based in Tibet but their headquarters were in Shigatse, some 200 miles to the west. Unbelievable as it seemed to some of the hotel expatriates, who considered that there could be no town on earth more primitive than Lhasa, the Swiss couple stationed in Shigatse regularly came on trips to Lhasa to see the big city of bright lights and shops.

Overworked and underfunded, the three NGO's were stretched to the limits to push ahead with their Tibetan projects. Village schools were built, TB inoculations given out by the bucketful, local doctors were trained and wells were sunk in waterless villages. It was a rare example of aid organisations working together in providing meaningful help to the local population.

It was a stark contrast to the aid effort in neighbouring Nepal, from where stories regularly drifted up about the immense bungling of foreign aid projects. The entire economy of Nepal depends on overseas aid and the opportunities for corruption and mismanagement on a large scale are enormous.

We occasionally saw the effects of foreign do-gooder organisations in Tibet, who would sail through, handing out wads of money and Toyota Landcruisers to the first who asked. The only effect this had on the local population was that certain minor officials suddenly had enormous amounts of spending money and some very nice cars to go shopping with.

The expatriates of the NGO's in Tibet were frequently in the hotel, meeting visiting diplomats who were looking for suitable causes to give foreign aid to. They looked forward to the charade of the National Day celebrations about as much as we did.

The only foreigners who really enjoyed the banquet were the English teachers. Six Americans lived downtown in the harshest conditions of any foreigners in Tibet, teaching English for practically no salary except for meagre pocket money and biannual airfares to Hong Kong.

They were a peculiar mix of people. Some were genuine teachers with a taste for adventure but others had ulterior motives. It did not take long to distinguish the real ones from the fakes: their uniforms gave it away. You know those people who knock on your door and ask you if you've read Revelations recently? Have you ever wondered what they wear when they don't have suits and briefcases? Well the answer is dungarees and lumberjack shirts. Some of the so-called teachers had entire wardrobes of dungarees and lumberjack shirts, sported suspiciously sensible hair cuts and smiled intensely at everyone in sight. A real give away.

At the table nearest the door was a group of foreigners who I was sure that I had not seen in Lhasa before. It would have been hard to miss them. They wore a selection of dark purple corduroy jackets with flapping lapels over butterfly collars on nylon shirts. Flared drip-dry trousers of the non-crease variety draped over dirty training shoes. Their flat hair styles, sticking to the sides of their faces over long side burns, gave telltale signs that they used the same shampoo as Heather and with the same frequency. But large bushy moustaches and round European eyes, ended the similarity. I asked our translator who they were. 'Please enjoy yourselves. We warmly welcome you,' she twitched at me for an answer.

I found out later, from Harry (who had also made enquiries), that they were six Romanians who had set up a beer factory in Lhasa, as an overseas aid project of the Romanian government. They were living on the factory site, beneath Sera monastery, and were about to return to Romania, having just completed the installation of the bottling plant. Green 70 cl beer bottles were imported from China, together with the hops and the machinery. Tibet provided most of the labour force and the water. It was another great leap forward in the modernisation of Tibet, this time with help from their modern Romanian comrades.

The words 'Lasa Beer' appeared on the label, with writing in Tibetan and Chinese, surrounded by two jumping fish – an auspicious Tibetan symbol. This led to many a suggestion about the contents but despite the flavour varying from bottle to bottle, the beer sold well, particularly to Khampas. It was predominantly watery, sometimes with a hint of a noxious chemical, perhaps a detergent concentrate, and occasionally it was so strong that it knocked you off the kebab stand. We tended to drink it with the excuse that we were supporting the local economy, and all the expatriates at table six requested a Lasa Beer from the waitress who came to take our drinks order.

Suddenly, there was an ear-piercing screech in the banquet room. The loudspeaker behind my chair had leapt off the floor as Mrs Chen shrieked into her microphone. We all turned to Derek, the Chief Engineer. He always needed a push to get him into action and had a store of unimaginative excuses for not being able to do things.

'There's nothing wrong with it.' he shouted across the table. As Derek was hard of hearing from working most of life in ships' boiler rooms it was no surprise that he found the noise level bearable. However, the rest of us had no intention of spending the evening sitting inches away from the interpreter's amplified squawks, so he reluctantly agreed to adjust the volume. Derek waved to one of his Engineering Department staff who was standing by the doorway in the opposite corner of the room. He pointed to the loudspeaker and made a turning motion with his hand to indicate that the volume needed to be lowered. The man in the Engineering Department uniform waved back to Derek, nodded, and ran out of the door.

Derek, who liked to tell anyone who had the misfortune to be stuck in one of his monologue conversations, that all of his staff understood him perfectly, was somewhat put out by this. 'He must have gone to get something,' he stammered.

The volume remained at full blast.

Mrs Chen, a Han-Chinese lady from the Foreign Affairs Office who they wheeled out every year for the occasion, continued her preamble to the top table introductions, unaware of the decibel level at table six. She used the standard Chinglish phrases for official parties: 'We warmly welcome all our guests. We warmly welcome you to enjoy yourselves. We warmly welcome you to celebrate.'

Her peculiar pronunciation and an unfortunate lisp, led to the 'Tibet Autonomous Region of China' becoming the 'Tibet *Anonymous* Region of China,' and this curious turn of speech, interspersed with 'we warmly welcome you to your comings' was well received by the foreigners.

Derek was relieved when the engineer he had sent to turn the volume down reappeared by our table. 'You see,' he shouted, 'I don't need to speak Chinese, these people understand me.'

The man from the Engineering Department handed him a microphone, a length of electrical cable and a spare plug socket. 'No, no, that's not what I wanted. Noise. Down. Turn it down!' He pointed to the loudspeaker. A waitress approached our table, straining under the weight of a tray fully laden with Lasa Beer bottles. Seeing the commotion where Derek was sitting she carefully made her way around the back of the table, concentrating on keeping the tray steady just as the General Manager had shown her. Stepping forward to lower the tray onto the table, her left foot came down squarely on the electrical cable that led to the loudspeaker. A noise similar to the crackle of gun-fire shot from the sound system as the plug snapped out of its socket and our loudspeaker was silenced.

It was too late for Derek to stop the words coming out of his mouth. His exclamation of 'TURN IT DOWN!' coincided precisely with the moment of silence created by the unplugging of the loudspeaker and a pause in the introductions from Mrs Chen. All heads, including the Vice Governor's, turned to our table and a mortified Chief Engineer shrank in his chair. The military commanders glanced over their shoulders and the General Manager kept a fixed angry stare at our table.

'Please enjoy yourselves,' our translator continued as if nothing had happened. The living Buddha smiled and the startled waitress poured out Lasa Beers as the head table introductions resumed.

Mrs Chen read out the name of each of the guests at the head table and the VIP stood up to return a polite clap to the applauding crowd. The situation was complicated by the audience not knowing whether to applaud after the Chinese introduction, or after the English introduction. The interpreter didn't know whether to wait for applause and then translate, or translate and then hope the applause would follow. The result was a table-load of embarrassed VIP's who received a constant trickle of feeble applause, rendering it impossible to hear exactly what each of their titles was. Snippets of translation could occasionally be made out over the din: 'The Deputy Chairman of the Standing Committee for Internal Affairs of the Tibet Anonymous Region ... Please warmly welcome the coming of the Vice Chairman of the Political Bureau of the Party of the Tibet Anonymous Region . . .'

When the introductions were over, the speeches began. They were always terrific. A copy in English would be circulated to the foreigners present so that we didn't have to rely on the spoken words of the interpreter to understand the wonderful statements being made. Chinglish, the pidgin English version of Chinese and English combined, is funny enough as a language but Communist Chinglish is an art form in its own right. It is an extraordinary language that ignores negatives, conveniently forgets atrocities and speaks only of good things. Figures, particularly exceeded quotas and increased production percentages, are scattered liberally throughout Communist Chinglish to add a scientific weight to the language, to prove beyond all doubt that it is certainly the truth being told. Mastering this language is even more important than learning Mandarin Chinese for the foreigner who wants to succeed in China. Who would have thought of calling the armed invasion of Tibet the 'peaceful liberation,' or describing the gunning down of innocent Tibetans in the Barkhor as: 'winning great victory against the splittists in the anti-split struggle?'

No one dares to laugh out loud and the Chinese and Tibetans all nod their heads in agreement with what is being said. They do not even listen to the words. The speeches are always the same and as they are not permitted to disagree with what is being said, it is better just to sit there quietly and go along with whatever the speech writers are saying.

The most powerful politician in Tibet, Mr Mao Ru Bai – the Vice Governor – took the stage to deliver the National Day message. Mao Ru Bai was an articulate speaker and had the baby-kissing appearance that would even have made him a successful politician – if voting had been necessary to be in power. His receding hair-line and permanently shining forehead gave him an unusually distinguished appearance compared with his political peers who always looked as if they had just come off the back of a yak. He smiled continually and oozed understanding and compassion, even when uttering harsh words about the *splittists*. He gave short bursts of speech and glancing across at Mrs Chen, twitched his cheekbones while pausing for her to translate.

The start of the speech never altered: 'Cordial greetings to all the workers, peasants, herdsmen, intellectuals, cadres, soldiers and to Tibetans residing abroad.'

In fact, pretty much, 'a big hello to everyone.' The main part of the speech would deal with the great leaps forward against the 'splittists', regardless of how recently the last riots took place, and would highlight all the wonderful changes that had occurred since the Chinese had taken over in Tibet. The Cultural Revolution and the destruction of over 6,000 monasteries was temporarily overlooked. No mention was ever made as to whether new fire extinguishers had been ordered for the police station.

There were also some warnings for Western spectators. The 1991 speech contained this frightening sentence concerning the movements of the Chinese: 'Strong socialist China now erects like a giant in the east of the world.'

Some interesting facts concerning Chinese policies in Tibet were also revealed:

'Since the peaceful liberation, under the correct leadership and kind attention of the central committee and state council [oops, they forgot to mention the Cultural Revolution here] we have scored great victory of democratic reform, and established a new political power – the people's democratic dictatorship.'

The speech following the National Day message is always read by the Nepalese Consul General. He speaks in English, but his Nepalese accent is so strong that little of what he says in intelligible. Luckily the wording of the speech follows the same format as Communist Chinglish, so that the interpreter is able to understand and all the Tibetans and Chinese nod in agreement with whatever it is that he is saying.

The speech runs around the monotonous theme of the good cooperation between the two great countries. It is true that it has been a long time since Kukri-wielding Gurkhas invaded Tibet, even Chinese speech writers would have a hard time describing the Nepalese excursions into Tibet as entirely peaceful and the Nepalese Consul General carefully avoided the subject.

It was after 47 minutes of speeches, with the boredom threshold long surpassed, that the flies started to drop out of the sky. The fly spray had been used in such quantities that not a single *diptera* in the room had a chance of survival. Chef paced up and down his buffet, pinching them out as they landed. The Nepalese Consul General droned on in the background as we watched the first fly crash-land on table six. It had landed on the rim of the living Buddha's glass of Lasa Beer and teetered dangerously from side to side. We watched it in eager anticipation: it was 50:50 whether it would fall into the glass or onto the table.

'Ten yuan the glass,' whispered Harry.

'Ten yuan the table,' Derek replied.

The fly carried on its walk around the rim. Harry tugged the table cloth. With one final rub of its front legs it stood back and dropped straight into the glass. The living Buddha was unperturbed. He pulled it out with his finger and placed it gently on his napkin where it would dry out. The next fly to hit the table, made an impressive spiral nose-dive, landing directly in front of our translator, who pretended to ignore it. But this one was closely followed by an entire squadron of the innocent insects, who bumped noiselessly onto the table in their last seconds of life.

Beyond boredom is that dangerous zone where your eyelids take over control of your body. Regardless of the message from your brain that this is not the right place or time to fall asleep, your eyelids close and your head lolls forwards. You only realise this has happened when you jerk your head back, opening your eyes wide and staring out at the person opposite you. But even the intense embarrassment is not enough to save you from your eyelids taking control again and your head drooping forwards. Several at table six had entered this zone when Mrs Chen shrieked into her microphone to announce that the Nepalese Consul had finished his speech and that we would shortly be warmly welcomed to start the buffet.

The guests of the head table and the tables nearest the door set off first and a queue 30 feet long and three people deep formed across the centre of the room. Unfortunately the person at the head of the queue had not realised that you should start a buffet from one end and then move along it, from the hors d'oeuvres, soups, main course, through to the desserts. Instead, he had walked to the middle of the long buffet table and was now at a loss as to whether to turn left for the main courses, or right for the starters. The rest of the queue had to follow him and soon the congestion at the buffet table became chaotic, with hungry banquet guests going both ways, colliding as they attempted to cross the large queue which now firmly blocked off the middle section.

Our table six translator was still saying 'please help yourselves, please enjoy yourselves, warmly welcome you to enjoy yourselves' and the living Buddha was going through one of his long silent phases, when we were warmly welcomed to enjoy the buffet and asked to join the queue into the melee. The military commanders were already pushing their way back through the line, with plates piled high in triumph as we joined the end of the queue.

There are many deep-rooted misconceptions between Chinese and Westerners but none deeper than the Chinese idea of how to tackle a Western buffet. Some mischievous Westerner has told the Chinese that there are special rules to follow when attending a Western buffet and these rules are now taken to be unbreakable:

1. You are to use *one* plate only. A bowl is optional for soup but only if it can be carried at the same time as the one plate used for the buffet.

2. You are allowed *one* visit only to the buffet table and on no account are you permitted to return.

3. You *must* absolutely stuff yourself but only in accordance with the limitations of rules 1 and 2.

With these false rules firmly implanted in the minds of everyone who attends a Western buffet, the line up at the buffet table becomes a competition to see who can load up his plate highest. As we stood in the queue we watched Mr Pong (from a safe distance) make his way along the buffet table. He was an expert at Western buffets and had broken out of the 'T' formation that was stuck in the middle of the table and moved along to the beginning of the hors d'oeuvres to stock up his plate. First, a few slices of imported cold meats and tomato salad. Next a bowl of turtle broth and a slice of bread balanced on the plate. He made room for a spoon from each of the hot dishes: a scoop of spicy aubergine, a pile of frogs' legs, a dollop of mashed potato, a pork chop, a spoon of hacked chicken splinters, sliced beef with pepper, a yak steak – just enough space for an extra scoop of frogs' legs, some cabbage, a piece of cauliflower and just a bit more room on top of the pile for two croquette potatoes. The dessert was always the trickiest part and showed the experienced Western buffet diner from the beginner. Mr Pong expertly balanced a large slice of sponge cake on top of the flattened peaks of mashed potato and smothered it with a generous helping of yak yoghurt. A black banana was curled around the rim of the plate and, content that he could fit no more on top, he negotiated his way through the crowd back to his table.

Eating from the mountain of food on the plate is interrupted periodically by a very Chinese custom which is as alien to us as buffet dining is to them. It is the custom of *gambay*, which can be translated as 'bottoms up.' Banquet drinking is a serious business and revolves around a particular alcohol called 'Mao Tai'. Every few minutes someone at your table will suddenly blurt out 'Gambay' and everyone at the table has to stop whatever they are doing and drink a small glass of Mao Tai. It is one of the most insidious drinks known to mankind and although they claim that the deceptively colourless liquid is a rice wine, it has a smell and a taste that bears a striking similarity to distilled cow dung – or at least to what you would expect distilled cow dung to taste like. If you hold your breath and swallow the tiny glassful in one go, you are spared the foul taste and only feel the burning sensation as it slowly dissolves your intestinal tract. It is incredibly powerful and can render the most solidly built person incoherently drunk within minutes.

Unfortunately banquet drinking is a matter of honour and no one is allowed to escape. A refusal is a sign of weakness and a loss of face for the work unit. As few can drink much of this toxin without being seriously ill, cheating is rife. A common trick is to keep the Mao Tai in your mouth, pretend to wash it down with a drink of something harmless such as orange juice but when the glass of orange juice is at your lips you discreetly spit the Mao Tai into the orange. This has the disadvantage that your glass of orange fills up over the evening which is a bit of a give away and it also means that you taste the vile liquid while it is in your mouth. The best way of cheating is to fill your Mao Tai glass with water. This is a very common practice and if you are challenged to a *gambay* by someone approaching you with a glass, it is more than likely that they will have filled it up with water before coming over to your table.

Cheating goes to the extent of bribing waitresses to fill personal Mao Tai bottles with water so that the other party guests will see your glass being poured from the bottle and will believe it is the real thing. I once saw an entire table cheat by pouring Sprite into their Mao Tai glasses. They would have got away with it, but the bubbles in the Sprite would not go away and they had to tap the glasses continuously on the table in an effort to dislodge them. Cheating is a risky business and those caught in the act bring disgrace to their unit and must pay the heavy price of drinking at least one full glass of the authenticated liquid.

The real Mao Tai comes from a small village in the south of China and, as with wine from the Champagne district of France, labelling is strictly controlled. There are many fakes and imitations and the Mao Tai connoisseur can apparently tell the difference between the real cow dung distillate and its imitators.

Considering that one bottle of Mao Tai costs twice as much as a worker earns in a week, banquet drinking is also an extremely expensive pastime. Fortunately, none of the individuals have to pay for the excesses, as it is always the work unit that hosts the banquets.

The use of Mao Tai for official banquets had been curtailed by the Beijing government in one of their major austerity drives. It was calculated that if every government banquet were to reduce the amount of Mao Tai drunk, a saving of millions of yuan could be made. But as Lhasa is an Autonomous region, the officials turned a blind eye to the Beijing rules. Judging by the amount of Mao Tai consumed at the National Day banquet, they would soon be turning a blind eye to everything.

Although Westerners find the *gambay* custom extremely difficult to follow, it has been easy for the Tibetans to adapt to this particular whim of the Chinese. According to Tibetan tradition it is very impolite to leave a party without showing the host that you are drunk.

Fortunately, the National Day Banquet does not linger on all night and the *gambays* come to an end as abruptly as they started. Shortly after the last frog's leg has been chewed and the mountain on the plate reduced to a pile of bone and debris spat out onto the table and the floor, the VIP guests thank everyone for a wonderful evening and then make a quick exit. Within a matter of minutes the rest of the room empties. There is no question of staying on with coffee, *petit fours* and liqueurs and no one is asking for any more Mao Tai. Conversation amongst the expatriates is left to how well we cheated with the *gambay's*. 'I had fourteen,' Charlie chuckled, 'only three real ones!' Derek was not so lucky, he had been caught cheating and had been forced to drink the real thing. It was just as well there would be a day off work on National Day.

I made the mistake of crossing the lobby on the way back to my room and was confronted by a group of American guests demanding to see 'someone who spoke god-damned English!' Even though I had cheated with all my Mao Tai *gambays*, an encounter with seething guests was all I needed after the National Day banquet. One of their party had been struck with altitude sickness and they had been trying to call their insurance company in America to fly out a helicopter. Just where they thought a helicopter would come from I didn't have the heart to ask. 'We've been locked up here all day and I've just about had it with you!' blasted one of the group.

It fell into the familiar pattern of complaining guests. They feel stronger in packs and one of the mob eggs the others on.

'Go on Bert, you tell him. Tell him we weren't allowed to the Barkhor today.'

Bert told me that they went to the Barkhor anyway and were sent back by the police.

'Yeah, the police! Tell him about that guy we saw with a machine gun. I mean Christ, what sort of a place do you run here?!'

All their pent up frustrations and petty problems come pouring out in the lobby because at last they have found someone who is wearing a suit and speaks English. The Chinese in Tibet, military on the streets, his office hasn't contacted him, his wife has a headache, he doesn't know if his shares have gone up or down, he should have booked Aspen again, and it is all my fault.

The ring leader of the group pointed his finger at me and with his head tilted slightly to one side and his face wrinkled as if there was a bad smell under his nose, he hissed menacingly:

'I need to make that phone call *right now*.'

6

A Day Off With The Vultures

Telecommunications between Lhasa and the outside world were far from perfect. Each room was equipped with a large orange telephone which sizzled when it was touched. The sizzle stopped when the receiver was picked up but two seconds later, exactly when the receiver would be next to your ear, a piercing screech of feedback would scream down the line causing temporary deafness in one ear. The screech took several seconds to die down to a low buzz and then you could dial the number of the Lhasa hotel operator. When the operator picked up her phone you could give her the number that you wished to call. She would ask a series of questions in a set sequence that had been memorised by heart. A heavy Chinese accent shot the questions out in short staccato bursts which crackled down the line:

> What is your room number?
> What country you want to call?
> What is the number you want to call?
> Who do you want to speak to?
> You wait in your room.
> I call you back.

A reply out of order to any one of the questions and there was no chance of your call being made. If you had answered all the questions in the correct order, the operator would make a call to the Lhasa city telephone operator repeating the message in Tibetan or Chinese.

If the line was not busy, the Lhasa city operator would then call the Beijing operator and give her the same information in Chinese.

The Beijing operator would then call the number that you had requested and place the call back to the Lhasa hotel operator via the Lhasa city operator.

Did you follow that? The telephone operators rarely did. Opportunities for error were endless and it was exceptional if a line was ever connected correctly. The line from Tibet to Beijing was constantly busy and unforgiving guests ruthlessly harassed the operators into making impossible calls to countries that the operators didn't even know existed. It was a lonely and thankless job. They spent day and night shifts in a cold room, surrounded by nothing but reams of interconnecting wires, flashing lights and junction boxes. They were housed in a separate block of concrete away from the main hotel buildings and only saw the interior of the hotel when they were summoned in for a reprimand. Between calls they would sleep, be chatted up by the security guards and slurp from their jam jars of tea.

The Lhasa city operators were far worse and seemed to spend most of the daytime and certainly all of the time after 9 pm asleep. Beijing operators were generally quite efficient but it was already very doubtful that your call would get that far.

The pack of angry guests who had cornered me in the lobby had been waiting for their call to the insurance company for over eight hours. Their ring leader glared at me, his lips curling downwards and his eyes narrowing. His skin grew pale, highlighting the little lumpy bit on his nose. He had not been particularly impressed with my detailed description of the workings of the Lhasa telephone system. One of his complaints was that no one at the reception desk could tell him the hotel fax number. I informed him that this was probably due to the fact that there were no fax machines in Tibet.

'No fax?!' the ugly guest shouted at me in disbelief.

I might as well have told him that a herd of flying yaks was coming in to land behind him, waiting to whisk his message away. 'That's impossible!' he blurted out at me.

It is surprising how often it is the tourist who wants to live in the quaint old Tibet where time has stood still, who also wants to be able to fax his office immediately.

'Let me get this straight. You don't have a fax.'

'No.'

'There is no other fax in Lhasa.'

'No.'

'The phones don't work.'

'Not terribly well.'

'There are no other phones in Lhasa better than here.'

'No.'

'You can't get me a helicopter.'

'No.'

Even the most stubborn guest gets the message in the end and the irate American finally lifted his arms up in the air, asking for help from the heavens. As if in answer to both his wishes, and mine, a man in a white coat rushed across the lobby towards us. It was Dr Grubby, the hotel doctor. I was hoping he would manacle the guest and drag him away, but unfortunately he just came to announce the good news that the guest's wife only had the usual first-day-at-high-altitude headache. There was no need for panic, calls to insurance companies or helicopters.

Dr Grubby was an affectionate man with a warm smile and an excellent knowledge of altitude sickness but sadly his appearance did nothing to convince foreigners of his medical abilities. He spoke a smattering of English which is why the People's Number One Hospital had assigned him to run their clinic in the hotel. Although he was a fine doctor, personal hygiene was not one of his strong points. Unintentionally, this worked to his advantage; his permanent patchy stubble and creased white coat with nauseating stains frightened most guests into staying healthy. His success rate, in so far as it could be measured, was remarkably high as very few patients ever ventured into his clinic for a second time.

Dr Grubby's advice to the angry Americans was to return to their rooms and try out the hotel's oxygen service. The guests backed away, staring at Dr Grubby in wonder.

'It's alright,' I reassured them, 'this is the doctor from the People's Number One Hospital. He is the top high altitude specialist in Lhasa. He is very good. Really.'

They didn't reply but turned down the corridor that led away from the lobby and ran off in the direction of their rooms. 'Slowly!' Dr Grubby called out after them, 'Don't strain at high altitudes. Bad for the heart!'

He shrugged, foreigners were very strange people to deal with.

It was one of the most peculiar claims to fame of the hotel – no fax, no touch dial telephone – but nearly every room had a private supply of piped-in oxygen. A branch pipe from the hotel's main supply arrived in each of the superior rooms beneath the bedside table. The gaseous mixture of oxygen-enriched air, bubbled through the metal pipe into a small glass bottle of water, and when a tap on the bottle was turned, the mixture carried on through a green rubber pipe and out into the room. A slight dose of oxygen in the room had little effect, so the guest, or 'patient' as Dr Grubby referred to all hotel guests, would have to hold the green rubber pipe up to the nose to benefit from the oxygenated air bubbling out of it.

For the rooms without mains oxygen supply, an oxygen pillow could be ordered. This consisted of a canvas bag, similar to a small inflatable mattress, which was filled with oxygen from a canister in the Housekeeping department. A rubber tube sticking out of the canvas bag was crudely tied in a knot to maintain the pressure on the bag and the knot could be untied when oxygen was required. Although some guests treated the oxygen as if it was pure, clearly this was not the case, otherwise the hotel would have been blown sky high when the first guest, or patient, lit a match. We often though of trying to produce a richer oxygen mixture and giving it a go.

It was the Japanese and Taiwanese groups who took their oxygen particularly seriously. For some completely unknown reason, these guests suffered from the highest 'drop factor.'

Harry and I calculated the drop factor on how many guests of a group checking-in one afternoon would not make it to the lobby the next morning for the first excursion of their tour. Bets would be placed in the evening after studying form at the group buffet and the final drop factor would be revealed at half past nine the following morning, when the guests gathered in the lobby to await their local guide and tour bus. The drop factor for Japanese and Taiwanese groups could be as high as 20 percent but as there is no known correlation between age or fitness and altitude sickness it was impossible to predict an accurate figure.

Japanese and Taiwanese guests are generally more aware of the health hazard at high altitude and there is a theory that the very action of worrying about high altitude sickness is enough to bring on the first signs: a severe headache and nausea. It is possible that these symptoms are entirely self-inflicted. The paranoia is taken so far that some Japanese groups even arrived with special wrist straps, that monitor oxygen levels in the blood stream, so that it could be seen which group members would drop first.

It was when a party of 30 Taiwanese guests appeared in the lobby each in a synthetic scarlet track-suit, topped with a fluorescent yellow baseball cap and carrying personal oxygen bags with the tubes taped up their nostrils that I decided I had to get out for a day. Nothing to do with the altitude but staying in the hotel for long periods was not conducive to mental stability.

The only real escape after the excitement of the Barkhor and the great monasteries of Lhasa was the lure of the surrounding mountains. I had survived the depths of boredom at the

National Day banquet by gazing out of the window at a conical rock formation and planning imaginary routes to the summit. The peak was on the south side of the Kyi Chu, or from where I was sitting, just to the left of the Vice-Governor's head, above a cluster of aerial masts on the staff quarters. I had found that I was not alone in my longing for escape into the mountains. Mark Waite, the quintessential Englishman who ran the Save the Children Fund in Tibet, had also been warmly welcomed to attend the National Day banquet and between cheating at gambays we had arranged for an assault on what, for lack of a better name, we termed 'the big one.'

The only day it could be tackled was on a Sunday. Every other day of the week was a full day of work and even Sundays were not always sacred. Heather calculated a duty roster at the beginning of each month, when she would chart evening and weekend duties for all the hotel expatriates. A Sunday towards the beginning of November was set aside: Heather promised not to put me on duty for that day, and Mark gave himself permission to take a day off from saving children.

Very early on a cool Sunday morning, while the guests slumbered in their beds, we met by the north gate of the hotel. The air was decidedly crisp and our breath left small vapour trails across the hotel car park. The giant green sign of Holiday Inn had been silenced for the night and none of the city street lights showed any signs of working. There was still a glow around us, not enough to light the hotel forecourt, but strong enough to lift our eyes upwards until we were craning our heads back like Chef doing a turtle impression. Diamonds on blue velvet pierced the night sky . . . thousands, millions, billions of them, twinkling away as if there was no tomorrow. The Great Bear, the Seven Sisters, Orion; the constellations I remembered from home, shone brilliantly all around us. The Milky Way bellowed across the sky ceiling in great clouds of stars, so close that you could reach up and touch it.

Mark had arranged for Dasang, a Tibetan driver who had use of a Beijing jeep, to meet us at 4:30 am at the north gate but at 4:45am there was still no one to be seen. The hotel security guards slept silently in the sentry box and even the pack of dogs in the hotel grounds had not yet woken. As we turned the corner to the front entrance of the hotel, we came face to face with three Japanese guests standing in the forecourt with their heads pivoted skywards. At first I assumed this was some kind of altitude acclimatisation technique – perhaps they had inserted the tubes too far.

They talked excitedly and pointed across the heavens, stabbing the sky with their mittened hands. I recognised them as the three Japanese scientists who had checked-in on Saturday afternoon. Harry had bet that none of the three would have made it to the lobby by breakfast time but he had underestimated the staying factor of Japanese with a mission. They were preparing for their journey to Yambajing, some 90 miles north of Lhasa, where they would be housed in one of the most gruesome government guest houses on the Tibetan plateau. Their mission was to set up what the Chinese called 'an ultra-high energy cosmic ray observing station.' It was to be the highest cosmic ray observing station in the northern hemisphere, with the advantage over their sea-level colleagues of having 13,000 feet less atmospheric dust to penetrate before being in touch with the heavens.

They returned to the warmth of the lobby and headed for the breakfast room. Mark and I followed them to the lobby, where we could wait in the warmth for our driver to arrive. At least I had expected the lobby to be warmer than the hotel car park but for the first time I experienced the curious Lhasa phenomena that the temperature inside the hotel lobby was even cooler than the temperature outside. The night receptionist stood huddled behind the reception desk wearing a purple anorak and a woolly hat. I asked him why it was so cold.

'No heating,' he beamed at me in a Tibetan smile.

The first set of tour guests of the morning shuffled across the lobby in search of the breakfast room. The buffet breakfast was served from 5am onwards so that guests could eat before leaving for the early CAAC flight and could avoid the horrors of the CAAC lunch-boxes given out on the plane. They saw the receptionist and walked over to him to complain about the cold.

'No heating,' he beamed back at them, 'Yes, really, no heating, it is true,' he continued.

I was about to step in when I heard a low rumble in the distance and the splutter of a cold engine approaching the hotel car park. The pack of dogs that had been curled up asleep between the revolving doors, started growling and the security guard at the hotel entrance woke from his slumber. A Beijing jeep with one headlight swung into the hotel forecourt.

'Dasang-la,' Mark called out, 'he is our ride to the mountain.'

I left the grumbling guests in the lobby to the cheerful explanations of the night receptionist, and climbed aboard the Beijing jeep. Dasang greeted us with the Tibetan smile which is forthcoming whatever the time of day and no matter how low the temperature may be. His face was the typical rugged face of the Tibetans, shaped by the severe conditions of scorching sun and freezing nights. The deep creases in his forehead folded even deeper as he questioned whether we really wanted to go to a mountain at five o'clock in the morning. He had found it hard to understand why these strange Westerners should want to do such a thing, but Mark assured him he would be paid well and that was reason enough for him to rise at this ungodly hour and bring out his work unit's Beijing jeep on his one day of rest.

I had thought Toyota Landcruisers were rough enough on the Lhasa roads but they were the height of luxury compared with the rattle of a Beijing jeep. Known by the NGO's as 'boneshakers', Beijing jeeps have a remarkable lack of suspension which is all the more noticeable when they are driven at take-off velocity by Tibetan drivers. We sped through the town of Lhasa, grinding through the gears as we approached the Lhasa bridge, swinging into a westward turn and off the tarmac onto the dirt track along the south side of the Kyi Chu. A quarter moon hung over the horizon revealing the outline of the distant mountains and we relied on this weak moonlight together with Dasang's one head lamp to guide us along the dirt road.

Without warning, the track ended with a 6 foot drop into a hole scooped out by mud diggers. Dasang just managed to see the shadow of the excavated pit by the light of his head light and skidded to an impressive halt on the brink of the crater. We didn't recognise the Tibetan words he used but the meaning was clear enough. By day, mud diggers plundered the river banks, carting away barrow loads of mud to shape and dry into adobe bricks for building walls and houses. The last set of over enthusiastic mud-diggers had dug straight through the main road.

Dasang wound his way between a minefield of craters and axle-scraping stream beds, before he eventually found a track that led us back up the river bank and straight towards a military camp. Mark and I exchanged glances. The National Day alert had passed without incident, but foreigners were not exactly encouraged to go prying inside military camps. Security was still a top priority of the Chinese and two foreigners found in a secret military instillation before dawn would have a lot of explaining to do. Dasang continued straight through the gate without stopping. Two armed guards, standing to attention on sentry posts, saluted as we passed. Our Beijing jeep was exactly the same make and model as those used by the military, however, a glance at the number plate would have shown that we were in a civilian car.

Dasang told us in sign language that he knew there was an exit through the far end of the camp. We drove on past bleary-eyed soldiers who stood around the entrance to their single-story barrack huts. Some stood shivering with enamel wash bowls, while others bent over standpipes with foaming toothbrushes. Mark and I held our heads back in the dark shadows of the jeep as Dasang swung into the main courtyard and his one head lamp panned across a long row of howitzers. A thought crossed our minds that the only fate worse than being caught in the middle of a Chinese military camp before dawn, would be to find ourselves in the middle of Chinese live ammunition howitzer manoeuvres on the mountain-side just after dawn. We peered out of holes in the hood of the jeep: the mounted guns were well wrapped up for the cool weather and looked like they were going to stay that way for some time. As we neared the camp exit a group of young Chinese soldiers approached the jeep. Mark and I sat in silence. Dasang kept his speed up and as we passed through the gates the soldiers stood to attention and saluted.

With the mud-diggers' craters and the military behind us, we could at last relax as much as the Beijing jeep's suspension allowed us to, for the drive on to the Tibetan village of Lu. Mark had calculated that we should start the trek from the village of Tsugar, which lay somewhere to the south of Lu, away from the river. All we needed to do was turn left when we arrived at the cluster of huts that formed the village of Lu. Dasang tried several left turns but all ended in cul de sacs, in a maze of low stone and mud walls. Heaps of dried yak dung stacked in herring bone patterns lined the tops of the walls and the roofs of the squat houses were piled high with winter fodder (gathered from the recent harvest).

Cockerels crowed in the pre-dawn, aware that night was drawing to a close. At the third dead end, surrounded by pigs and chickens, Dasang knocked on the door of a cowshed to ask for directions. Although the village cockerels were crowing, no one in the village seemed particularly anxious to wake up and it took Dasang some time before finding a friendly villager who pointed the way to Tsugar – where Mark and I would start our trek. Dasang squeezed his Beijing jeep between the whitewashed walls of two cowsheds and we drove uphill at a gravity-defying angle towards Tsugar until he admitted that the jeep would go no further. We arranged that he would return for us to the same spot in thirteen and a half hours time at 7pm.

The cockerels may have known that day was around the corner but there was no sign of it in the night sky. The quarter moon had dipped over the horizon and we were left with the light from the stars and two pocket torches to guide us on the first part of the ascent.

We stumbled across the pebbles of a stream bed and found a small track leading up the main gully. Mark had planned the route while driving along the Lu road on trips for SCF and had estimated that we needed to follow the gully to the south, turn up the third grassy knoll to the right, arrive at a hanging valley high between the peaks and that our goal – the big one – would be at the end of the hanging valley. Simple.

Despite our determined paces and strong step, we soon lost the track – a habit which was to be a hallmark of all our expeditions together and instead followed the stream, which he estimated would lead us up towards the hanging valley. In the dark it was hard to make out exactly where we were going and when, at long last, we arrived at the foot of a grassy knoll, we were more than happy to start climbing up, away from the deafening noise of the stream. When first light came, at 7:45, we made a discovery. We had started our climb up a grassy knoll too early and were nowhere near the mountain where we had expected to be.

We should have been directly beneath the hanging valley but instead we faced a craggy mountain-side of rock outcrops and boulders, half a mile to the east. Neither of us wanted to waste the hard-earned height which we had gained. We would just have to approach the hanging valley by traversing the boulder scree. Walking became increasingly difficult as we rose in altitude. Each step higher took its toll.

The start of a walk in the mountains always has the effect of opening up the mind. The triviality of all the petty problems of work is brought to light and mundane worries and concerns are left far behind. The mind is free to ponder matters of greater significance, and many a global problem has been solved by trekkers in the first hour of their day.

By 6:30 am Mark and I had sorted out the problems of Tibet, the country had been peacefully unliberated, the Dalai Lama was back in the Potala Palace, global warming had been stopped and there was never to be war anywhere again. But after several thousand steps higher into the rarefied atmosphere – with previously unknown muscles now strongly objecting to being brought into use – the mind focuses on something that becomes an even greater concern than the destruction of the world: the placement of one foot in front of the other. Approaching 16,000 feet talking is limited to short bursts between heaving lung fulls of air and the mind slips away from conscious thought. A methodical rhythm sets in. Breathe. Step. Breathe. Step. Breathe. Step.

A party of Himalayan Griffon vultures, the largest raptor of the Himalayas, circled above us as we stopped for a rest. We were the intruders on their mountain and they eyed us with curiosity. We took off our rucksacks, and unpacked a thermos of coffee while they quartered the hill-side around us, unafraid of our presence. These vultures are used to humans, as every day they gather at dawn for their human breakfast.

The Tibetans have a method of disposing of their dead which may seem slightly unconventional in Western culture but in reality is a highly practical method: bodies are taken out at dawn, laid out on a large rock, cut up by a specialist butcher into tiny pieces and fed to the vultures. This is known somewhat romantically as a 'sky burial'. The vultures sit around the sky burial rock in a strict pecking order and it is said that they are so well behaved that they will take pieces of meat from the butcher when he calls them forward by name. The vultures in Tibet have as much incentive to go out and search for dead mice on the mountain-sides as the pigeons of Trafalgar Square need to search for wild grain.

There are other burial options in Tibet but they are not so popular. 'Water burials,' following the basic technique of dropping bodies into the river, tend to be only for the poorest and for very young children and fortunately for those living down stream, water burials are not very common. At the top end of the range are cremations but these, due to the scarcity of wood and good burning yak dung, are only reserved for the highest dignitaries and lamas.

On the face of it, the sky burial may seem a bit gruesome, but in fact it is a highly ecologically sound method of disposing of the dead. What better way for the body to be returned to the earth than directly as vulture droppings? In these days when we should be looking after the planet, the Tibetan system of interaction between man and nature certainly wins over our selfish Western method of wasting good land to house the dead in wooden boxes.

More birds are becoming urbanised in the West; kestrels nest in tower blocks, gulls on roof tops but I doubt we will see a new breed of Urban Griffons circling over the undertakers of our cities.

The Himalayan Griffons lost interest in us when they saw that we were still moving. 'You'll have to wait!' we called after them as they soared higher, catching a ride on a thermal to the rugged cliff tops above us. We made the coffee last as long as possible to delay the next part of our route. We had arrived at the point where we could walk no further but had to scramble across the boulders that would lead us to the hanging valley. Giant slabs of rock, cemented together by earth that had settled between them over thousands of years stood in our path. Recharged from the coffee, we shouldered our packs and climbed onto the first slab of granite.

After only five paces we were exhausted again. The altitude meter read 17,000 feet (5150 m) and our breathing told us that our lungs were requiring far more oxygen than when we had started the walk. We had been following the pattern of resting for ten minutes in every hour but the gaps between the rests grew shorter and the rests grew longer. The boulders, which we had estimated would take 30 minutes, took us two hours to cover. Mountain hares were our only companions, darting beneath boulders when they saw us approaching. The

Himalayan Griffons had settled higher up against the rugged cliffs, where they would remain for their afternoon siesta to digest breakfast.

At one o'clock we jumped from the last slab onto the top of the grassy knoll directly beneath the mouth of the hanging valley. A few paces higher, over frozen turf which cracked under foot and we stood at the valley entrance. The sight was breathtaking: A giant with a butter knife had scooped out a perfectly rounded hollow from the top of the mountain range and dragged his knife along to the top of the grassy knoll. Okay, so it could also have been a glacier that made the shape, but in Tibet you are allowed to explain natural phenomena in any manner of supernatural ways.

The sunburnt pasture of the hanging valley, neatly cut in two by the line of a frozen stream, gave out into boulder moraine and then to the jagged rocks of our goal. What we had gazed at longingly from the National Day banquet, as a speck on the horizon over the shoulder of the Vice Governor of Tibet, now stood before us, larger than life, with ice between the boulders glistening in the strong sunshine.

We stopped for a long rest, sitting amongst the dead flower heads of gentians and primulas that must carpet the pasture in vibrant colours in the summer. The city of Lhasa was way below, spread out before us in a living map. Flickering gold in the sunlight revealed the site of the Jokhang temple roofs. Beyond the gold, tiny dots of army trucks moved along the straight line of the road to the military hospital. Just to the right, the freshly white-washed triangle of the cluster of buildings forming Sera monastery stood out against the parched foothills.

The summer rains had long since departed and the Kyi Chu river was drying up to its winter trickle. Swirls of sandbanks and pebble beaches stretched away to the west, past the monument to the unknown road builder and between military camps to the river junction where the Kyi Chu flows into Brahmaputra. The gold and ochre of the Potala palace could be seen rising from the valley floor next to Chagpori, the iron hill, where the Tibetan medical college once stood. The college had been a centre of heavy fighting in the 1959 'uprising of the reactionary upper strata' and has since been replaced by an attractive television mast, bringing the benefits of Chinese television to Tibetan nomads and yaks. Another great leap forward.

We looked out at the mountains across the Lhasa valley and saw that we were now at the same height as the summits of the neighbouring ranges. A sense of achievement came over us. Were we the first people to have climbed to this remote hanging valley? Had any human footsteps trod amongst the gentle grasses which lined this high altitude meadow?

'Tashi Delai!'

Our glory was short lived. As we gazed out at the view a small Tibetan boy shouted down to us from the far end of the hanging valley.

'Tashi Delai!' he called out again. He ran down towards us, followed by a herd of yaks which appeared from among the boulders on *our* mountain. It was hard to say who was more surprised: Mark, myself, the Tibetan boy, or the yaks.

Where had he come from? Where was he going to? He talked to us incessantly, probably asking much the same questions as we had for him, but we understood little of what he said. In our limited Tibetan we told him we were English. He smiled, as if this explained everything, and with a wave he disappeared around the corner of the mountainside as quickly as he had appeared. The yaks followed, nodding their heads as they walked but keeping their eyes fixed on us, until they too were over the edge of the hanging valley and on their way down to the lower pastures. The sound of the yak bells carried on the wind long after they were out of sight. Piles of steaming yak dung were a constant reminder to us that we should not be so vain to have imagined that we had 'discovered' the place. There was really nothing to discover about it. The hanging valley had been there since the time of the last Ice Age and the Tibetans had been grazing yaks on these high pastures long before Westerners even realised that Tibet existed.

As we reached the end of hanging valley, where the pasture gave out into the boulder scree that formed the cone of the mountain peak, our breathing became longer and our conversation stopped altogether. It took one hour and 20 minutes to near the top of the mountain. I could have quit at any time. Every boulder left me gasping for breath and taking a 30 second rest before I could face the next one. I came to terms with the fact that I would never be able to climb Everest. I thought of Greg and Dave and the teams that had been there this climbing season. Had they made it to the top? I had heard news of a fatality in a Japanese group and a mountaineer returning via Lhasa had seen the partially cremated body of a climber at Base Camp. I winced at the thought and looked across at Mark.

He was facing the same stage of breathlessness as me, and the best we could do was to nod to each other to show that we were still hanging on. We were so close that despite our exhaustion we couldn't possibly turn away and with the top just a few yards away a final burst of energy carried us up to the summit. It had taken seven and a half hours. We had reached 18,090 feet (5,480 m).

The view was stunning – the whole of the Lhasa valley spread out to the north and ripples of mountain ranges flowing away to the south. There was not a patch of green left from the summer and the fresh snows of the winter which settle briefly on the hills of the Lhasa valley had not yet arrived. Snow caps shone far in the distance from the mountains over 20,000 feet (6,000m) but around us all was barren rock and sand. We were sitting higher than the summit of Mont Blanc but looking out over a dry and arid landscape.

We placed two white scarves on the lichen-covered cairn and opened our rucksacks for lunch. 'What is a cairn doing here?' Mark asked between deep breaths.

It was another sign that we were far from the first to be standing on this rocky outcrop. Perhaps it had been the site of an important religious ceremony or some bored yak herder had gathered up some stones to pass the time. Whoever it had been, we were honoured to have shared the experience and the view with them, on their mountain.

A Himalayan Griffon drifted effortlessly past us, carried over on a thermal to the valley to the south. We unpacked our lunch, trying not to think of what the vulture had just been eating. There is something about high altitude which has the effect of dampening the appetite and we stared at our table cloth spread with Chinese spam, flattened dry bread rolls and desiccated apples for some time before starting. Even the Swiss chocolate, donated by a generous Kuoni tour leader was not appreciated as much as at lower altitudes.

Thirst was continually on our minds. The deep breathing to pull in lung-fulls of the thin air left us with parched mouths and it was a battle to drink enough to satisfy our needs. We had already emptied a thermos of coffee and two cans on the way up. For lunch we opened our third can of Jan Li Bao, the Chinese fizzy orange and honey drink which the label on the can claims to be good for athletes.

The sun was strong on our faces but the wind was cold and after an hour at the top, we reluctantly bid farewell to the cairn and the flat slab of granite that had formed our lunch table.

The descent was much quicker than the climb up but no easier. We took the route through the hanging valley and over the edge to the grassy knoll which we should have taken on the way up. Once we were on the knoll, we discovered that it was not so much grassy, as we had expected but was covered in dwarf rhododendrons. The bushes were pruned back to the frozen earth, as Tibetans harvest the rhododendrons as a crop. The dried stalks are sold in the Barkhor to pilgrims and city folk who have not had the time or inclination to climb up and get their own. It is used in the incense burners around the

Barkhor and other holy places as a way of sending offerings to the deities.

It was dusk by the time we reached the valley floor, where we were joined by our yak-herding friend, who was singing loudly while he walked his yaks back to the village. He shouted to them between bursts of song and collected suitable stones for his yak-hair sling. If any yak slowed, or made the mistake of rising up the mountain-side instead of following the stream to the bottom, he would spin his sling shot in the air and let loose the stone with such velocity and precision that it would crack on the ground behind the heels of the yak and send the animal galloping down hill to join the rest of the herd. He grinned at us whenever he sent off one of his sling shots, clearly very proud of his startling ability. Just a pity shooting the sling isn't an Olympic event, or the Tibetans would be in contention. He was in a good mood and sang with a full voice. It wasn't often he would have a good tale to tell around the yak-dung fire about two foreigners he found at the top of the mountain: 'Strange people with sickly white skin, they didn't know where they were going and they couldn't even speak properly . . .'

As we reached the spot where we had started thirteen and a half hours earlier, we saw a trail of dust in the distance with a tiny Beijing jeep at the head. Dasang was on his way to collect us. But before he could reach us, the inevitable rent-a-crowd appeared from the village.

No matter where you are in Tibet, as soon as you stop for five minutes, a crowd of small Tibetan boys and girls arrives from nowhere. They sit in a tight group some 20 feet away, watch all that you do, whisper comments to each other and giggle. Word had spread fast that these two strangers who had passed through in the morning were by the side of the track and small children came running from all directions to join the crowd. The boys are generally the braver ones and some called out to us. Whenever we replied they all bowed their heads in shyness and the girls hid behind the boys. Never mind the Chinese television beaming down from the antenna at

Yak-butter tea girl taking time off from churning tea at Pabungka.

Tibetan Opera at the Shoton Festival in Drepung Monastery.

Ceremonial horns above the thangka wall
at Drepung Monastery for the Shoton Festival.

Young monk playing with a friendly beetle
in the summer above Ganden Monastery.

Harvest time at Lake Yamdrok – the 'Turquoise Lake'.

Nun with Dalai Lama photograph
and reincarnated naughty monks.

Khampa lady at celebrations for the enthronement
of the Kharmapa. Tsurpu Monastery.

Kongpo lady spinning large prayer wheel at the Barkhor.

The rickshaw taxi rank outside the Holiday Inn Lhasa.

The Potala Palace in the crisp, clear air of winter.

Young girls collecting yak dung on the slopes towards Kamba La.

The entrance to the Jokhang Temple in the centre of the Barkhor.

The giant thangka unveiled for a few precious hours at dawn on the first day of the Shoton Festival. Drepung Monastery.

Tibetan children with the author beside ruins on the shore of Lake Yamdrok.

The ruins of Lhalu House, formerly one of the 'five beauties' of Lhasa.

Chagpori, we were the evening's entertainment. We pointed to top of the mountain and in sign language told them that we had just been there. They thought this was just the most stupid thing anyone could want to do and they rolled about on the grass in fits of laughter.

Dasang pulled up in his Beijing jeep and the crowd backed off slightly. He lifted out the back seats and from a bumpy holding area over the rear suspension pulled out dish after dish of Tibetan cuisine: rice in yak butter and sugar, flat bread, yak yoghurt, yak meat with boiled potatoes and a thermos of yak butter tea. The hospitality of the Tibetans is legendary, usually unexpected and when it concerns yak butter tea, regrettably unwelcome.

Although some foreigners claim to like yak butter tea they cannot possibly be telling the truth. They say that it is an 'acquired taste' but what deprivations you have to undergo to acquire the taste they do not say. To capture the taste of real yak butter tea, the only way is to follow the steps of preparation as it is made in Tibetan cuisine:

> 1. Boil water in a blackened pan over a yak dung fire. This does not impart any flavour into the water but impregnates your clothes with the smell of charred yak dung and creates the right ambience for a good cup.

> 2. Take a Chinese tea brick and break off half into the water. Stew for far too long.

> 3. Add several tablespoonfuls of salt.

> 4. Add a dash of soda.

> 5. Pour this delightful mixture into a wooden tea churner. Go to the shelf and find the bowl of last year's rancid yak butter. Scoop out a handful and throw into the tea churn. Wipe hands on apron. Churn

the liquid and rancid yak butter until the lumps have melted into the tea.

6. Pour the broth into a Chinese thermos flask and wait for unsuspecting foreigners to arrive.

While the majority of foreigners find the taste particularly nauseating, yak butter tea forms the staple diet of the Tibetans, together with *tsampa* (ground barley). It is an essential part of Tibetan cuisine and any Tibetan will tell you that it is not wise to start to the day without a good bowl full of yak butter tea. It has been claimed that Tibetans can drink up to 50 cups a day.

Such facts matter little when you are confronted with a freshly poured bowl and an eager host who is beaming a beautiful smile and beckoning you to take a drink. Of course once the yak butter tea is poured, it is considered extremely discourteous to leave the bowl untouched. This is where the problem arises, the Tibetans are such an incredibly friendly and hospitable people that offending them must be avoided at all costs. The host is continually hovering around, trying to fill up your bowl, smiling and telling you to drink.

Sipping it is no good, as you keep getting the taste and an automatic refill, so I tried the technique of downing it in one. This is a failure, as despite making your host beam from ear to ear, he then fills up the bowl to the brim again and you are left with the same problem that you started with – except that you already have a belly full of the hideous mixture.

I discovered that the answer is to keep putting the bowl up to your lips while not actually drinking any. This at first confuses the host as he still keeps trying to fill the bowl after every sip. Then, at the end of the party, when getting up to leave, you hold your breath and down the bowl in one. In this way the host is only upset that he could not have been more hospitable, but this is better than leaving him feeling insulted. As an alternative you could always try to like yak butter tea – but that was an area where I had to admit defeat.

The rest of Dasang's feast was delicious. Yak meat is not as bad as it sounds, and while being rather chewy, is full of a flavour similar to good beef. Our appetites had returned and while we disappointed Dasang with our slow drinking of his yak butter tea, he was clearly pleased with our enjoyment of his food.

The children kept their distance, watching how we ate, and cheered when an elderly lady approached us from the village bearing a glass and a kettle of *chang*. Fermented from barley, *chang* is the main party drink of Tibet. Its alcohol content is very low and the first few glasses can be consumed without any noticeable effect, apart from feeling rather ill. The colour is cloudy green and the taste somewhere between cider, mead, a rough yoghurt and Robinson's Barley Water. It was a wonderful return from the mountain-side and our impromptu party went on until night drew in and a chill came over the ground. The children chased our Beijing jeep all the way to the village of Lu and waved until we had disappeared into the military camp.

Dasang and Mark dropped me off at the hotel and I crossed the lobby without being noticed by any guests. It was late and I was looking forward to a good night's sleep. As I pushed the door open to my room, a note on the floor put an end to my thoughts of eight hours of rest.

I set the alarm for 5am.

7

From Missionaries to Mao Tse Tung

'Why don't your staff speak English?' was a question which was asked by menacing guests throughout the day. It became very tiresome and although it was extremely tempting to reply, 'Why don't you speak Tibetan or next time stay at home, you complaining old bat?' this answer was not really acceptable in an international hotel. Instead a polite, 'Oh, I am terribly sorry, we are constantly looking for ways to improve the service to our guests and thank you so much for bringing this matter to our attention' usually surfaced.

The last straw on the pile of 'lack of English' complaints came from an investment banker who had been invited to Tibet to discuss important financial projects with the local government. We had special instructions to provide red carpet treatment and the General Manager escorted him and his wife personally to the best suite in the hotel. The financier was concerned that his wife, who would be sightseeing while he was meeting with government ministers, may suffer from altitude sickness and he looked around the suite for the piped-in oxygen supply. He found the bottle beneath the bedside table and followed the explanations on how to release oxygen into the room, but no oxygen-enriched air bubbled through the water as the instructions had told him it would. He called the operator to ask for someone to check the oxygen. 'Yes,' the operator responded, and he replaced the receiver on the telephone set. He waited patiently in his suite for an engineer to arrive. Fifteen minutes later no one had appeared, his wife was complaining of a headache and he paced the large suite, wondering why the service was so slow and trying to remain calm. He called the operator again to ask for the oxygen. 'Yes, wait a moment, I check for you,' was the abrupt reply.

Another quarter of an hour passed, and still no one had arrived – his wife's headache was worsening and his own temper turned from a steady simmer to boiling point. He snatched up the orange telephone receiver, recoiling when the feedback screeched in his right ear, dialled 2222 for the operator and demanded to know why there was no oxygen. The operator gave him a terse reply, he had been wasting her time: 'Yes, I checked for you, but there is no Mr Oxygen staying in the hotel. No guest of this name.'

There was no escape from the fact that the hotel needed an English teacher. The investment banker made his opinion clear to the General Manager who in turn shouted at anyone who might have been remotely responsible for the VIP's problem. Derek was called to the General Manager's office and reprimanded for the faulty engineering. Charlie was asked why his chambermaids had not found the fault and Harry was interrogated at length as to why he had not checked the equipment personally when assigning the room for the VIP. Only sending a receptionist to check a VIP room was not good enough. I heard the blast from outside the General Manager's office, where I had also been summoned: 'How do you expect a Tibetan who has only lived in filth and squalor, surrounded by inefficiency and incompetence, to check if the room is correct for one of Europe's top bankers?'

Harry was also officially liable for the telephone operators, so was held doubly responsible for the complaint. By the time I was to see the General Manager he had forgotten what he wanted to see me for, and exhausted from shouting and thumping the table, he waved me away again. Harry sent Dr Grubby up to the suite to check if the banker's wife needed anything for her headache and she declared that she had made an immediate recovery. Dr Grubby never had to see a patient twice.

The banker had pinpointed the weakness in the hotel's Blue Dot System of English – it didn't work. The Blue Dot System had been pioneered by the first foreign staff of Holiday Inn Lhasa and it had started as a great success. Each employee was awarded blue dots on his or her name badge to indicate the level of English spoken. Three dots denoted 'good English,' two dots 'some English' and one dot 'a little English.' The vast majority of the staff had no dot, signifying 'no English whatsoever. Nothing. Don't even bother to ask me anything because I will just stare at you.'

The Blue Dot System was very popular with hotel guests as they had an idea of who would be able to reply to their questions and who it would be a waste of time approaching, but unfortunately the staff saw the Blue Dot System as a way of being forced by the management into the unthinkable – *working*. Much better to stand at the back of the reception desk and wave people away because you have no dots, rather than be in the front line and have to work occasionally. Even worse, when a guest did talk to you, it was always something difficult: 'Where can I send a fax? Why is there no heating? Why isn't there a newspaper? Why are my photocopies black? Why are we locked in the hotel today? What do you think of Human Rights in Tibet?'

In the time of Communism, when everyone was equal, it was impossible for the management to give real financial or career incentives to the staff with dots. Career advances could only be made according to who you were or who you knew in the *Party* – it was unheard of to pay someone more for working harder. That would have been extremely unfair. Consequently, the staff scratched off the blue dots as soon as they were awarded and there was a real incentive *not* to learn English.

The complaint of the investment banker had come as a severe embarrassment to the local government and consequently had led to a serious loss of face. It was the right moment for us to push the hotel owners, who happened to be the local government, for permission to employ an English teacher. The usual red tape and refusal to add extra foreigners to the hotel staff was abandoned and authorisation was given immediately. It had been a victory for Party B, and the General Manager sent a telex to Hong Kong requesting that an English teacher be hired as soon as possible.

The answer came sooner than we had expected. A young couple had just asked at the head office if there was a teaching position available at the Holiday Inn Lhasa. According to the recruiters in Hong Kong, they were 'very nice' and 'very keen' and even more important, they would accept a 'very low' salary. This should have sent alarm bells ringing but instead, the two new recruits to the expatriate staff were booked on CAAC flights via Chengdu through to Lhasa.

I listened to the alarm clock from the warmth of my bed, peeping from under the blankets to check that it really was 5am. The note under my door from the General Manager had told me that the English teachers were arriving on Monday morning, and I would have to go to the airport with Dorje to pick them up.

I tried sleeping in the Landcruiser but with Dorje at the wheel there was little chance. I clung on to the door handle and the dashboard in an attempt to stay on the front seat. Dorje drove with dipped headlights but put them on full beam if he thought another truck or car might be coming our way. It was an interesting driving technique practised by all who drove on the Tibetan plateau: blinding oncoming drivers to announce their presence. I thought of explaining that in the West we tend to drive on full beam and dip our head lights when a car approaches, but after considering the sign language involved in the dark at 70 miles an hour, I decided it was better just to keep myself wedged onto the front seat and let Dorje concentrate on the road ahead.

We passed an upturned Beijing jeep at one of the worst bends on the Kyi Chu road. White painted cubes of rock protruding 6 inches above the tarmac are set along the centre of the road around the bend in an attempt to force drivers to keep to the correct side. Clipping one of these stones sends vehicles spinning over into the path of oncoming traffic, bouncing on their roofs and occasionally rolling completely over into the river below. Dorje slowed as we passed the flattened jeep. Four Chinese soldiers' hats, stacked one on top of another next to a pool of blood, stood as the grim evidence of what had happened to the jeep's occupants. There was no one around, whatever had been left of the soldiers had been taken to the nearest military hospital. Dorje shook his head, and put his foot down to speed away from the scene. Carnage on the airport road was nothing unusual and by daybreak the debris of the night's accidents would litter the roadside.

The Lhasa airport was the usual chaos. Toyota Landcruisers, Beijing Jeeps and tour buses vied for poll position in anticipation of the race back to Lhasa. I left the car and strolled down to the runway where the tour guides gathered with their scraps of paper. They huddled together their eyes skywards trying to spot the first of the two 707's which were due in.

'Hello Mr Alec,' said a friendly voice. 'My name is Renchen. How do you like Tibet?'

I had heard of Renchen from the few guests who had been fortunate enough to have him as a tour guide but I had not met him before. Some unfortunate guests paid their thousands of dollars only to be greeted by a newly arrived Chinese recruit. Their knowledge of English was often poor, their knowledge of Tibet even worse and their lack of respect for the culture diabolical.

'Tibet is beautiful,' I told Renchen and he grinned back at me. The crowd stirred, a plane had been spotted and soon the mighty roar of the 707 engines came hurtling down the runway towards us.

I watched the passengers leaving the plane, gasping the fresh, thin air of the Gonggar valley. Families of Tibetans with their bundles, worried Chinese soldiers arriving for tours of duty, small groups of bewildered tourists, and then, there they were: two sets of dungarees and lumberjack shirts bouncing down the steps. The penny dropped. Sensible hair cuts bobbed across the runway in the early morning breeze.

'Hi there. Thanks so much for coming to the airport. It's so wonderful of you!' Nancy introduced herself. 'My, isn't Tibet wonderful! Gee, we just love it and we've only just arrived! We have twenty four suitcases to collect, but this one I took on the plane with me.' Nancy giggled, clutching her precious bag, 'It's our Mr Smiley stickers!'

I shivered. Undercover missionaries had penetrated the capital of Tibet. But it was not the first time that the Tibetans had been confronted with bible-bashing visitors and as history has shown, not even the deepest atheism of the Cultural Revolution could dampen the Tibetans' beliefs.

Some 300 years before Nancy and her husband Bob had bounced down the steps of the CAAC plane, two Jesuit missionaries, Albert D'Orville from Belgium and Johan Grueber from Austria, had walked into the Barkhor with the very same intentions. Travel was somewhat slower and tougher in the mid-1600s; it had taken them three years to walk to Lhasa from China. During the continuation of their journey overland to Rome, D'Orville succumbed to the rigours of seventeenth century travel and went on to meet his maker in India. I often wonder if they were nauseatingly nice people but somehow I imagine D'Orville and Grueber to have been fire-breathing, God-fearing types, and not burdened down with bagfuls of Mr Smiley stickers.

In the eighteenth century Capuchin missionaries arrived on the scene and a rival mission was set up in Lhasa to compete with recently established Jesuits. The Tibetans in general were extremely tolerant of other religions and even today, although there are no Christian churches in Lhasa, a mosque to the east of the Barkhor beckons the Mohammedan traders and settlers from Xinjiang and Qinghai provinces. There has only been the occasional case of foreign missions being burnt down to the ground and the occupants slaughtered and this has generally been restricted to the outskirts of Tibet, where bandits and easily incited peasants roamed the land.

The missionaries in Lhasa were accepted by the Tibetans but the conversion en masse of the Tibetan people was taking longer than the early Jesuits had anticipated. In fact only seven were recorded. Competition between the Jesuits and Capuchins intensified and the Pope had to be called in to decide who should be given conversion rights for Tibet. The Capuchins won, although it made little difference as by 1745 the Chinese persuaded the Tibetans to evict all foreigners from Tibetan soil, under the pretext that if foreigners were allowed into Tibet, their precious Buddhist religion would be destroyed forever. Quite ironic considering what the friendly Chinese later tried to do to Tibetan Buddhism.

The Tibetans were constantly warned by the Chinese about the dangers of foreigners and in contrast to the present day, the Tibetans became fiercely xenophobic. Soldiers patrolled the remote passes and the approaches to Lhasa on the look out for the foreign explorers, eccentrics, missionaries and madmen who attempted all manner of disguises to reach the Holy City.

The British in India found the closure of Tibet particularly infuriating, as by 1860 they had mapped the entire Indian sub-continent and were now expecting to carry on with their divine right to map making beyond the Himalayas and into Tibet. A great blank area on the world map with the word 'unexplored' emblazoned over it was a lure that no adventurous member of the Empire could resist. It was simply inconceivable that by the latter half of the nineteenth century the British did not have an accurate latitude and longitude bearing for Lhasa. Someone had to go there to take measurements. The Russians had been attempting from the north, an American from the east, the French from any direction they could. The British tried from the south but despite many ingenious attempts, no disguise was good enough to allow an Englishman to cross the Tibetan frontier and reach the forbidden city.

The English devised a cunning plan to send in the only alternative: loyal British subjects. Indian pundits were recruited from the southern slopes of the Himalayas and trained in surreptitious map-making techniques. Nineteenth century James Bond gadgets were designed in a fashion that Q would have been proud of. Sextants were concealed in the false bottoms of pilgrims' carrying cases and mercury was hidden in the caps of walking sticks. Even the roll of printed prayers inside prayer wheels was substituted with note paper, which would be used to make jottings of illicit observations.

Codenames were given to each of the pundits for maximum security and training in serious began. The spies learnt to walk in evenly measured paces and to keep record of their steps on fake rosaries using 100 beads instead of the holy number of 108 beads. One bead was counted for every 100 paces and thus the beads of an entire rosary would represent 10,000 paces. By counting every step of the way into and around Tibet the pundit 'AK' mapped out his track of nearly 3,000 miles by recording over five million paces.

Of all the incredible feats performed by these brave and selfless men, the most astonishing story must belong to Kintup, codename 'KP.' If he had dreamt that the spy world was to be a 007 whirlwind of women, romance and excitement in luxury hotels with open expense accounts, he would have been disappointed. He set off for the Tibetan frontier in August 1880, disguised as the servant of a Mongolian lama with the mission to solve the riddle of the Brahmaputra. It was a puzzle that vexed every Englishman in India and caused many a sleepless night for members of the Royal Geographic Society. The great Tsangpo river raced along the northern side of the Himalayas and the even greater Brahmaputra raced in the opposite direction along the southern edge of the Himalayas and out into the Bay of Bengal. But were the two related? Did the Tsangpo turn the corner at the end of the Himalayas and become the Brahmaputra? If it did, where and how? That damned blank area on the map was simply intolerable – the region had to be explored.

The answer to the riddle was expected to come from the spy team of Kintup and the Mongolian lama who would launch 50 marked logs into the Tsangpo river in Tibet every day for ten days. The Brahmaputra on the southern side of the Himalayas would then be checked by British officers to see if the marked logs floated down. Elementary.

Kintup and the lama entered Tibet without any hitches, but the plan went disastrously wrong when Kintup discovered that the lama had given up the idea of map-making, taken all the money for the expedition, disappeared towards Mongolia and sold him as a slave to a ruthless petty official in the remote town of Tongkyuk Dzong. This left Kintup in an awkward position, to say the least. After seven months of forced labour he escaped, only to be captured again by the official's men. The traditional punishment for runaway slaves was amputation or at least a permanent crippling by severing tendons in the legs. However, Kintup was fortunate to be bought off his captors by a kind Tibetan abbot, who treated him well and allowed him temporary release from slavery to make pilgrimages. Over the course of three years Kintup used his pilgrimages to continue with his British secret service orders to solve the Brahmaputra riddle. He cut logs, marked them with the special tags and visited Lhasa to ask a Sikhimese trader to take a message back to the British in India saying on which date he expected to launch the logs. The following year the kind abbot released Kintup for good behaviour from his slavery and he could finally launch his logs into the river. Savage tribes blocked the direct route back to Sikhim and so he returned on foot via Lhasa, arriving home some four years after setting out.

His homecoming was not the glorious welcome he deserved. His mother had died, his note had never arrived, no one had looked for his logs and none of them had ever been recovered, the riddle of the Tsangpo/Brahmaputra had already been solved in his absence and to top it all, no one believed his tale.

It took a further 20 years after Kintup had returned until Westerners would walk in the streets of Lhasa. Many had tried to reach the Holy City but all had been turned back by the xenophobic Tibetans, the Chinese, the bandits or by the forces of nature, which surround the Tibetan plateau. These forces were to prove no obstacle to the British who, determined to protect the Empire in India and to keep the Russians at a safe distance, eventually invaded under the pretext of wishing to sign a treaty on trade. Their entry was not entirely peaceful but anxious not to be seen as an invading force the intrusion was sportingly called an 'expedition.'

Tragically there was heavy fighting on the way, leaving many Tibetans dead and dying. The wounded Tibetans prepared to face death as the British troops swept out over the battlefield after each fight. Treatment of prisoners in Tibet varied from region to region, but it invariably led to a nasty end. Khampas preferred decapitation, while the most feared captors were the *Glak-lo Nagpo* (the 'black savages') of the lower Tsangpo area, who were said to *eat* their prisoners of war. The reaction by the British was somewhat different and totally incomprehensible to the Tibetans. Immediately after every skirmish the invaders rushed around the battlefield picking up all the wounded on stretchers and spent the rest of the day with them in the hospital tent trying to sew them up again and restore them to good health. It made no sense at all. What was the point of shooting someone in the morning and then patching him together in the afternoon?

Colonel Younghusband, who led the expedition, marched his men through *Pargo Kaling*, the western gate of Lhasa on 3 August 1904. The gateway formed a magnificent entry to the city, framed in the centre of a rock curtain joining the two hills of Lhasa; *Mepori* crowned with the Potala and *Chagpori* with the Medical College. Over the stone gateway stood a large *chorten* – a geometric cone containing sacred relics.

The gateway and the *chorten* have long since disappeared – blown apart by the Chinese in their programme of road modernisation. Strings of prayer flags now mark the spot where the gate once stood and an elderly Tibetan with beer bottle bifocals sits cross-legged on the pavement carving the Tibetan characters for 'Om Mani Padme Hom' on slabs of stone. This phrase, roughly translated as 'hail to the jewel in the lotus' is the most popular prayer of Tibetan Buddhism. *Om Mani Padme Hom* is said to 'open heaven and close hell' and is chanted ad nauseam as every utterance gains a further merit point towards the big day when all the brownie points are added up and the decision made as to whether the next rebirth will be up or down.

Younghusband was fascinated by the faith of the people and while waiting for the trade treaty to be signed, he and his officers studied the religion, culture, fauna and flora of the capital, as well of course taking time for the mandatory map-making. The unexplored area on the map was becoming smaller but there were still some tantalising blank spots requiring investigation. In particular, the lower reaches of the Tsangpo where it was rumoured that waterfalls greater than Niagara existed in the homeland of the fearsome 'black savages.' Colonel Waddell, the Chief Medical Officer of the expedition, learnt more enthralling information on the 'black savages' from the wounded Tibetans who he had brought back to health. Apparently, as well as eating their prisoners of war 'the *Glak-lo Nagpo* at their marriage festivals, kill and eat the mother of the bride if no other person is forthcoming.'

The 650 British soldiers and 4,000 Indian infantry and camp followers pitched their tents on the dry plain north of the city towards Sera monastery. Younghusband and the expedition headquarters were stationed nearer the Potala at Lhalu house, a residence of one of the wealthiest families in Tibet – which coincidentally had also produced two reincarnations of the Dalai Lama.

Lhalu House with its vast gardens, fine stonework buildings and large courtyard, was known as one of the five beauties of Lhasa. Parties were held on an island in the large pond in the grounds and it was said that the best *chang* in Lhasa was brewed from the estate's barley and the pure water which flowed through a crystal clear stream beneath the house.

Tibetan dances were held in the courtyard of Lhalu house and the British put on durbars and gymkhanas to woo the Tibetans into friendship and hurry them up with signing the trade treaty. They seemed to enjoy the festivities, although there were some areas where the different cultures could not understand one another. Betting was popular at the gymkhanas but Younghusband reported that the Tibetans found it hard to see why only the first person over the finishing line should receive a medal yet everyone had completed the race.

It took Younghusband a month and a half to persuade the Tibetans to sign his trade treaty before he could check-out of Lhalu and take the British and Indian troops back over the Himalayas, leaving Tibet to its own devices once again. Chinese empires came and went and after the fall of the Manchus in 1913, the Tibetans could at last consider themselves independent. They allowed the British to make several explorations, including one by Colonel Bailey who traced the course of the Tsangpo towards the land of the black savages. He took with him the only notes of the area, those made by Kintup nearly 30 years previously, and found them to be astonishingly accurate. On his return to India, Bailey searched for Kintup who had been dropped from the secret service after his epic journey. He discovered that Kintup was living in obscurity as a tailor in Darjeeling and immediately campaigned that Kintup be awarded a government pension. Instead he was granted a 1,000 rupee reward. It turned out to be far more than he would ever have received as a pension, as he died only a month after receiving the money.

Life in Tibet continued without the strain of the Manchu governors, known as Ambans, and the Chinese oppressors were quickly replaced with Tibetan ones. Unfortunately, the power struggles, corruption and incompetence of the Tibetan government in these years of de facto independence did nothing to prepare Tibet for the inevitable move into the twentieth century. The 'good old Tibet' searched for by romantic Westerners was little different to medieval Europe, with absolute power in the hands of a few who were guided solely by their own personal interests. Government jobs were bought and sold, human rights were nonexistent and mass exploitation was the order of the day. Political opponents could be stabbed, decapitated, have their eyes gouged out, sent parcel bombs or poisoned. Traditionalists will be pleased to know that some of these old habits still exist in present day Tibet. It is said that decapitation remains a favourite of the Khampas, while poisoning is regarded by the more cosmopolitan city folk as a relatively safe way of ridding oneself of an unwanted spouse or adversary.

Ganden, Sera and Drepung, the three great monasteries of Lhasa, housing a combined total of over 20,000 monks, gripped the nation in the Middle Ages. Any changes proposed by farsighted nobles were immediately stopped by the leaders of the monasteries, who permitted nothing to come between them, their way of life and young monks.

This may seem a rather bleak picture yet it is generally accepted that the Tibetans were surprisingly happy with their lot. It was not all sodomy and decapitations and life continued auspiciously with a spin of the prayer wheel, a cheerful chorus of 'Om Mani Padme Hom,' a ready smile and much laughter. A tough but pious life would lead to gaining more merit and therefore a good chance of a successful reincarnation next time round so individual hardships were simple to bear.

Some even went in the fast lane to Nirvana by volunteering for unimaginable deprivations. 'Brickie' hermits believed they were taking the ultimate short cut to enlightenment by voluntarily being bricked up in small caves. There are stages on the way for the faint of heart or for those wishing to give it a trial run before committing themselves for the big one. First a six month sentence, or a three year three month and three day sentence, but the only direct way to Nirvana, without passing *go* or having to suffer the tiresome circle of rebirths, is the full self-imposed life sentence, where they would stay not just for a few hours or a few days but for life. Their only contact with the outside world was the daily knock on a small wooden shutter just large enough to pass a small bowl of food prepared by the hermit-keeper. But solitary confinement until death was not enough for the brickie hermits to reach Nirvana, they also had to keep to their vows of silence and not to look out from behind the wooden shutter, however tempting it must have been to have just a quick peek at the view from the cave, as total darkness was also a prerequisite for the Nirvana road.

If the brickies had been permitted radios in their cells, they would have learnt of the storm clouds gathering to the east and the imminent danger which threatened not just their extreme lifestyle, but the very existence of all life on the Tibetan plateau. The Buddhists were in for a shock.

The small group of foreigners living in Lhasa had been listening anxiously to the events taking place in mainland China. The expat community included the British under Sir Hugh Richardson, who maintained a British Trade Mission in Lhasa for nine years. Heinrich Harrer and Peter Aufschnaiter, the Austrian and German who had completed a Herculean escape from a British internment camp in India to reach Tibet and set up residence for seven years, were also present. All were about to leave.

The Communists had been victorious in the fight against Qiang Kai Chek in mainland China and on 1 October 1949, Mao Tse Tung announced the foundation of the People's Republic of China: a land without oppression or serfdom, a land where no one was induced to brick themselves up. His next target for liberation was fairly obvious, and in 1950 he sent his triumphant PLA troops to free their Tibetan comrades from oppression – the 'peaceful liberation' began in earnest.

Lhalu Shape, who had been stationed in Chamdo in Eastern Tibet, returned to Lhasa and was replaced by the young Ape Ngapoh Renchen. The Tibetans had been used to fighting: against themselves, the black savages, the Nepalese, the British and the Chinese warlords, but never before had they faced such totally unfair battle tactics as used by the Communists. It was a dirty war. Prisoners were asked to speak up about the injustices they had suffered, were lectured on equality and the benefits of the proletariat distributing and sharing in the profits of the land. To top it all, the prisoners of war were sent free after the lectures, with a silver coin each to take back home. It all sounded quite good, and on 23 May 1951, a 17 Point Agreement was signed by Ngapoh to the effect that Tibet would be part of the motherland and that the Chinese would allow the religion, government and Dalai Lama of Tibet to carry on as before.

Just how Communism was going to be put into effect while the old government and clergy remained in power was not entirely clear and the Chinese soon started to break the agreement, point by point, so that they could push ahead with reforms and bring Tibet in line with Beijing. Robert Ford, an English radio operator working for the Tibetan Government in Chamdo was amongst the first to find out the true nature of the 'liberators' of Tibet. He was detained for five long years in Communist prison camps undergoing 'thought reform' treatment until he could convince his captors that he had been converted.

By 1959, the Tibetans had seen enough and a widespread uprising led by Khampa warriors tried in vain to turn the tide against the Chinese. Any pretence of sticking to the agreement was thrown out of the window and the Chinese ruthlessly crushed what their speech writers call 'the reactionary clique of the upper strata,' using means that were anything but peaceful. The feudal system was shattered by its very antithesis – Communism in a big way. The 16 year old Dalai Lama and an estimated 100,000 Tibetans fled into exile over the Himalayas to an uncertain future. The nobility had little choice: fight and be killed; leave Tibet and start a new life; or stay in their homeland and do the best they could for their country under the new regime.

The Chinese used the nobility who stayed to run the country, as a nobleman apparently converted to Communism was a good role model for the rest of the population and the ex-nobility could still command the respect of the people. Even today, when it is widely assumed by the outside world that the Han Chinese have total control in Tibet, a large proportion of Tibetan ex-nobility, the next generation from the negotiators of the 17 Point Agreement, have a say in the direct running of the day to day life of the Tibetan people.

Nobles who had not welcomed the change so rapidly were exposed for their sinful ways. Lhalu house, where Younghusband had stayed at the turn of the century and where lavish parties and the best chang of Lhasa had flowed during the years of independence, was confiscated for Lhalu Tsewang Dorje's role in the uprising. The Communists gave the land to the peasants with the slogan 'crops to the cultivators' and held ominous 'serf parties' in the courtyard of Lhalu house. These were the basis of the Communists' attempt to eradicate the feudal system. An American journalist who was strongly pro-Communist, witnessed the serf party at Lhalu house, walked through the deserted rooms of the mansion and wrote of the 'disorderly evidences of power and sex and religion and foreign contacts.' It must have been terrible.

According to the journalist, Lhalu was called into the courtyard and made to stand bowed down with his torso at right angles to his legs. A crowd of nearly a thousand Tibetans sat cross-legged in rows, cajoling Lhalu, mocking him and calling out: 'Confess! Confess!'

Any one of the crowd was free to stand up and shout his or her accusation at Lhalu. A man crippled with a twisted back slowly raised himself from his cross-legged position and waited patiently for his turn to call out his grievance. 'Lhalu, do you remember me?' Lhalu, trembling slightly, remained silent. 'You forced me to sell my two horses and my wife's jewellery and turned me into a beggar! I lost everything I had worked for and became crippled because of you.'

It was a common claim that all aspiring peasants, who started to accumulate wealth by fair means and lay the foundations of a Tibetan middle class, were systematically 'beggared' by the nobility. Being beggared by the nobility was even worse than the other common complaint of being buggered by the clergy, as 'beggaring' condemned an entire family to life on the streets with no hope for them or future generations of ever climbing back up the ladder into Tibetan society.

There was just one other form of life on par, or possibly lower, than beggars: the *Ragyapas*. It is a paradox which still exists in the Buddhist community in Tibet today: Buddhists cannot kill but as they eat meat, someone has to kill it for them. This is where the Ragyapas come in. They were considered so unclean, so base, that they were not permitted to reside in the holy city but instead lived as outcasts by the western gate of Lhasa in what Waddell described in 1904 as a village 'built of the horns of yaks and sheep and other offal.' The work of the Ragyapas was not limited to abattoir attendants and butchers, they were also the sky burial specialists and purveyors of human thigh bones and skulls to the clergy.

The Ragyapas were not complainers by nature and there are no records of them attending the serf parties. They were considered socially unclean and unmarriable by anyone other than a fellow Ragyapa but they performed a function that kept them in full time employment.

The old man with the twisted back sat down again as the crowd shouted, 'Confess! Lhalu, Confess!'

Another serf was quick to take up a new accusation: 'Lhalu, you flogged my husband to death and killed my sons by taking them as slaves and putting them to hard labour!'

The serf party carried on all day under the watchful eye of the 'tribunal' and the newly formed Peasants' Association. Several incensed peasants made dashes at Lhalu to beat him but all were rugby-tackled to the ground by their comrades: Communism aimed to take over by persuasion, not by force.

At one point a man came running into the courtyard with a sackful of papers. The cry 'Burn the debts! Burn the debts!' rose from the crowd.

The papers were the notorious feudal debts which were carried by each family of serfs from generation to generation. The debts to their masters were calculated at exorbitant interest rates leading to a serf inheriting debt and leaving even greater debts for his offspring who would in turn leave even larger debts for their offspring. It was a vicious circle similar to the Third World debts of today only these were about to be written off forever by means of a giant bonfire in the Lhalu courtyard. The peasants were free at last from oppression. Or so they thought.

Tibet had to change but the price they were about to pay was far worse than anything the Tibetans could have imagined – and the Tibetans have pretty vivid imagination. Hot on the heels of the serf parties and the genuine wish of the Chinese for equality and egalitarianism, came Mao's 'Great Leap Forward.' This leap into collectivisation and growing wheat instead of barley had disastrous effects for the Tibetans. Just when they thought it couldn't get any worse came the dreaded Cultural Revolution. All those centuries of warning the Tibetans against outsiders because foreigners would destroy the religion now came full circle as the Chinese themselves started the systematic destruction of Tibetan Buddhism.

The initial good intentions of Communism have long been forgotten by those in Tibet who remember the lunacy of collectivisation and the horrors of the Cultural Revolution. The entire Chinese nation was decimated in Mao's reign of madness and in Tibet the madness was particularly savage. Although the Potala Palace was saved, apparently by the orders of Zou En Lai, it is claimed that the fanatical red guards raised over 6,000 monasteries to the ground. Monks were killed, imprisoned or forced to sleep with nuns.

Today, less than 50 years after the 'peaceful liberation' and 20 years after the end of the Cultural Revolution, the country which had managed to remain in the depths of the Middle Ages, is being thrown into the deep end of the twentieth century. Present day Tibet is a melting pot of Buddhism, Communism and capitalism. Portraits of Marx, Engels, Lenin and Stalin hang on the walls of the government bookshop near the Barkhor, where posters of Chairman Mao Tse Tung are still on sale to the party faithful, and to Tibetans who don't yet know that Chairman Mao died a long time ago and doesn't count for anything any more. Collectivisation is over.

Monasteries and nunneries are being rebuilt as the Chinese leaders admit that there were 'some mistakes' during the decade of the Cultural Revolution. Although still severely restricted, Tibetan Buddhism has survived and the temples and shrines are packed once again by pilgrims and the devout of the city. But where Communism failed to eradicate Tibetan culture, capitalism is now taking over. The new economic policies of China, allowing private enterprise throughout the nation, have led to a complete transformation of Lhasa in just a matter of years. For the first time in their lives, the new generation of Tibetans are not forced to take on a government job but can now set up their own business, be hired or fired, work hard and make money. The old street fronts with their dilapidated Tibetan buildings, unchanged in appearance for centuries, are being torn down and row after row of monotonous concrete boxes erected.

Each box is built at relatively low cost by the unit which owns the land, and rented out to one of the thousands of eager new businessmen. Sadly, only a small number of Tibetans seem to be benefiting from the economic boom, instead it is the Han Chinese who arrive in droves to open noodle shops, hot pots, jeans shops, toy shops, plastic flower shops, beauty product shops, hair salons, fluorescent nylon clothing shops, discos, bars and karaokes. Lhasa is the Wild West, a frontier town where prices are high, life is tough and there is money to be made.

The Han Chinese are not physically sent by the Beijing government, as some claim, but vast numbers are sucked into the economic vacuum of business opportunity in the boom town. They bring in cheap Western-style goods which are bought by eager Tibetans anxious to take part in the 'progress' and follow fashion.

A modern Lhasa girl has been brought up wearing the long Tibetan cloak made of home-spun wool; the *chuba*. The design and fabric is the same as the *chuba* worn by her mother, her grandmother, her great-grandmother and way back down the generations, beyond when the first missionaries met them in Lhasa. Now, for the first time, the beautiful, increasingly fashion conscious Tibetan girl can buy fluorescent pink nylon trousers with shiny buttons and zip pockets, a polyester blouse with disco sequins and a white collar which will show up in the UV lights of the Lhasa nightclubs. Times are changing, and much as Westerners (myself included) would like to see every Tibetan wearing traditional costume, it is the Tibetans themselves who are making the change.

It is a depressing thought that, as multinational companies push their concepts of the 'global village' and marketeers steer the course of global consumer needs, in a few hundred years all of humanity, from pole to pole, will be dressed in jeans, T-shirts and baseball caps, drinking Coca-Cola, eating at McDonalds and staying at Holiday Inns.

Well, perhaps not so soon. *All of humanity* was certainly not flooding in to the Holiday Inn Lhasa. Winter was setting in and visitors were becoming scarce. Harry read out the statistics in the Morning Meeting. Occupancy was taking a nose-dive.

'Today twenty three percent. Tomorrow twenty percent. The day after fourteen percent.'

After the boom of the summer months it was the first time occupancy figures had dropped below 20 percent. This was serious. Occupancy below 20 percent meant that the heating would not just be switched off at night but there would be no more heating at any time anywhere in the hotel until the following year. The oil which fired the central heating system was strictly rationed and the year's supply had practically ran out. Switching on the heating could only be justified when the hotel achieved an occupancy of 20 percent. The temperature was decreasing day by day and the prospect looked bleak for those of us who would be staying on throughout the winter. A solution did come but not one that any of us around the table at the Morning Meeting would have dared suggest.

8

The Miss Tibet Fiasco

Virtually the only guests checking-in to the hotel by mid-November were the last groups of mountaineers returning from the Himalayas. Everest, or *Chomolongma* as the Tibetans refer to the world's highest mountain, was the most popular peak but we also had groups who had been on Cho Oyu, Shishapangma and the Japanese favourite: Namche Barwa. At 25,446 feet (7,756 m) Namche Barwa was the highest unclimbed mountain in the world and the Japanese kept throwing themselves at it, determined to score a 'first.' The death toll was high, but to their great credit – if you happen to think it credit-worthy to risk your life for the sake of standing on top of a large piece of windswept rock and ice – they did eventually succeed.

The 'Cowboys' were the last team of the season to arrive back from Everest: 16 Americans, bearded, sunburnt, exhausted and filthy – but all alive. None had made it to the summit but all were in good spirits. They had every right to be. Climbing Everest depends on an equal amount of phenomenal skill and luck, and this season even the most skilful teams had been defeated by bad luck. Each team told their own version of being stuck a few hundred metres from the summit waiting for a 'window' to appear in the blizzards which constantly sweep around the peak.

Curiously, the distance they reached from the summit diminishes in direct proportion to the length of time spent in the hotel bar, the number of Tsing Tao beers consumed and the chances of scoring with easily impressed tourists.

The 'windows' on Everest never came that season and each team had to return to Base Camp without having planted their flag or taken the triumphant 'here I am standing at 29,028 feet' photo. Tragically there had been two fatalities. It was usual for the majority of mountaineers to return untriumphant but after this season the gap in numbers between those making it to the top and those remaining dead on the mountain grew smaller.

The teams arriving back in the hotel headed first for the showers and then for the bar. Some tried it the other way around and we had to tactfully explain to them that they should experiment with soap and hot water before entering any of the public areas of the hotel. Not all the guests appreciated the smell of ripe mountaineer. Then there was the other odour particular to mountaineers and trekkers – the smell of burning yak dung – gained from happy evenings sitting around a yak dung fire. They thought they could wash it out of their clothes but even the Holiday Inn Lhasa laundry, which could reduce a perfectly good garment to shreds of unrecognisable fibre, could never remove the smell of burnt yak dung.

Once safely back in the hotel bar, the mountaineers played guitars, drank the hotel out of proprietary brands of liquor and partied late into the night. They were a fun crowd. The hotel became alive again and the corridors buzzed with stories of mankind's battle with the forces of nature.

There exists a friendly rivalry between groups of climbers and although individual famous mountaineers are hero-worshipped, each team is quick to point out the deficiencies of the other. One team in particular had become the butt of all the Base Camp jokes – a group of Frenchmen who called themselves, 'Everest Express.'

They had been training at high altitude in the Alps and had planned to jet into Kathmandu, storm over into Tibet, rush straight onto Everest and be at the summit in seven days. They intended to be fully acclimatised from training in the Alps and so the climb on Everest would be *très simple*. But a week after crossing the border into Tibet they were still at Base Camp, suffering from jet-lag, altitude sickness and arguing about food. The other teams renamed them, 'Everest Escargot.'

The expeditions returning to the hotel brought windfalls in the form of their surplus food supplies, or at least what remained of the supplies after pilfering by the notoriously dishonest Base Camp yak herders. The General Manager eagerly inspected the lorries as they came in to see what could be scrounged for the hotel's Delicatessen. The Cowboys produced a particularly bountiful supply of dried bacon bits, hot chocolate powder and 15 boxes of nearly post-sell-by-date fruity nut bar. In fact these leftovers, together with a few cans of Chinese spam, was about all there was in the Delicatessen. Several grumbling guests pointed out that 'Delicatessen' was, perhaps, a slightly over-optimistic name for a shop with little more than spam and the mountaineers' leftovers, so in order to keep them happy, the shop was given the new name of 'Picnic Corner.'

The mountaineers were good business all round. The hotel was the first taste of the comforts of Western civilisation after two and a half months on a mountain-side and they made the most of it. Unfortunately they did not take enough rooms to hit the magic 20 percent occupancy figure but they spent well in the restaurants, on their attempts at using the telephone, their sacks of yak dungy laundry and especially in the bar. The only drawback was that you had to sit and listen to their stories.

There can be few people with a greater ego than a climber who has attempted the highest peak in the world. Later I was to discover there is one worse – those who have actually made it. Yes it is deserved. He or she has diced with death and won but all the same, the endless tales of death-defying acts and heroism repeated ad nauseam in a loud voice become very wearing.

My stories of climbing the mountain across the river seemed rather tame in comparison. Instead of 'climbing the big one,' I started referring to it as a 'trek on the mountain' and then more accurately as a 'walk on the small hill.' After I had suffered listening to an over-ripe mountaineer, who could hardly get his head through the door to the bar, talking loudly to the assembled crowd of adoring tourists,

'. . . the yaks had gone over the crevasse, my oxygen gave out on me at 27,000 feet, I was left with frostbite and had to carry the Sherpa with snow blindness . . .'

I thought it best not to mention my hill walk again.

The mountaineers had all left by the end of November and quiet settled in once again to the hotel. Occupancy dropped to single figures and the General Manager, weary after four long years, started looking forward to the arrival of his replacement. We were told that an Italian would be on his way to Lhasa in December.

Winter, although bleak in terms of hotel occupancy and temperature, is without doubt the best time to visit Lhasa. Don't believe the guide books. Don't believe the tour operators. Yes, it is *freezing*, but it is also fantastic. Snow is uncommon in Lhasa and when it does fall it is just enough to give a delicate veil of white over the surrounding hills. But it soon melts. There is not a cloud in the sky, not a drop of rain and each day is blessed with over eight hours of strong sunshine. The air is crisp and pure and a high factor sun cream needs to be used if you want to avoid acquiring the Tibetan weather-beaten look. Although it is hot in the sun, take one step into the shade and the temperature plummets.

Fortunately my room in the hotel was south-facing. Now I could see why Harry had told me this was so important when I arrived. However the Sales Office faced north. Not a single ray of sunlight passed through the windows.

The temperature had now dropped to low single figures – the correct temperature for a walk-in refrigerator – and even my thick woollen suit, which had been so uncomfortable in Hong Kong, was not sufficient to prevent me from shaking as I sat at my desk.

I went down to the Barkhor, my usual haunt on a Sunday afternoon, to look for a pair of long johns. I had purchased one of the first mountain bikes to be found in Lhasa, a cheap Chinese version with dodgy brakes, which saved me the hassle of bargaining with the rickshaw drivers every time I wanted to leave the hotel. Cycling has the extra advantage that you can stop and look and explore, instead of just being bumped along on the rickshaw wondering what it is that you are passing.

It was some time before I realised that along the route to the Barkhor from the hotel, just past the government book store with the Stalin posters, was a building once described along with Lhalu House as one of the five beauties of Lhasa. *Yutok Sampa* – the Turquoise Bridge. It was hard to believe that it had once stood as a roofed bridge over a major stream running through the marshes around the Barkhor. Frank Ludlow, a member of the British Trade Mission stationed in Lhasa in the 1940s wrote that in this same spot, wild bar-headed geese, 'used to waddle across the road in front of my pony just like tame geese.' Before the Communists arrived in Lhasa, all life was treated as sacred and wild animals showed no fear. Blue sheep grazed on the fields in the Lhasa valley, Brahminy duck nested in the windows of the Potala Palace. How different it is now, when both Chinese and Tibetans go hunting and the former marshland around the bridge is now a concrete urban sprawl.

At least Yutok Sampa was still standing, but it was in a bad state of repair. It looked like a long barn, about 40 feet long and 15 feet wide, with a row of open windows at each side and a large opening at either end. The walls were stout, built of stone and supported rows of blue painted beams, which in turn held up the magnificent roof that gave the bridge its name. Centuries of exposure to the Tibetan weather had produced a deep blue-green colour that glowed from the earthenware tiles.

I cycled on, hoping that one day it would be restored to its former glory.

The Barkhor in winter takes on a completely different complexion to the summer months. In November, after the harvest is over, the Tibetan buildings receive their annual white-wash. No need for paint brushes or rollers, the white-wash is simply flung against the walls from buckets. It is a spectacular sight but should be observed from a distance as everything in the vicinity; bicycles, tables, chairs and people are white-washed from head to toe.

The villages in the valley and the Tibetan houses of Lhasa positively shine in the strong winter sun. But it is not just the buildings which take on a new and brighter appearance – so too do the people. The tourists have vanished, the Chinese who can find an excuse to leave have returned to the 'mainland' and the town is filled with newly arrived Tibetans for the winter pilgrimage. Yak hair tents appear along the roadside by the river and the sterile Chinese parks are turned into lively Tibetan campsites. The nomads bring in goods to trade in the markets and the Barkhor comes to life. While Lhasa is becoming depressingly cosmopolitan, the glimmer of hope for Tibetan culture lies in these people from the far flung corners of the great country.

For many of these villagers, the winter visit to Lhasa is a once in a lifetime pilgrimage. The Barkhor is a moving mass, continually turning clockwise and humming with the chant of 'Om Mani Padme Hom.' The pilgrims turn prayer wheels, cunningly clever devices which allow thousands of 'Om Mani Padme Homs,' to be said at the flick of the wrist.

A prayer wheel consists of a roll of paper covered in 'Om Mani Padme Homs' inside a drum on the end of a short stick. You hold the stick in your hand and spin the drum in a clockwise direction. A small weight is attached to the drum, which helps to keep it spinning when the correct momentum is reached. Each spin of the wheel sends the entire prayer contents of the drum skywards – so gaining high merit points for the life to come. In addition to these hand held prayer wheels, each *kora* has large fixed wheels at certain points which should also be turned by the passing pilgrims. Each temple has a line of them, fixed top and bottom by a metal spindle, and spun by pushing a yak buttery wooden arm which is fixed to the base of the drum. The largest wheel I have seen was taller than a Khampa, and I can only guess at how many millions of prayers must be delivered when this is turned. Serious merit points.

The Tibetans are certainly ingenious when it comes to ways of scoring large amounts of merit in one simple move. There are also versions of prayer wheels which are turned by paddles in streams and smaller paper models, which are suspended above yak butter lamps and turned by the rising heat. It will not be long until there is a battery version and an enormous marketing opportunity for Duracell. But thankfully, the majority of Tibetans who crowd the Barkhor in winter and form queues at the great monasteries of Lhasa, are still untouched by the commercialism of the twentieth century.

They arrive in their traditional clothes: mighty Khampas with *chubas* and hair braided with red or black tassels; wild-looking nomads from the north wearing *chubas* made of turned out sheep skins; Kongpo people from the east with their small rounded hats and square capes. Even the Lhasa folk dress differently in the winter time. Thick *chubas* are worn and each man proudly wears a flower pot-shaped hat decorated with golden brocade and lined with rabbit fur. The pot has three large flaps and the de rigueur Tibetan wears one side flap folded in, with the front and other side flap sticking out like the peaks of baseball caps. Ladies have shorter hats of the same material but with four flaps. Some of the men wear an even more macho fox fur hat. These look as though an entire fox is curled up on top of the head, with its head and tail dangling at the back. So much for all life being sacred.

Each Tibetan who catches your eye around the Barkhor will immediately smile and beam a reply to your *tashi delai's*, the universal Tibetan phrase for, 'Hello. How are you? Good to meet you.' Some stick their tongues out in greeting. They find foreigners amusing – our funny clothes, big noses, ugly blue eyes, pale skin and the funniest thing of all – body hair.

As I asked in sign language at a stand around the Barkhor for a pair of long underpants I felt a tug at my sleeve. I looked down to find a young monk, eight or nine years old, pulling at the hair on the back of my hand, grinning all over and saying 'po' to his friend. This caused fits of giggles and the two of them ran off dodging in and out of the moving human line of pilgrims which circled the Jokhang temple. They peeped at me from behind the *chubas* of the crowd still laughing and pointing. 'Po', I discovered, means 'monkey'.

After several 'may-ohs' and 'putchidao's' at the Chinese stands I eventually found a pair of Chinese heavy duty winter underpants. Our staff, including Jig Me, wore tracksuits beneath their suits, but these always stuck out at the bottom of the trousers and looked rather stupid. I cycled back with my new acquisition.

All had seemed peaceful at the Barkhor. The Chinese were relaxing. There had even been a recent sports rally where everyone had been waving 'PROGRESS & UNITY' banners. The Chinese told themselves that those nasty splittists had been crushed and everyone was happy in the New Tibet. But this was just the lull before the storm.

The storm broke on International Human Rights Day when a group of nuns and monks followed the circuit of the Barkhor around the Jokhang temple, waving the Tibetan flag and chanting 'Free Tibet!' The Chinese have different ideas on handling demonstrations to Westerners. There are no peaceful pleas for calm, not even water cannons or rubber bullets – the answer comes immediately with AK47's. The Tibetan monks and nuns, guilty of nothing more than expressing their thoughts were gunned down in the square by nervous Chinese soldiers. The Tibetans answered in the now traditional way and the Barkhor police station was set on fire again.

There was pandemonium at the hotel. Party A banned us from going outside, foreign tourists were deported and there were restrictions placed on new arrivals. Chinese soldiers were kept on patrol around the Barkhor and as calm returned to the streets the control on tourism slowly eased.

Among the few foreigners allowed in was a Mr Ernesto Barba, the new General Manager. He seemed pleasant enough. A suave Italian looking ten years younger than his 60 years of age. Long dark hair swept back over strong handsome features. His clothing was from the leading couturiers of Italy and his manners, on first impressions, were impeccable. He had the worrying habit of taking you by the arm and of tugging at your earlobes when you came up with a good idea, but this we put down to the warmth of his southern Italian origins. Chef was not so sure. Being typically Germanic, he liked discipline and private body space and took great exception to having his earlobes interfered with. Fortunately he did not have many ideas which Barba liked, so did not have to undergo too much stress.

After a brief hand-over period the former General Manager bid us farewell and left for the warmer climes of Southeast Asia. He was thin and pale; exhausted from the strains of running the hardest hardship posting of Holiday Inn. He gave us a wry smile and wished us luck. Perhaps he knew something we didn't about Barba, 'the crazy Italian.'

I was not too concerned at the time. One of Barba's first acts was to promote me to being the Asia-Pacific region's youngest Executive Assistant Manager in charge of Sales and Marketing, and to boost the Sales Department by bringing in a Belgian girl, Conny, as Sales Manager. Few expatriate women had worked in Lhasa and Conny's arrival was a welcome change to our male-dominated team. She was bright, beautiful and most important of all, she immediately fell in love with Tibet. Some expats succumb to the altitude in the first few days. Others who have come with the wrong expectations leave without even unpacking their suitcases. But Conny's reaction to her first visit to the Barkhor was the same mixture of wonder and excitement that I felt every time I was there, and I knew that she would survive.

The first days with Barba passed without incident although we were soon to discover that he was no ordinary man. He had come to Lhasa as part of his studies of oriental religion. He hated Holiday Inn. 'Alec, when I signed the contract, I held my nose!' he chuckled to me in his office.

But the smile soon left his face. He sat behind his desk with a crossword book and sheets of paper onto which he was pasting blackened photocopies of Buddhas and Bodhisattvas.

'Alec, what are we going to do here? Is it really this cold? What is this *Party A, Party B* nonsense? Who is Jig Me?'

As with all new recruits, he was having trouble coming to terms with the system. I left him with his Chinese glue pot and headed back to my office.

'Mr Alec! Mr Alec!'

Tashi shouted across the empty lobby. 'Here, I have a note for you.'

I took the crumpled piece of paper from him and read, 'SOS. The People's No.1 Hospital. Greg.'

Greg! He should have been out of Tibet weeks ago. I knew from the other mountaineers who had passed through Lhasa that the two Canadians had not made it to the top but I had assumed that they had carried on with their plans and had left Tibet via Kathmandu. Was this some sort of hoax?

I asked Tashi to find Dorje and tell him that we had to go quickly to the hospital. Dorje was delighted with the news and appeared almost immediately at the wheel of his Landcruiser, revving up the engine in the hotel forecourt. We sped through the streets, the accelerator pedal pressed to the floor. Cyclists were forced off their bikes, pedestrians into skips and several of the Lhasa dogs came very close to their next incarnations. We screeched to a halt at the hospital gates, dropped some yuan in the shoe-boxes of the chanting monks and set about finding Greg.

We peered into room after room of sickly Chinese and Tibetans until we came to Greg's cell. It was sparse, with a concrete floor and the usual decoration of green paint half way up the walls, with the top of the walls and the ceiling a cobweb shade of white. A table stood between two beds, with three pots of bottled tangerines and various medical paraphernalia. Oxygen cylinders and a drip feed stood in the corner. On one of the two beds the cheerful CMA guide sat bolt upright and on the other lay Greg. He was hardly recognisable. He had lost a lot of weight, grown a scratchy beard and although his skin was scorched red from his time on Everest, his lips had turned blue. He was attached to several bottles and had oxygen tubes taped to his nose. He smiled when he saw us and gave a sigh of relief.

Despite the physical pains of his illness, he seemed to be in far more trouble with the psychological trauma inflicted on him by the guide. Between gasps of oxygen he complained of being fed only on a diet of bottled tangerine slices and being stuck in the hospital with no idea of when he would ever get out. He was desperate for some other form of nourishment and I promised to bring him some soup from the hotel. Between gasps of oxygen he told me his story.

He had climbed with Dave to within 800 yards of the summit but the weather closed in on them. They too had waited for a 'window' but it never came and reluctantly they had returned through their advanced camps back down to Base Camp. Dave had carried on to Kathmandu and as Greg hadn't been feeling too good, he had decided to return to Lhasa with the CMA guide. This was his mistake. He expected to be staying at the Holiday Inn but the guide had told him the hotel was fully booked (if only!) and had taken him to one of the Chinese hotels where he had fallen seriously ill. After a week in bed his condition deteriorated further and after shaking the rats out of his clothes, the guide brought him to the People's Number

One Hospital. He had the very unfortunate combination of pulmonary edema and haemorrhoids.

The doctor had told him that if his breathing became any worse he would slit his throat and insert a tube direct to the oxygen bottle. This had done nothing to calm Greg's nerves. His breathing was certainly irregular. The only real cure for his altitude sickness was to get him out of Tibet, to a lower altitude and more familiar methods of health care. The weekly flight from Kathmandu had stopped for the winter, so we persuaded the guide to purchase a ticket for Chengdu as soon as it was medically safe for Greg to travel.

Between the gasps he also expressed his grave concern about the guide's motives in consistently wishing to 'lend a hand' applying the haemorrhoid cream. For macho mountaineers, this thought was even worse than the life-threatening pulmonary edema.

Chef prepared special thermos flasks of soup and Greg slowly regained his strength, enough for him to be able to take the plane to Chengdu, accompanied by a doctor from the People's Number One Hospital and the friendly CMA guide.

I was sitting in the hotel bar after the mountaineers had gone, frightening a group of elderly American ladies with the vision of Greg in the hospital and details of what can happen to you at high altitude, when I suddenly felt myself turning white. The ladies were facing me, listening attentively, gulping down their over-priced bottles of Evian water and it happened. There, behind them, clinging onto the water pipe against the wall, stood an enormous rat. I tried to remain calm. I have no problem with rodents but the thought of being stuck in a tiny bar with a herd of stampeding tourists, whose eyes were already wide with fear over the horror of high altitude sickness, filled me with dread.

'And so Greg recovered fully.'

I brought an abrupt end to the story. 'Goodness me, is that the time? We really must all be leaving the bar straight away or we will be late for dinner. Bring your drinks and follow me. Keep looking this way. That's right, this way ladies, keep looking this way.'

Then Laba, the barmaid, broke my cover. 'Zizi!' she screamed, pointing behind the ladies who I had managed to bring half way to the door.

'Look Mr Alec. *Big* zizi!'

'Yes. Thank you Laba.'

The ladies turned around and there was a moment of stunned silence. The rat looked at them. They stared at the rat. I looked at the ladies. Laba giggled at me. To my great relief the silence was broken, not by hysteria but by one of the group asking very calmly, 'Does *zizi* mean rat in Tibetan?'

After all, these were ladies from a Smithsonian Institute tour. I had underestimated them. They wanted to know what species it was and two of them debated whether it was as big as the one they had seen in their room in the floating hotel in Vietnam.

This particular 'zizi,' which Laba had been so kind to point out, was one of the first rats of the winter to make it into the hotel. They followed in droves. At night they ran along the air-conditioning ducts above the bedrooms, and every evening as I brushed my teeth, I heard the patter of tiny feet on the ceiling tiles above my bathroom. In reverence to Manuel's 'Siberian Hamster,' the expats referred to the rats as 'Himalayan Hamsters.' Any guest reporting having seen or heard a mouse or rat was informed that they were very fortunate to have witnessed a rare Himalayan Hamster. This excuse was very thin and hardly ever worked. The Smithsonian Institute guests were not taken in by it and it certainly was not worth using when George Schaller was around.

The rats were a seasonal problem. All summer long they had been breeding and stuffing their little faces in the barley fields of the Lhasa valley. Now that the crop had been harvested and the temperature was dropping, they headed to the hotel kitchens for warmth and food.

There was nothing new about the winter rodent invasion. As a child, the Dalai Lama had befriended the mice living in his room in the Potala Palace. He snuggled under his blankets and happily watched them as they ate the offerings and climbed over his bed clothes. This is understandable, considering that the Dalai Lama is the incarnation of the Bodhisattva of Compassion, but generally the hotel guests were not so welcoming to these little four footed visitors. One of the long-staying guests was lent a mouse trap which produced a record-breaking eight mice.

Tu Dian reluctantly set the remainder of the traps in the kitchens and in the bar, but the rodent numbers continued to increase. Public sightings were becoming embarrassingly common. Meals were hurried at the management table in case a rodent was spotted. If it was, the trick was to leave the table as quickly as possible, without telling the others why you were going. This meant that the last expat at the table would have the explaining to do when the guests stormed up and asked why rats were roaming around the restaurant. As the numbers increased, meal times became intolerably short as we scrambled to leave our seats. Action had to be taken.

After a lengthy debate in the Morning Meeting, where Barba received his halitosis baptism from Mr Pong, it was agreed that war would be declared on the rats. Heather translated the ultimatum into English: 'We shall summon rat-catchers from Chengdu and put medicine down for the rats.'

This was a very odd concept. Medicine for rats? I made a note never to take any Chinese medicine while I was in Tibet.

On a predetermined date little piles of pink rice, tainted with 'rat medicine' were placed outside each door along every corridor of the hotel. The kitchen floors were covered in medicine, the store rooms, the garage, the staff canteen and the telephone operators' chamber. There was not a room untouched.

Conny, the new Sales Manager, was given the task of writing a letter to each guest telling them not to touch any of the pink rice piles which were there entirely for the good of the guests and from our commitment to maintaining the highest possible standards of service. None of the guests complained.

By early morning, there was no more pattering of tiny feet along the air-conditioning ducts. The effect of the medicine had been catastrophic. The highest head count came from the staff canteen, where barrels were loaded with the bodies of 224 dead rats. Before I could stop them, the rat-catchers wheeled the open barrels across the courtyard from the staff canteen and straight through the lobby. I chased after them to intercept any guest who might become disturbed by the sight but fortunately there was no one around. The rat-catchers were on their way to the kitchens, which had the next highest toll. When the bodies from the store rooms were added, the total for the hotel came to over 440. It was a sad day for the rodents of the Holiday Inn Lhasa.

But Barba was still not pleased. The rodent problem was temporarily solved but the cold was getting unbearable. 'We have to get that twenty percent occupancy.' He was thinking aloud at the breakfast table. 'We need to do something different. Something sensational. We need to bring the press in.'

'You know journalists aren't allowed here Mr Barba,' Harry answered. 'They were banned after the rioting.'

'I don't care! They can fire me! You think I want to stay here? I have an idea that's going to get the heating on! I *like* being fired!'

He stood up to shout this last sentence and brought his fist down on the table harder than all of the previous General Manager's table thumps put together. The guests paused with their breakfast and turned to face our table. This man was not normal. He glowered at them. 'You want to complain to the manager?' he shouted.

No one did. He ran his hands through his hair, sat down again and started telling us calmly why he had been sacked from every major hotel chain in the world.

'At Sheraton it was for sleeping with the owner's daughter,' he chuckled. I had not worked with an Italian before and did not realise that this would mean having intricate details of his previous sexual experiences relived second by second at the breakfast table.

'At Hilton it was even better. I opened the Okinawa Hilton but was fired after the opening party. It was a great party. Everyone enjoyed it. I put hash in the cakes. Can you get hash in Lhasa?'

None of us answered. Mr Liu gave his forkful of food an extra examination and decided not to continue with breakfast.

We were late for the Morning Meeting and Jig Me gave us a condescending look when we entered the meeting room. Barba announced his idea to the assembled managers; 'I am going to hold the first ever Miss Tibet contest!'

The Tibetans and Chinese looked blankly at him. Heather had trouble translating. They still looked blank when it was said in Chinese. Chef chuckled. I groaned. I was getting the measure of Barba. He would come up with the crazy idea and Conny and I would have to make it work. While Conny had the dubious task of staying with the crazy Italian to plan the Miss Tibet arrangements, I left for Hong Kong to hold a press conference at the Foreign Correspondents Club.

The journey on CAAC was as eventful as ever. The departure from Lhasa had been fine but the descent into Chengdu is engraved on my memory. The old Boeing dropped though the cloud over Chengdu, undercarriage down, patchwork of rice fields beneath us, the airport buildings are coming into view through the mist, closer now, coming in to land, concrete runway beneath us, another plane is on the runway. ANOTHER PLANE IS ON THE RUNWAY!

Fortunately the pilot had the same reaction. He slammed the Boeing into a 45 degree ascent on full thrust. The seats shuddered as the engines roared and the oxygen masks all popped out. The Tibetans thought it was hilarious and stood in the aisle talking in loud voices while the pilot circled again and came in to land once the runway was clear.

The CAAC flight from Chengdu to Hong Kong was less nerve-wracking. Chengdu has a growing number of foreign-managed factories and the flight to Hong Kong is used regularly by expats on their way out of China for 'R & R' (Rest and Recuperation). All the expats on board were in good humour. This could have been caused by the sign on each seat, which should have read, 'Your life vest is under your seat,' but instead proclaimed, 'USE BOTTOM CUSHION FOR FLOTATION.'

The in-flight magazine was equally entertaining. There was an article about a pilot, Mr Liang Luxin, 'the owner of civil aviation first grade safety medal.' Apparently, Mr Liang Luxin has, 'flown safely 10,645 hours in 30 years, is boundlessly loyal to our Party and flies for more than 300 days a year.' This is what they call safe!

A drink advertised on the back page looked interesting; 'Guoguang Fushoule – a high grade tonic wine with low alcohol.' It could cure all sorts of ills but advertised its main ingredients as gecko and dog's kidney. I crossed it off my shopping list.

The plane glided effortlessly between the apartment blocks of Hong Kong and came to a perfect landing on the runway stretching out into the harbour. Perhaps Mr Liang Luxin was flying us today, clocking up a few extra hours of safety in the sky.

Inside the aircraft was CAAC, outside was Hong Kong. It was always exciting sensation. From drab Communism to vibrant capitalism. You could say whatever you wanted, think whatever you wanted and buy what ever you wanted. A taxi took me to the Holiday Inn Golden Mile – paradise after months in China. The sheets were soft and white, there were no Himalayan Hamsters, no yak burgers, no Party A. There were yellow bananas. Everything smelt different, tasted different. But I was not here to relax, I had to keep my appointment at the FCC.

At 5pm I faced the press of Hong Kong.

'We are organising the first Miss Tibet contest in history,' I announced to the packed room, 'you are all invited.'

They scribbled notes.

'But none of you can come.'

They stopped writing.

'At least none of you *journalists* can come. But over there I think I can see a housewife, and over there a teacher and over there a technician.'

It was painfully simple. Every visitor to Tibet had to apply for a permit and one of the questions on the application form asked for the profession of the traveller. All you had to do to get a permit was write any answer other than 'journalist.' Suddenly we had 75 enrolled on the tour. It was an immediate success. The travel arrangements from Hong Kong for the Miss Tibet extravaganza were put together by an excellent tour operator and by the time I returned to Lhasa, 120 seats were sold.

Barba had been working hard on the plans for the evening but had not actually sought any permission for the event. Jig Me kept insisting that no further arrangements could be made until a meeting was held with the 'parties concerned.' This sounded ominous to those of us who could read the warning signs, but Barba was in a bullish mood. He shouted at the Morning Meeting, 'it will just be one of those rubber stamp schmucks. Give me a few minutes with him and then I can get on with the preparations.'

The 'rubber stamp schmuck' turned out to be a delegation of 20 people. There were representatives from the Public Security Bureau (PSB), the Foreign Affairs Office (FAO), Tibet Tourism Bureau (TTB), Tibet Cultural Bureau (TCB) and Tibet Television (TTV). Barba proudly announced that I had been in Hong Kong and the major press and television stations of the world had been invited to witness the great event. The PSB solemnly reminded him that journalists were not permitted to enter Tibet. The FAO stated that they had received a request from NBC television to film the event. Barba bluffed; 'We have eight TV crews already on the way to Lhasa! You can't stop it now!'

Heather translated. Jig Me was furious. He was responsible for the behaviour of the expats and was rapidly losing massive amounts of face amongst the powerful elite of Lhasa.

'We can stop anything,' said the PSB man. The meeting grew tense. A small man wearing a blue Chairman Mao suit stood up and asked what a beauty contest involved. Heather translated Barba's reply. The man in the Mao suit stated that there could be no contest as such because that would be unfair. Instead, a rally with banners saying some good Party slogans and some dancing would be more appropriate. The rep from the Cultural Bureau stood up and gave a 15 minute speech about dancing. Heather diligently translated. Now it was Barba who became furious.

'Do you think the world's press are going to come here to see a bunch of Commie dancers? That's it. I cancel everything.'

9

The Race to Resign

Barba had no intention of cancelling Miss Tibet. He was doing what he was best at – bluffing. He called another meeting with Jig Me and the group of Communist cronies and this time tried another strategy. 'There will be no press, just a group of housewives and teachers from Hong Kong.'

With this new, toned down approach, he won the support of Mr Hu from the Tibet Cultural Bureau and so started the preparations in earnest. A great extravaganza was planned, with a picnic at 14,000 feet, a barbecue with roast yak on Jarmalingka island, a surprise buffet on the roof of an isolated monastery, and then the grand finale – the Miss Tibet Gala evening, with music from a Filipino band, especially flown in for the occasion.

With two days to go before the arrival of the guests, Mr Hu asked for a meeting with Mr Barba. He wanted to show Barba his gala performance. Jig Me acted as mediator.

'No, no, Jig Me,' said Barba, 'you must be translating wrong. You mean that he wants to see *my* gala performance.'

'No, *he* has prepared the gala performance. You cannot do one.'

It was quite a surprise. Two sets of preparations had been going on, each oblivious to the other's work. Barba's blood surpassed boiling point. I have never seen anyone capable of summoning up greater anger. Everything about him oozed rage; his facial contortions, the little beads of sweat that appeared on his forehead, the maroon colour which spread across his face, his stammering voice and the vast array of imaginative swear words accompanied by Italian sign language. He stood up from the table and shouted, 'You mean that this little *Communist* has prepared a show. Am I, described by Playboy magazine as "the Felini of the hotel industry", not able to produce a show good enough?!'

It had been a great insult to Barba's gigantic ego. But Mr Hu realised that he too was being severely insulted and hurled abuse back in Chinese. Jig Me visibly aged ten years and Barba stormed out of the meeting.

Later in the afternoon, a compromise was reached. Barba would view Mr Hu's show in the evening to give it an appraisal. He laughed all the way through it.

'Call this a show? Chinese girls, prancing around to disco music twenty years out of date!'

Mr Hu thought Barba was enjoying the performance and made him an offer – he could have the show for $15,000. The atmosphere became electric and Barba shot to his feet. He was just saved from assaulting Mr Hu by Jig Me's very simple solution. Mr Hu could have his show on one night and Mr Barba could have his on another. With careful scheduling, Mr Hu's evening show was put on at a time when the hotel was practically empty and Barba's was kept as originally planned for the last night of the Miss Tibet tour.

The group of 'housewives' and 'teachers' had no difficulty reaching Lhasa and on the day of their arrival, occupancy hit the magic 20 percent. It was the first time in the history of Holiday Inn Lhasa, that a day in December had reached this prized figure. Derek was triumphantly given the order to switch the heating on. Barba had achieved his goal although he was a little disappointed that he had not yet been fired.

Conny and I took the group to the Barkhor on their first afternoon. Some of the 'housewives' carried suspiciously large home video cameras, and many of the 'teachers' took note pads with them wherever they went and looked everywhere for

Tibetans who could speak English and tell them about human rights.

We were starting to gain too much attention for a normal tour group and we bundled the 'tourists' through the crowd of 'You how much?' Khampa girls and back on to the tour bus. You never knew who to trust at the Barkhor. Any one of the harmless looking Tibetans or Chinese could be an informer. No matter how much Barba was savouring the risk of being fired, I was enjoying working in Lhasa and had no intention of being deported for organising his group of illegal journalists.

Back at the hotel, the guests complained of the cold. The long-awaited heating was completely ineffectual in the massive marble-lined lobby. The staff had the annoying habit of leaving doors open at either end of the hotel, turning the corridors into wind tunnels. We tried all sorts of methods to keep them closed but nothing worked. The heating however, did have an effect in the rooms, and when I opened the door to room 3205 I was hit by the heat of a sauna and a rather curious smell. I looked around my room but couldn't find anything out of place, so I decided the smell must be coming in from outside.

The tour was going superbly. What they saw, where they ate, what they did, had all been carefully planned to bring them on to a new and more thrilling high each day. The momentum gathered at breakneck pace and they returned to the hotel on the final afternoon of the tour in eager anticipation of the *grand finale* – the Miss Tibet election itself.

Three hours before the election was due to start, the small man in the blue Chairman Mao suit who had been at the initial meeting reappeared at the hotel. He announced that the Filipino band was forbidden to play Rock 'n' Roll, that the lead singer of the band was not to look too sexy and that the election had to be cancelled. There could be no Miss Tibet. We would be allowed to continue with the show, but the Tibet Cultural Bureau would provide the pre-selected contestants and the title from now on would be the 'FASHION PARADE EVALUATION.' Conny was ordered to take down all the posters and signs which read 'Miss Tibet' and change everything to the 'FASHION PARADE EVALUATION.'

That evening, as I changed into a dinner jacket for the gala evening, the smell in my room became unbearable. It was not just in my room but in all the rooms. There was a tinge of it on the air in the corridors and it worsened as you approached the coffee shop.

It suddenly hit me. I recognised the smell. This was the same odour that had spread through my garage back in Jersey when I had baited a mouse trap and then forgotten to look at it for a few weeks. The difference now was that this smell was not just from the body of a tiny dead mouse – this was the rat population of the hotel which had been poisoned in the air-conditioning ducts. The rat-catchers from Chengdu had long since gone, having only picked up the bodies which were out in the open. No one had thought of the air-conditioning ducts, where the corpses had initially been preserved in the dry, chilled atmosphere. But now the bodies were being blasted with hot air and were rapidly defrosting and decomposing. The stench throughout the hotel was excruciating.

The heating was immediately switched off. The windows in the Everest Room were opened wide and Derek ran around the hotel instructing his Engineering Department staff to block off all the vents. A bend in the air-conditioning ducts above the coffee shop produced the bodies of thirteen rats. No one knows how many lay out of reach in the five stories of the hotel.

Once the temperature had been lowered the smell started to decline. I put on several layers of T-shirts and my thick woollen long johns under my evening suit and went to the Everest Room, to see if there was anything I could do to help with the final preparations.

The Everest Room was usually home to the notorious group buffet but tonight Barba had transformed the area into a Hollywood set. He had ordered a Tibetan tent village to be constructed in the hotel grounds outside the Everest Room, so that yaks grazed on the lawn by the windows. Charlie, who was responsible for the grounds of the hotel as well as the housekeeping inside, kept prodding the yaks away from the flower tubs but to no avail.

Inside, gigantic *thangkas* – Buddhist paintings on scrolls – hung from each wall and a vast stage had been knocked together by Derek's engineers (which would serve as the catwalk and set for the Filipino band). An arch spanning the width of the stage had been created by the hotel's Art Department and emblazoned with Barba's favourite phrase: 'The Best is Yet to Come.'

All references to 'Miss Tibet' had been painted out at the last minute and there was still a smell of fresh paint. No one complained as it made a change to the smell of defrosting rats which hung in the corridors.

The panel of judges and VIP's took their seats at the head table. For each of the ten foreign judges that Barba had asked for, the authorities had insisted there be two locals – so the table stretched from one end of the room to the other. Us mere mortals sat at the round tables.

Conny took the stage as hostess for the evening. She was stunning, dressed in a beautiful black velvet ball gown, which definitely had not been made by Communist tailors. Her big brown eyes sparkled with excitement and she kept up a beaming smile despite the mayhem behind the scenes. Barba had donned his impresario outfit and lurked in the background, wearing a pale lilac shirt and a blue silk neckerchief beneath his dinner jacket. From behind the 'Best is Yet to Come' banner, he shouted commands and directed the players of the evening.

Conny was ordered to commence. She welcomed the VIP's and the first act of the night – a Tibetan yak dance. This becomes rather tiresome after you have seen it a few times, but the first occasion is always very impressive. To the fast beat of a drum and the sound of crashing cymbals, a yak herder enters the restaurant with two pantomime yaks in tow. He cracks his whip on the floor and skips from side to side. The yaks also jump continually to the rhythm of the drumbeat while, still skipping, the yak herder pulls out two white silk scarfs, *khatas*, and places them on the floor, one in front of each yak. The drum beat quickens and the yak herder skips even faster and shouts at the yaks. Between dancing from side to side, the yaks try to scoop up the silk scarves on their horns. Several attempts are made and the yak herder has to shout louder and crack his whip even harder until finally we are all put out of our misery when the yaks each hook the scarves onto their horns. This brings cheers and rounds of applause and a great sense of relief that it is finally over for the poor men inside the yak costumes.

As the yak herder led his animals away, Barba shouted his commands to the next act. The Filipino band came on stage and the waitresses appeared from the kitchen bearing plates with the first course, while dancing the Chinese 36 steps. It was an amazing sight. Thirty waitresses following a carefully choreographed dance routine, while carrying bowls of vegetable soup.

Discos were big business in Lhasa. New ones were opening in town virtually every day and the hotel was home to one of the hottest nightclubs of Lhasa. Every night over 600 Chinese and Tibetans crammed into the Holiday Inn Lhasa disco to hear the latest from Boney M and Abba. During the Cultural Revolution dancing had been suppressed in China as being something inherently bourgeoisie. After the fall of Mao, dance halls opened up across the country and the population, both young and old, took immediately to this newly allowed form of pleasure. Couples waltzed the night away to the sounds of old Chinese folk songs, moving Communist propaganda ballads which they had all learnt when they were in the Red Guard and they waltzed too to the new disco imports from the West.

The discos became the places for girls to meet boys. Waltzing close with a partner in the dark of a nightclub, particularly when inhibitions are subdued by alcohol, has always been a good way to find romance. But as in all nightclubs, the atmosphere can become tense when charged with alcohol, love and lust.

Khampas were not allowed into the Holiday Inn Lhasa disco carrying their daggers and Chinese soldiers were not permitted to enter with revolvers. Despite the efforts of the hotel Security Department, fights were fairly common. I was once called down by Dr Grubby who was refusing to treat a patient in the clinic. It turned out to be a bloodstained Chinese soldier who was sitting on the couch, waving his handgun at anyone who came near. On another evening a bullet hole was left in the glass door as a memento from an unhappy customer. Fortunately, there were not too many of these.

Despite the occasional dangers, dancing was a popular past-time in Lhasa. It was not used exclusively for romance. Girls danced with girls and boys waltzed with boys. The disco was particularly popular with the young Chinese soldiers and they would often dance together in their uniforms, arm in arm to the slow numbers.

After the Chinese waltz, the next favourite dance was synchronised disco. The most complicated of these was The Thirty Six Steps. One person would start and soon the entire dance floor would be a solid mass moving in perfect coordination. Bend the knees three times, kick with the left leg twice, walk forward three paces, right foot first, kick forwards with the left leg, turn, kick back with the left leg, side step three paces to the right . . . and so it went on for 36 steps.

The waitresses at the Miss Tibet gala evening were doing superbly. No one seemed to mind if the soup was little bit cold and half of it was in the saucer. Barba crammed the evening full of surprises. A Tibetan magician made bowls of noodles from paper, the entire Housekeeping Department dressed in their brown Mao-style uniforms came on stage and sang Communist propaganda songs. There was even a Miss Foreigner in Tibet competition. Barba had chosen his favourite foreigner, Mary-Anne Bishop, who had been in Tibet studying Black-necked Cranes. A horse drawn carriage came in, pulling a pair of enormous weighing scales. Poor Mary-Anne had to sit on the scales and receive as her prize – her own weight in yak cheese. As the horse departed, it stopped in front of the head table, lifted up its tale and dropped a huge pile of steaming dung on the dance floor. Everyone roared with laughter. Everyone that is, except for Charlie, who had to scoop it up.

Finally, the great Miss Tibet election itself. The girls, all pre-selected by the Tibet Cultural Bureau, paraded along the stage wearing costumes from different parts of Tibet. Who knows what the judges were doing, or even if their votes were counted.

The 'housewives' and 'teachers' ran to the front of the stage with their 'home videos' and souvenir snap cameras and after some confusion, Conny announced the winner as a Miss Droma wearing a costume from Gyantse. Gesang, the head of hotel security, rode into the Everest Room on his motor bike with side car and Miss Droma was driven away to the sound of the Filipino band. Never mind that Miss Droma was a married 26 year old mother and pregnant with her second baby. No one would know.

The exhaust fumes from the motorbike filled the room and several guests became nauseous. The hall emptied. The evening had been a great success and Barba's ego swelled to Everest dimensions.

The next morning the hotel also emptied and we were left alone again. The day after a big party always has a strange feeling to it. The corridors which had echoed to the laughter of happy guests in their dinner jackets now stood empty, the only sound being the whistling of the wind. All the excitement was over. None of us had been fired. The hotel was freezing again. Charlie tried in vain to stop a large icicle from returning to the urinal opposite the coffee shop, but within a few minutes of breaking it off it would be back again.

Barba was exhausted, and left for Christmas vacation. So too did the rest of the expats. I was left alone, with the 'English teachers' Nancy and Bob, which was rather a depressing thought and with Conny, who I had the task of training in the Sales Department. This was a far more enjoyable prospect.

Thankfully, I had not seen much of Nancy and Bob since their arrival in Lhasa. Tashi would come back from the English lessons and tell me more than I wanted to know about them. They seemed to treat the lessons more like Sunday School junior class than adult education. Tashi asked me if it was normal that the staff should be made to play the games of small children. They had been told to tie balloons to their feet and then jump around in the courtyard (or 'playground' as Nancy and Bob looked at it) and try to pop their colleagues' balloons. Nancy shrieked with laughter at every pop and gave away her precious Mr Smiley stickers to the winners.

It was a strange concept to me. The Tibetans had a wonderful religion of their own which had seen them through untold hardships and deprivations and yet, Nancy and Bob were intent on converting them to Nancy's particular off-beat brand of Christianity.

Not surprisingly, their methods were having little impact on the local population. Tibetan Buddhism had withstood the extremes of the Cultural Revolution – it could certainly withstand Mr Smiley stickers. With the Chinese, who were caught between the atheist principals of Communism and the overpowering spiritualism present everywhere in Tibet, Nancy and Bob had a better chance. They focused their attentions on a Chinese boy who had left his job as a receptionist as he was bullied by the bell boys. They renamed him 'Jacob' and concentrated all their efforts on him. Thankful that they were easing off the Tibetans and had left the expats unmolested, I put aside my personal thoughts on their business in Tibet and acted as Christianly as possible by promising to invite them to the hotel Christmas dinner.

I was determined to save something special for Christmas. Since Chef had left on vacation, the variety of food, which had never been good at the best of times, reached its lowest ever levels. There was virtually nothing to buy in the local market, the stores were bare and Mr Han, the local Purchasing Manager would not be going on a purchasing trip until the spring.

Cabbage and spam became the only supplements to yak meat. Fried spam, diced spam with cabbage, boiled spam strips on a bed of cabbage, spam cut into imaginative shapes to pretend it isn't spam with cabbage. The choice was becoming very depressing and my diet grew progressively unhealthy. To mark the occasion, I taped the chorus of the Spam song from Monty Python in the middle of a section of Vivaldi's Four Seasons. Every so often, 'Spam, Wonderful Spam' would blurt out over the PA system and startled guests would look up from their food. A few seconds later they would go back to their plates of spam as Vivaldi's 'L'Inverno Allegro' blasted through the squeaky in-house music system again. Had they been dreaming? Tibet had a profound effect on many visitors. They returned to the West with unanswered questions on spiritualism, the meaning of life, and whether they had really heard the Spam song while they were eating.

I sat in the coffee shop, decided against the special of the day, which was yet another enticing combination of spam and cabbage and instead ordered a large plate of chips. After 20 minutes a small plate arrived with ten miserable chips.

'No, no,' I said, 'I ordered a *large* plate of chips.'

The waitress sighed visibly, returned to the kitchen, and came back into the restaurant with the same ten chips on a large plate. After all, that is what I asked for. They really must think we are stupid.

The coffee shop kitchens were kept warm by the stoves boiling cabbage, but the steam also caused some of the salt cellars to clog up. I asked Zhang Li to put a few grains of rice in the salt pots to dry them out again. She looked at me with a completely bewildered expression. I explained again. 'Oh, yes Mr Alec,' she said, the penny finally dropping.

One of the greatest problems with the staff was that they had no interest in thinking, or coming up with any new ideas. We would give our big speeches about 'we are all Holiday Inn together, working as a team, all for Holiday Inn' and they would just look at us blankly. They thought it was a very peculiar notion that they were expected to work hard just because they worked for Holiday Inn.

Conny and I tried to change this attitude in the Sales Department. We gave our staff a sheet of paper each and asked them to write on the left-hand side what they were doing at the time and on the right-hand side what they would like to be doing. We thought that secretaries might want to be more involved in PR or take on more responsibility with the local agents or go on sales trips abroad. A week later, not one of the staff had filled out any part of the form. I asked Tashi what was going on. I explained that we wanted to develop the staff, train and motivate. Tashi shrugged his shoulders. 'It doesn't matter what we write Mr Alec. We have to do as you say.'

So this was the system. Good old Communism. It was no use thinking for yourself because you always have to do what you are told.

In the coffee shop the salt cellars had gone from bad to worse. No matter how many I tried, I couldn't get a single grain of salt out of them. I opened one up. Zhang Li had put *cooked* rice inside. True, I had not told her that I wanted dry rice grains. So how was she to know?

Christmas approached and a steady trickle of guests came through the hotel. These were the expats from companies in China who had fallen for the direct mail shot (that had gone out in the envelopes with the stamps on the reverse). They loved Lhasa, but complained bitterly of the cold. There was no hope of the heating being switched on again and the temperature inside the hotel dropped to below zero. On the coldest day in the office the thermometer on my desk sank to minus eleven degrees Celsius. I opened the door in the morning to find that a water pipe had burst in the ceiling above the sofa and our filing cabinets. Clusters of icicles hung from the ceiling tiles in great cascades of frozen stalactites. The filing cabinet was a block of ice and files left out overnight on the sofa had to be cracked open.

I wore my Chinese long johns, layer upon layer of T-shirts, my thickest suit and then a down jacket. I walked around like the Michelin Man and just kept my teeth from chattering. Charlie had leant us a small electric fan-heater which had no effect whatsoever on heating the office, but was quite good at keeping the feet warm. I had brought in two lap-top computers from Hong Kong when I came back from the Miss Tibet promotions and these also needed warming with the fan-heaters to start them up in the morning. Any coffee which Conny and I had left in the cups would be solid ice if we forgot to clean the cups out. This was seriously cold. I could see why the other expats had all found a reason why they absolutely had to take their leave over the Christmas period.

Christmas Day itself felt special in Lhasa even though life outside the hotel continued as usual. Herds of yak were driven along the roads to the market, and the Barkhor, as vibrant as can be, was packed with pilgrims. Inside the hotel, I carried on with my plans to celebrate Christmas. I asked Tu Dian to decorate the coffee shop and we went through the Christmas dinner menu for the handful of guests who had chosen the Holiday Inn Lhasa as their Christmas home.

I also invited the local travel agents to the lunch and accompanied by Tashi, visited their offices to hand them the invitations personally. This was a mistake. I had not been inside their offices before and it would have been better if I had left it that way. We called first at the office of China Youth Travel Service (CYTS). Their previous manager had been banished in disgrace for allowing a journalist on a tour in Tibet. The new manager, a Mr Zhang, had been sent to Lhasa from Beijing and I wondered what he had done wrong to be sent here. More to the point, where had they sent the previous manager? What place did the Chinese consider to be worse than Tibet? Mr Zhang didn't know the answer and quickly changed the subject.

He said that he was always shown around travel agents' offices when he went abroad, so he would show me around his.

Mr Zhang's offices were on the second floor of a large rambling Tibetan house which he said had belonged to a noble family. They wouldn't have recognised much now, apart from the beautiful stone work of the exterior. Large rectangular blocks of granite were hemmed in place by smaller slithers of granite and covered in the ubiquitous whitewash. Concrete stairs led up the outside in an obvious post 1959 addition and then it was hard to tell what was new and badly decorated and what was original but falling down. Mr Zhang proudly showed me the various offices: the guides office with the group code numbers chalked up on a large blackboard, the accounts office with piles of papers covering the desk and the floor and then his office, complete with frilly nylon settee covers and jam jars of tea.

From there everything went down hill: the scramble over piles of mountaineering gear at the office of TMA in the Himalaya Hotel, the dingy office of Lhasa Travel in the Sunlight Hotel to the filthy office of China International Travel Service (CITS) Xigaze branch in the Tibet Hotel. I thought this was as low as you could go until we walked a few doors down the corridor in the Tibet Hotel, to the office of the CITS Shannan branch.

We knocked on the door. There was no reply but we could hear noises from inside, so Tashi nudged the door open. The time was 12 noon. There were two beds in the office. One was unmade. The other had one of the office 'workers' in it, stretching and yawning loudly. The one who was standing up was not in much better shape. Hair standing on end in typical post-siesta style, one trouser leg of the crumpled, crimplene suit rolled up to the knee. He burped loudly in our direction and we were hit by the stench of yesterday's garlic.

The entire office was an absolute pit. Piles of soiled clothing lay heaped in the middle of the floor. Piles of rubbish in the corners. A rotting black and green banana skin stretched tentacles of mould across the carpet. We had to wait for one of them to look for some important papers, which he thought might be in one of the piles, or in a draw, or perhaps in a pocket somewhere. I picked up a new brochure of the CITS Shannan Branch. In English it described their services; 'It is expensive but worthy of it, while it is inexpensive but beneficial to it.' I thought about this for quite some time. No. It really doesn't make any sense.

While waiting, Tashi asked me for some words in English. I pointed out objects in the room: video, photocopy, photocopier and finally – lost for pleasant words in that airless, odour-filled room – I introduced him to the meaning of the word 'disgusting' and we left.

Holiday Inn Lhasa, despite the first impression of some of our guests, was heaven on earth compared to the other hotels of Tibet. Back in the safety of the Holiday Inn, Tu Dian proudly called me to the restaurant to show me the decorations he had prepared for Christmas. He had dug up a stunted, half-dead conifer from the hotel grounds and covered it with fluffy cotton wool and the remains of last year's Christmas baubles.

For some reason, Christmas baubles were highly prized by the staff and each year a significant proportion were stolen. Sometimes they even took the imitation snow. The tree stood by the doorway, where the security guards could keep an eye on it, and in the centre of the room, on a table with Charlie's best red table cloth, was Tu Dian's *piece de résistance* – a cage containing four large white rabbits.

Tu Dian was so pleased with it that I hadn't the heart to tell him that rabbits were associated with Easter and not really a necessary addition to the dining room at Christmas time.

'Well done Tu Dian,' I said, '*Yagadoo.*'

Believe it or not, *yagadoo* means 'good' in Tibetan. It is tempting to say 'yagadagadoo', but as the Flintstones have not made it to Tibet, this falls rather flat with them. Tu Dian was happy. Fifteen of us sat down for the Christmas dinner. A select crowd of the local travel agents, a group of Germans from Beijing who were wearing red hats with white bobbles, two Belgian engineers who had come out to install a PBX system at the Lhasa telephone exchange, Conny, myself and the dreaded Nancy and Bob. We sat there around the table, in sub-zero temperatures with tinny Christmas music blaring over the PA, staring at the white rabbits.

A Himalayan Hamster shot across the doorway of the coffee shop. Fortunately the food arrived before any of the guests noticed it and then all concentration was on eating. The meal was excellent. A Tibetan bean soup for starters. Imported cold cuts of meat as second course followed by roast Chengdu chicken and not a piece of cabbage, yak or spam in sight. Dessert was a very passable creme caramel. Conny showed the chefs how to make a delicious mulled wine and we even celebrated by using Chinese Dynasty wine as the main ingredient, which has the rare distinction of coming out of a bottle with a cork. Most Chinese wines are peculiar chemical brews, held in the bottles by screw tops and if left over night in a glass, they tend to separate into a clear liquid and an evil looking purple substance.

Just before dessert, the rabbits started becoming frisky. The cage rattled as the rabbits thumped away at making baby rabbits. Not all the guests found it amusing and reluctantly I asked Tu Dian to take them away.

The Tibetans loved Christmas because it signalled the start of the New Year party season. The parties would extend through Western New Year, into January or February for Chinese New Year and on until the most important of all – Tibetan New Year, which could be as late as March.

Between Christmas and New Year there was a party every night. The Foreign Affairs Office winter party, the CITS party dining on highly suspicious items in their refrigerator restaurant beneath the Potala Palace and worst of all – the 'Advanced Workers' party. This demonstrated all that Communism stands for: a group of various workers from units involved with tourism were presented with 'Advanced Worker' certificates in front of a bored, clapping crowd. We sat in our overcoats in the filled-in swimming pool of the Tibet Hotel, which had been turned into a nightclub, while the 'Advanced Workers' paraded around the dance floor. There was an engineer from our hotel, although what 'advanced work' he had done, nobody could tell me.

They held their banners high as we listened to the inevitable speeches. Everyone nodded and clapped when they thought they should. We were served warm beer, inedible cold meat and bowls of sunflower seeds. Grisly bits of yak meat accompanied slices of unidentified animal organs on chipped plates. I left mine untouched and spent my time trying to master the art of eating sunflower seeds. I assume that this sport is an import from China, but it has been widely accepted by Tibetans. You have to pick up a handful of sunflower seeds, pop them one at a time into your mouth and then, without the aid of your hands, crack the seed open between your teeth, spitting out the seed case on the floor while swallowing the seed kernel and talking simultaneously. If you are good at this you can build up the speed of emptying an AK47 in the Barkhor and the floor by your chair will be covered in a crunchy coating of empty sunflower seeds. I was never very good at it but it kept me amused while the speeches were going on.

New Year's Eve was the excuse for yet another party. The Tibet Tourism Bureau had the bright idea to call it the 'Visit Tibet Year' party. It was a good idea, it was just a pity that they had not told anyone about this earlier. Nobody knew that the following year was going to be 'Visit Tibet Year,' but such minor technicalities were unimportant to them. It was a similar case when CAAC started flights between Lhasa and Kathmandu. They had kept it secret until the first flight landed and were then surprised that the flight had been empty.

Promotion and even the basics of marketing were alien concepts to the Communists. This always baffled me as you would think that if they were so good at brain-washing a billion people into thinking that Mao was great and that the Little Red Book was essential to life, then they would know a thing or two about selling ideas, promotions and PR. This could however explain why the word they used for all the marketing activities we undertook was 'propaganda.'

'Making some more *propaganda*?' Tashi would ask as I warmed up the computer to type in the latest edition of the Tibet Travel News.

I was unable to avoid the Mao Tai *gambays* of the 'Visit Tibet Year' party and was very pleased when it finished abruptly and everyone went home. I tried to play Scrabble with Conny that night but it was a pretty boring way of spending New Year's Eve – finally we gave up and listened to the BBC World Service wish their listeners in Asia a very Happy New Year.

On our Western New Year's Day, Jig Me again gave the expats a day off. I slept in and only just made it to the buffet before the coffee shop closed at 10am. The tray of so called 'bacon' looked even more unappetising than ever. I fished around in the grease with the stainless steel serving spoon but all I could find were small cubes of hairy pork fat. There was some curled up spam in another dish which looked equally unappealing. The bread rolls were positively dangerous. They would have been better suited to the construction industry than as a food item. I was not going to risk my teeth on them, as going to the dentist at the Barkhor was not high on my list of priorities. I found Tu Dian and told him that this was not acceptable. I had become very good at these speeches. He bowed his head, frowned and nodded. 'Sorry Mr Alec. Tomorrow okay.'

I looked at the tray of scrambled eggs. At least it was still yellow, but it had gone fairly solid. I hacked off a corner and returned to my table where Zhang Li had poured me a cup of five-hour-strong Shanghai coffee.

To give the impression that the coffee shop was heated, each table was supplied with a small pot of burning alcohol – the type used to keep pans warm when served on the table. They did not generate any significant amount of heat but it was fun to pick them up and roll the alcohol quickly around the rim as this produced a great cloud of flame which leapt up to the ceiling. This game soon lost its attraction and I spent the afternoon with Conny climbing one of the small hills by the pointy mountains at the west end of the Lhasa valley. It was a beautiful day but by the time we returned to the hotel I was feeling rather ill.

The scrambled egg was taking its revenge. I just made it back to my room before exploding. Liquid came from holes I never knew I had. I have had food-poisoning many times in the past, from experimenting with unknown foodstuffs during my travels as a back-packer, but I had never been knocked out by anything like this. Shamefully, I told everyone that it must have been something I ate at the Barkhor – while only Tu Dian and I knew the real source. Tu Dian felt responsible for me and made special soups which Conny brought me but I could not keep them down. Jig Me wanted to send me to the People's Number One Hospital but I insisted that I would have to be dead before I went in there. Conny called for Dr Grubby but he was sick too. The flights to Kathmandu had been cancelled for the winter and the flights to Chengdu had been out of action for the last two days. 'Can you die from food poisoning?' I kept asking myself. Would I get a sky burial?

I was out cold for four full days. I was eventually brought back to life by rehydration packets which Sue, the new manager from Save the Children, had brought from her previous assignment in Africa. Conny mixed them up and told me they were, 'Delicious. Like lemonade.'

Both of these statements were untrue.

To make matters worse, I contracted a severe bout of flu. A nurse from the People's Number One Hospital came up to the hotel to give me gigantic syringe-fulls of penicillin. They were the syringes of horror movies. Enormous things with long needles which she filled up in front of me. With a sadistic smile, she then waved for me to roll over and jammed the needle into my backside. Slowly, ever so slowly, she emptied it into me. Twice a day. Alternating buttocks. There were no pills available – this was too simple a solution – if it was going to cure you then it had to hurt. Between the injections Conny nursed me back to health and I could see that there was more to beautiful Belgians than their chocolate.

I was still white when Barba returned. He laughed when I told him what had happened.

'You see Alec. I am a vegetarian. I do not even eat onions or mushrooms as they interfere with my meditation. This could never have happened to me.'

Barba had brought back a new member of staff – his Sicilian side-kick – Guiseppe Bonetti. It is hard to imagine a closer fit to the Italian stereotype. A Danny Devito look-alike with one sole objective in life – sex. Bonetti's idea of nirvana was not to break away from the endless cycle of rebirths but to find himself in one endless orgy.

He was a perfect companion for Barba. Each morning they could discuss in detail their conquests of guests or staff of the previous night. So much for the cryptic warnings I had received in Hong Kong about trying on shirts. The lessons learnt from the episode in the Palace Hotel lift were now largely forgotten. Bonetti was officially in Lhasa as Food & Beverage Manager and he struggled valiantly with Tu Dian, his local deputy and Mr Han the Purchasing Manager, to improve the food quality.

Chef returned to Lhasa and found a way to improve the desserts on the buffet table. The cakes never had soft centres but were always frozen solid. Guests would chip at creme caramels with their spoons, thinking they were cracking the caramelised sugar of a crème brulée. But it was not sugar. It was ice. Chef found that if the desserts were stored overnight in the refrigerator instead of being left out overnight, the problem was solved.

Although the cuisine started to improve, the traditional fight between Executive Chefs and Food & Beverage Managers soon resumed.

'How can you have a *German* chef?!' screamed Bonetti.

'How can I verk in ze kitchen ven I find Bonetti in here cooking his own pasta on my stoves?!' shouted Chef.

Morale was sinking to rock bottom. There was a day when we had no guests in the hotel. No one. Not a sausage. Four hundred and sixty eight rooms, 18 suites, two Presidential Villas and not one guest. Empty.

The wind whistled along the corridors and a lone sweeper from Housekeeping Department polished the marble floor in the lobby. One of the expats had brought a video of *The Shining* up from Hong Kong. That night we huddled around the television in room 3205 and watched the horror story about the family of a mad axe-man, who bore a striking resemblance to Barba, living in an empty hotel. They were in the depths of winter, cut off from the outside world, as all manners of horrific incidents took place. Was that noise just the squeaking hinges of the fire doors blowing in the wind or had a tricycle gone down the corridor?

'I put ze lights off in ze coffee shop,' said Chef. 'And now zey are on again.'

I still shudder at the memory of that night.

Barba was also becoming scary. His moods were less predictable and his rages greater than ever before. His wife had refused to come out to Lhasa with him and he took out his anger on whoever he saw fit. He abandoned the management table in the coffee shop and set up his own table in the winter sunshine out in the courtyard. He ordered one of Charlie's finest table cloths for his own table, while all the other tables remained bare. Bonetti was his personal chef and regardless of what the guests and other expats had to put up with, Barba was assured a freshly made Italian meal every day. He and Bonetti brought in their own supply of extra virgin olive oil, mozzarella and parmesan cheese. Any guest asking to eat what the manager was dining on was given a short answer, normally consisting of two words. Any guest making the mistake of sitting at Barba's table was sent running and waitress Zhang Li was given the task of keeping guests away. It was pitiful watching her trying to explain to a guest who had paid $200 to $300 a day for the privilege of being in Tibet, why he or she could not sit at the table.

'You no sit here. Here Mr Barba. Mr Barba Manager.'

No one could join Barba at his table except by personal invitation. The two exceptions were Bonetti, who provided him with food and entertainment, and myself, who told him what was going on in the hotel. Barba adopted me as his protege and each morning at his breakfast he taught me his ideology. Although this gave me a great insight into his marketing genius – it also meant that I had to sit and listen to his obscure beliefs.

One morning at the breakfast table, Barba sat in a pensive mood. 'Alec, to manage someone,' he scooped his freshly made doughnut in the bowl of yak yogurt and honey and looked me straight in the eye, 'find out their weakness. Then manipulate them.'

As soon as he had passed on this secret to success, I suddenly saw everything in a new light. This was how he treated all of us. Never mind Maslow's *Heirarchy of Needs*, or the trendy *Management by Objectives*. This was Barba's 'Management by Manipulation.' Now I understood why behind the picture of his wife by his bedside, stood a picture of Adolf Hitler. I had seen and heard enough.

Chef had also come to the end of his tether. He had taken enough insults about German cuisine and went to Barba to hand in his notice. I followed the same day. It was a well thought out and carefully worded letter. Life with Barba had become intolerable.

Barba climbed on top of his desk and shouted, 'How dare you resign?!' He looked at Chef and at me.

'*Nobody* is allowed to resign before me! *I* am the boss here. If anyone resigns it is me! HEATHER! Come in here and take down this telex to Hong Kong.'

Barba ran his hands through his hair and dictated the message from on top of his desk. 'Quick, Heather, Quick! Write!'

Heather trembled. She had seen him angry but never this angry. And never standing on top of his desk.

'To the Vice President, Holiday Inn Asia-Pacific etc etc. You can use my contract as toilet paper. I am leaving this no hope company now. Yours, E. Barba.'

10

House Arrest

Barba chuckled to himself as we bumped along in the back of Dorje's Landcruiser on the way out of Lhasa. He had caused panic at Head Office and considered this to be one of the highlights of his time with Holiday Inn.

'So Alec. We're all friends again now, eh?'

He tweaked my ear and burst out laughing. Whatever the medication was it must have been working. Dorje put his foot down as we crossed the Lhasa bridge, not in the direction of the airport but east, towards the monastery of Drak Yerpa. Barba had backed down from his resignation because ultimately he wanted to be fired, not to resign. As his character returned to his normal, just tolerable self again, Chef and I had tentatively withdrawn our resignations.

'I knew you weren't really going to resign,' he said to me. 'You have just been learning too many of the great Barba's tricks.'

'I still have the letter in the computer, Mr Barba,' I shouted back above the roar of the engine. 'I can easily put a new date at the top and print it out again.'

He smiled.

Dorje skidded on a patch of ice as we overtook a group of pilgrims and we called out for him to slow down. The pilgrims were packed in the back of a trailer drawn by a small, open tractor engine. One step above a rickshaw, these vehicles were the main public transport system of Tibet. We had passed many of them on their way to Ganden, which lay a few kilometres further up the road. The monks of Ganden had once played a central part in the Tibetan government, together with the two other great monasteries of Lhasa – Sera and Drepung. Ganden alone housed nearly 5,000 monks until the time of the Cultural Revolution, when each building was systematically blown apart by the fanatical Red Guards. The ruins stand out as a great scar on the mountain-side and are a constant reminder of both the power that must have been wielded from here in former times and the brutality that put an end to it. Today, Ganden is slowly, cautiously, being rebuilt.

Dorje paid no attention to us and sped past the pilgrims, through the stark winter scenery of the Ganden road. The Kyi Chu next to us had dried up to a trickle and the river bed had been turned into a vast stretch of sand dunes and pebble banks. Dead seed heads of Tibetan clematis hung onto the dry stone walls between the barren fields. There were no colours other than the desolate brown of the hills and the bright blue high altitude sky.

We left the Ganden road at a Chinese suspension bridge and crossed back to the north side of the Kyi Chu. Dorje was not concerned that the tarmac road had finished and he managed to keep up his speed along the dirt track, leaving a long plume of dust billowing out behind us.

As we passed through a cluster of Tibetan houses, we came across a group of little girls in the road, all carrying school books. They waved to us and Barba did his good deed for the day by asking Dorje to stop and give them a lift – presumably to the school in the next village. We piled them up in the back of the Landcruiser – seven smiling, shy, yak-buttery little things.

Meeting children from the villages was always one of the joys of going outside Lhasa. No matter where you stopped, children would appear from nowhere and come up to the Landcruiser. All have beautiful white teeth and rosy cheeks which glow as they smile at you. Their eyes sparkle through a tangle of matted hair and a skin which has not seen soap and water for a very long time. For some, the annual bathing festival in September, is the only occasion they have a complete dip. And in this climate, who can blame them? The back of their hands and their wrists are like black leather, encrusted with layer upon layer of dirt. Their clothes are mixtures of traditional *chubas*, nylon tracksuits and factory made polyester shirts bought from the Chinese traders. Whatever the original colour all eventually become a universal brown, engrained with dust blown up in the sand storms which sweep across the plateau every spring. Some of the children remain sewn up in their clothes throughout the year. In the dry climate and high altitude, there has been no need for the kind of hygiene that we subject ourselves to in the West. We have become victims of our own advertising campaigns. Does your shirt really have to be whiter than white? Does your washing powder have to remove all stains, even at low temperatures? These may be essentials in our Western society but for the Tibetan villagers they are ridiculous questions.

Through sign language and example, we asked our new friends to sing to us as we went along. They needed very little prompting and as soon as they had understood, there was no stopping them. Seven little voices shrieking full blast the Tibetan top ten village songs. It was a wonderful drive; bouncing along through the barren landscape with the Tibetan hit parade being screeched to us from the back of the car. Whenever we turned to look at them, they would instantly bow their heads, or duck behind the back of the seat – but they continued to sing.

We were wondering where their school was when we came to the turn off for the Yerpa valley, which turns north away from the Kyi Chu. They hadn't shown any signs of wanting to get out of the car. The track crossed a dried up river bed with patches of ice where the last of the summer water had been trapped in pools. We stopped to pick up a young monk who was taking supplies of *tsampa* (ground roasted barley) up to Drak Yerpa. He beamed smiles at us and against the background chorus of Tibetan song, we all said *tashi delai* to each other for the next five minutes. Dorje switched over to four wheel drive and took us up through a series of terraced barely fields, small villages and along the frozen stream bed until we reached the final village directly beneath the mountain-side of Yerpa. It had been Barba's idea to visit the remote settlement of Yerpa as a means of reconcilliation and to celebrate the withdrawing of our resignations.

For a Tibetan, Yerpa scores highly in the big time Buddhism league. Several of the key players in Tibetan history have stayed here – Atisha, Songsten Gampo and Guru Rimpoche. The caves of Yerpa are considered to be amongst the most important meditation and power centres of Tibet. Barba was already shaking with the 'good vibes' in the village at the bottom of the hill. What was he going to be like when we reached the caves?

It was a 40 minute walk up the steep slope and this seemed to calm him down again. He paused on the way up.

'Alec. Why did you come to Tibet?'

'For this Mr Barba. For adventure.'

'Adventure! Ha! Call this adventure?'

He was taking on his role as my mentor again and I could tell that a big lesson was approaching.

'A real adventurer Alec, is someone who travels through the four disciplines of life: the mind, the body, the soul and sex.'

We took a few more paces before stopping for breath.

'Alec, have you ever taken drugs?'

'No, Mr Barba.'

'Then you have never travelled in the mind. The body? Well physically you are here, so I suppose you might pass that one. The soul? What do you know about tantric Buddhism? About the secrets of the Mahayana way? While you waste your time in the Barkhor and in the hills looking at nature I have received my second stage teaching on the path to enlightenment.'

'Mr Barba. Buddhism is about compassion and wisdom, right? So if you are a Buddhist, how come you have a picture of Hitler by your bed and why did you threaten to break Chef's arms and legs when he wanted to resign?'

Barba exploded: 'I am a *student* of Buddhism!'

Somehow this was meant to explain everything. We walked up for the next ten minutes in silence, pausing only to regain our breath. The monk with his heavy sack of *tsampa* had already reached the caves and the group of schoolgirls were up by the first set of ruins. Just before we reached the strip of flat land with the ruins of Yerpa Drubde, Barba stopped and looked at me.

'And sex Alec. Do you ever tie your girlfriends up in chains?'

'Er, no, Mr Barba.'

'No. I didn't think so. You have so much to learn. I tell you what. I'm not going to stay here long Alec. I will be leaving as soon as I have finished my studies. Then, when I go, I shall leave you my chains.'

We walked on a few more paces until we reached the top of the first hill.

'I have a mirror too which you hang around your neck. And a mask. Have you ever . . .'

Fortunately he was interrupted by a new burst of song from the group of little girls who had come back down the hill-side to see why we were taking so long. The monk with the bags of *tsampa* waved to us from up ahead.

There was not much left of Yerpa Drubde, the old monastery. The Red Guards had made an even better job of it than they had at Ganden and a pile of rubble stood where the teaching college had once been. Robin accentors perched on the ruins, jut a few feet from us. The birds here were remarkably tame, as if they knew they were in no danger from the humans who lived here. From the hill where the monastery had once stood, a magnificent view opens up of the cliff-side above with its dozens of caves and small temples. Many have now been restored and the guide books we took with us were way out of date. Even as we looked inside the temples, major restoration work was being carried out. A set of new statues, each over five metres high was being built inside the main temple. The heads and bodies had already been completed – beautifully sculpted out of brown clay. The painting still had to be finished and bundles of straw and twigs poked out of the arms where the hands were missing. As with all Tibetan Buddhist art, seen in the right context, this was going to be awesome. Put on display in a show case in the West, it loses all of its power. It has to be seen against the backdrop of a stark and unforgiving environment in a land where the people believe in demons and Bodhisattvas and where Dakini walk across the sky. Apparently, Yerpa had been a good place for this, and it is said that a group of 80 yogis who lived here regularly took to the air, soaring around the valley.

It would certainly have been a handy way from getting from one cave to another. Barba stayed in one of the small temples to meditate, and I continued along the *kora* with the group we had accumulated – Dorje the driver, the monk with the *tsampa*, several recluses from the hill caves who had ventured out to greet us and of course the seven little girls.

The caves were fascinating and the monks proudly showed us around, pointing out many 'self-manifested' images. These are statues and carvings coming out of the cave wall, that *no one* has carved. They just 'self-manifested' out of the rock. Yes. Honestly. They weren't there one day and then they were the next.

We were also shown an extraordinary 'Om,' the Tibetan writing of the first character of 'Om Mani Padme Hom.' It was made of what appeared to be a seem of white quartz in black rock and this too had self-manifested. Quite something. If you choose not to believe in self-manifestation, just how *did* it get there?

The kora took us high up to caves along pathways jutting out of the cliff edge, and to grottos where the ancient masters had meditated. It was an incredible setting – these small caves and temples perched high on a steep slope with a view stretching down the Yerpa valley to the dry river bed and the snow-capped mountains beyond. If I was going to come back as a flying yogi, this would be the place for me.

There was silence except for the distant chanting of solitary monks in their caves and the incessant nattering and giggling of our seven little friends. I rested on the sunburnt grass near the stone seat, which the monks told me is the throne for the Dalai Lama when he visited, or for when he will visit. I slept for a while, thinking of the Dalai Lama sitting at this stone and imagining the great crowd of Tibetans there would be across the hill-side. How I hope that day will come.

The cry of Red-billed Choughs woke me, as they played in the air currents hitting the cliff-side above us. Barba meditated, Dorje chatted to a nun who was in her third year of isolation, and the little girls played in the ruins of Drak Yerpa. Through a combination of my fluent sign language and extremely limited Tibetan, I discovered that they were not *going* to school but were on their way back from school and had just been standing outside their own village when we picked them up. For all they knew we might have been taking them off to Kathmandu. What would their parents be thinking?

We moved on when the sun fell behind the mountains to the west, causing a dramatic drop in temperature. Himalayan Griffon vultures, with wingspans the size of golf umbrellas hoisted themselves skywards on the last thermals of the day, heading for their evening roost. We set off in great style – our little friends singing away full blast in the back of the car. One of the hot favourites was a musical version of 'Om Mani Padme Hom' – another ingenious idea, which means that you can even gain merit while you sing. We gave two other people a lift back down the hill. It was hard to tell who they were; pilgrims who had been along for the day, visiting monks or nuns, or residents going for a night out. At first glance, monks can be difficult to tell from nuns. They don't make it easy like Christian nuns do. As far as I could see, they wear the same colour robes, have the same sunburnt skin, the same cropped hair and exactly the same beautiful smiles. The give away to look out for is that Tibetan nuns sometimes wear a brown woollen cloth wrapped around their heads.

We dropped everyone off at their respective villages, with big waves from the seven little village girls. Slightly anxious that there may have been a search party set up in the village –a lynch mob on their way to find who had absconded with the daughters of the village – we asked Dorje to step on it. This was of course totally unnecessary; a) because Dorje always stepped on it and b) because he didn't understand a word we were staying. In the Tibetan vocabulary that I had picked up I had learnt the essential phrase for 'please drive more slowly' but I had never thought I would need to know the Tibetan for 'step on it, there is an angry-looking man with an axe approaching us at speed'.

Back in Lhasa, the celebrations for Chinese New Year were under way. I survived the inevitable party and managed to be in bed before midnight. A few fireworks were going off outside, but this was nothing unusual and I snuggled into bed trying to get to sleep. Suddenly, at midnight, yells and shrieks rang out from the staff quarters. Chinese fireworks lit the sky. Firecrackers were being thrown out of the windows of the army barracks across the road and the concrete walls of the staff quarters were lit by flashes from giant Chinese fire crackers, as the pounding thuds echoed between the buildings. The pack of dogs in the hotel grounds raced, terrified, barking and howling from their hide-outs as rockets, golden rain and Roman candles poured across their territory. Any thoughts of sleep were out of the question.

Tibetan New Year was a week later. The Tibetans follow the lunar calendar and divide the year into 12 months of 30 days each. Unfortunately, this doesn't quite work out, so just as we have to add an extra day every leap year, the Tibetans add a whole month every so often. And why not? It makes a lot more sense than having a year with months of 28, 30 and 31 days.

Every Tibetan at the hotel took leave for a week and the expats were also given time off. It was a wonderful occasion and we were invited from house to house by the Tibetan staff. It was a time for singing Tibetan songs and drinking chang and the streets were filled with happy, staggering Tibetans in their finest party clothing. They grinned and waved to us and called out 'tashi delai' with even more gusto than usual.

Traditionally the highlight of the New Year celebrations is *Monlam*, where monks from the surrounding monasteries descend upon Lhasa for the Great Prayer Festival. Some 20,000 monks and nuns would cram the streets of Lhasa and control of the city would be handed over to the Shengo – the head of the elite Drepung fighting monks.

The Chinese had rather dampened things down this year by cancelling the Great Prayer Festival. It was a strange notion – a bit like cancelling Christmas. I went down to the Barkhor but nothing was happening. There were fewer monks around than usual. A large flag was pinned to the front of the Jokhang temple and all the Tibetans passing by on the Barkhor were throwing *khatas* up to it. Khatas are the white offering scarves which can be simple muslin or made of pure silk inscribed with auspicious symbols. I had never seen khatas being offered to a flag before and I had never seen a flag like this one. Two snow lions stood either side of a white mountain and the sky was coloured in bands as though in a glorious sunset, of yellow, red, white and blue.

I walked up to the front of the Jokhang to take a closer look and suddenly realised what I was seeing – the forbidden Tibetan national flag. The prison at Trapchi is crowded with monks and nuns who have done nothing more than fly this flag. I returned quickly to the hotel but the thought of the flag and the act of defiance of the monk or nun who had put it there, knowing they would be caught and knowing what it would cost them, stayed on my mind.

After the Tibetan New Year celebrations, I set off to Europe for a sales trip. Each year I would visit tour operators at their offices and at the major travel shows, with the aim of persuading them to feature Tibet in their brochures. Once they were sold on Tibet, there was only one hotel they would be staying in – the Holiday Inn.

On my way out of China, I first visited Xian with Tashi, to make a presentation to a group of expatriates. After a night in Chengdu, arranged by the ever helpful Mr Li, we survived another death-race Chengdu taxi driver and arrived in record-breaking time at Chengdu airport for the early morning flight to Xian. We waited and waited. And we waited some more. No information was given as to what had happened to our flight. Three hours went by. I stared out into the grey mist that always hangs over Chengdu. It was so different to the clean crisp air of Lhasa, with the dazzling brightness of the Tibetan sky. Chengdu was always humid, miserable and grey. Another three hours passed with nothing to do. I paced up and down the corridor, careful not to slip by the spittoons. Another four hours passed by. In total ten and a quarter hours passed before a wailing voice came over the tannoy to announce the departure of our flight to Xian. As if a starting gun had just been fired, the Chinese immediately grabbed all their belongings, hurtled down the stairwell from the waiting room and spilled out onto the tarmac, racing towards the plane. I held Tashi back. 'What is the point?' I said. 'We all have boarding passes. We are all going to get on.'

I was determined that amidst this bedlam I would remain 'British', form a queue and approach the plane with some decency, instead of scrambling and pushing to get on first.

It was a strange plane – an old Russian Illyushin 18, secondhand from Aeroflot. These were christened the 'flying fossils' by the expats. 'So old they have an outside toilet'. Curiously, the baggage is stored with you in the main part of the fuselage, behind a section which is cordoned off with netting. The seats next to me were all taken and I looked around for Tashi. He was nowhere to be seen. I went back to the doorway, and found him at the bottom of the steps with five other passengers, arguing with the stewardess.

'Mr Alec!' Tashi shouted up to me. 'There are not enough seats. Too many tickets. She say I cannot come on!'

So this is the explanation for why everyone in China sprints, pushes and kicks to get on the plane. A boarding card is no guarantee that you have a place. Feeling guilty that it was my fault he had not made it on-board, I helped him argue with the stewardess. The pilot held the plane while we tried to sort something out. He was already over ten hours delayed, so another half hour wouldn't really matter. The stewardess came up with a solution. Tashi and one of the other stranded passengers could come on-board but there would be no seats for them, they would have to sit on suitcases in the luggage compartment.

Tashi made himself comfortable on some large sacks stuffed with garlic grass and one by one the four propellers of the flying fossil chugged up to full speed and the pilot drew away across the runway.

The show went well and as Tashi returned to Chengdu and Lhasa, I carried on to Hong Kong. I had brought with me a suitcase containing a sheepskin *chuba* which I would wear at the sales shows in Europe. I had worn normal *chubas* before but I thought an authentic sheepskin one would go down even better. I opened the bag in the Holiday Inn Golden Mile in Hong Kong and was knocked over by the stench. While the sheepskin had been fine in Lhasa at an altitude of 12,000 feet (3,600 m), in the dry air, here in the humidity of Hong Kong, it had started to deteriorate. I looked at it closely. There were still pieces of meat on it.

There was a bottle of 4711 aftershave in the room and I emptied this over the coat in the hope that it would beat the sheep smell. It didn't. I went outside to Watsons and bought a can of Odour Eater which I sprayed systematically over every part of the sheepskin until the can was empty. I hung the coat in the bathroom and closed the door. At least the smell was out of the bedroom. As soon as I opened the bathroom door, there it was again – dead sheep. The Holiday Inn cleaners refused to touch it and asked me how long I intended to keep it in the room. I asked at a dry cleaners but they sent me away, suggesting I try a furrier.

I had never been in a fur shop before. I rang the security bell of a very superior looking one on Nathan Road and explained my problem to the rather precious Chinaman behind the counter. In a very affected Eton accent he told me that he was well accustomed to dealing with furs from China and asked me to bring it in. Nothing I could say about the state of the sheep could dissuade him. He smiled to the two ladies in the shop who were trying on minks for the Hong Kong 'winter' season. 'We always please our very discerning customers,' he said, bowing to them and smiling obsequiously. They smiled back, flashing their heavy jewellery at us.

Ten minutes later I returned with the *chuba* stuffed into my suitcase and lifted it up onto the display counter. 'Errgghh,' he leapt back as the odour hit him and clutched his silk handkerchief to his nose. 'That is quite by far the most difficult fur I have ever seen. Quite disgusting. Disgusting!' The two women hurried out of the shop without saying a word.

A day and $200 later, the *chuba* was back on the shop counter. He had, as promised, tried to clean it. The wool was soft as silk but the smell was exactly the same. I tried to argue about the price but he told me that wool from the *chuba* had blocked his cleaning machine, causing thousands of dollars of damage. He was negotiating with his insurance company. He had also received complaints from his regular customers about the awful smell of their minks, which had also been cleaned in the morning. Perhaps even today their are some Barkhor dead sheep odours mingling at the high society dinner parties in Hong Kong. I would like to think so.

In Europe, even without my *chuba*, the sales were going well. On the second morning at ITB in Berlin, the largest travel show in the world, I met up with the rest of the Holiday Inn Asia-Pacific team.

'Have you seen the news Alec?' they asked me as I arrived. 'Dozens of Tibetans have been killed! The Chinese have closed Tibet!'

I rushed back to my hotel room and watched the events unfold on CNN. As I sat hunched up on the end of my bed I saw the Barkhor in flames, crowds of monks throwing stones, and yes, the police station on fire again. Martial Law was declared and all tourists expelled. No more would be allowed in until further notice.

I returned to Lhasa via Kathmandu, instead of through Hong Kong. There is a large Tibetan community in Kathmandu and I was told all sorts of stories about the conditions in Lhasa. Apparently rioting was still going on. One told me; 'Some Tibetans are still being arrested, I think *four to five* of them yesterday.'

Another picked up the story; '*Forty five* of them? Tibetans in trouble?'

The rumour gathered pace;

'Forty five Tibetans killed yesterday?'

A Tibetan told me; 'You know, it's disgraceful how the Chinese are oppressing the Tibetans. I have relatives there who do not even have proper bathroom facilities in their house. These Chinese are oppressing them so much.'

Just what kind of bathroom facilities he expected there to be in Tibet remains a mystery to me. As time goes by, the distance between the Tibetans from inside Tibet and those on the outside widens.

With the closure of Tibet to tourists, the flights from Kathmandu to Lhasa were not operating, so I took the overland route in. The first day leaves the squalor of the Kathmandu valley, up through the green and fertile foothills of the Himalaya to the border crossing at Zhangmu. The town itself lies on a steep mountain-side but before reaching it you have to pass the notorious Nepalese customs. They scrutinise every document, every piece of baggage to see if there is something they can confiscate. The previous year, they had taken a video player off one of our expats, as they said there was no paperwork allowing it out of China. They know that you are at their mercy and so you wait, being as polite as possible and wishing them 'Namaste', the Nepali equivalent of 'tashi delai'.

Once away from these nasty little officials and across the bridge you are in a no-man's land between Nepal and Tibet. There is a road here up the steep mountain-side but most of the year it lies in the bottom of the valley, washed down by the summer monsoons. A group of porters offered very reasonable prices to carry my suitcases up the hill. Business had not exactly been booming since the imposition of Martial Law in Lhasa and the closure of Tibet to tourists. It was a tough hike and I was glad of their services. As I struggled up, porters passed me with refrigerators strapped to their foreheads – this is the major trade route between China and Nepal.

The town of Zhangmu is perched precariously on the hill-side and every so often, large chunks of it fall off into the stream, several hundred metres below. The Chinese guards scrutinised my paperwork, visas and permit and passed me over to Dorje, who was waiting patiently for me with a Holiday Inn Landcruiser. As it was late, we stayed the night at the Zhangmu Hotel, which unfortunately, had not yet dropped off into the valley. The rooms were filthy, and all the rubbish from the hotel was strewn down the hill to the stream below.

I undressed in the bathroom and nervously, stepped into the shower. I stood in a small puddle of cold water and looked at the tangle of pipes, tubes, taps and electricity cables on the wall. I read a notice with the instructions for the water heater: 'Pull Lever A to Position B.' As I pulled Lever A, blue sparks shot out of the device and I leapt from the shower. I got dressed again. I could wait until Tingri, the next stop, for a bath.

We left the bamboos and lush vegetation of Zhangmu behind and followed the dirt track up, up and up. Even with Dorje at the wheel, progress up the tortuous track was slow. The trees became shorter and spindlier until they finally disappeared as we rose above the tree-line. The greenery fizzled out and we climbed ever upwards through a crack in the Himalaya and onto the Tibetan plateau. It was a sensational experience. To our left, across a brown plain, was the massive Shishapangma, to our right the mountain range which leads to Everest. We stopped at the 17,000 feet (5,200 m) Thang La ('la' means 'pass' in Tibetan) and Dorje called out the cry of all Tibetans as they reach the summit of passes; 'La! So so so so!'

I would have called it out too but I was having trouble with breathing, let alone shouting out of the window at the top of my voice. My heartbeat was racing and my head pounding. Despite the beauty of the mountain scenery I was very pleased when Dorje pointed out that we were approaching Tingri and the brand new Xegar Hotel. My pleasure was short-lived. There was no water, no electricity and in fact nothing but a great deal of filth in this unimaginatively designed lump of Chinese concrete. Everything, right down to the frilly pink nylon bed-covers, had been imported from eastern China. So too had the 'management.' Breathing was impossible in the festering toilets and no one in their right mind used them. Instead, the car park was used as a much less smelly option.

I persuaded Dorje that this was not a place fit for human habitation, and we left on a side road down to Everest Base Camp. There were no mountaineers about, it was both too early for them and in any case they had been banned from entering Tibet along with all the tourists. We struggled over the Pang La and the mighty range of the Himalaya stood before us. Dorje was not so keen on the road. He liked speed and was unhappy about the rough ride ahead, over boulder screes and icy stream beds where the track had disappeared. We drove over glacial debris towards Rongbuk monastery, thought to be the inspiration behind the mythical Shangri-La of James Hilton's novel.

Rongbuk lies just a few kilometres from Base Camp and the surprised monks made us very welcome. They lit the stove in the guest room and stoked it, not with yak dung, but with wood. There was not a tree for miles around and the fuel was a rare luxury, for which we paid a suitably high price. As night drew on, we settled down into thick sleeping bags which Mark from Save the Children had sent down in the Landcruiser with Dorje, in case we should need them. They had been bought from army surplus stores in Pakistan and had 'High Altitude Use' stamped on the label.

An icy wind blew through the cracks of the monastery walls and wild dogs howled in the starlight outside. Rongbuk is said to be the highest monastery in the world at 16,350 feet (4,980m) and it felt to me as if we were in outer space. My head pounded and my breathing grew erratic. After every few normal breaths I took an involuntary gasp. I shivered to the bone, fully dressed inside the thick sleeping bag. The temperature had dropped to minus 20 degees centigrade. The fire was still crackling in the stove but I calculated that it must be using up the little oxygen available in the room. I opened the door to allow in a fresh supply of oxygen.

I could hear a movement outside, above the noise of the wind. I peered out into the dark and caught sight of the starlight glinting in the eyes of a pack of dogs, as they pounced up the monastery steps towards me. I slammed the door shut just in time. I could feel the claws sinking into the wooden door as they growled and barked outside, snapping at the door handle. I was caught between my worst fears: freezing to death, dying of lack of oxygen or being mauled to death by a pack of savage dogs. This was certainly not my idea of Shangri-La. I spent the worst night of my life between gasping for oxygen out of the door, keeping the dogs at bay with a burning stick and stoking the fire to keep the warmth in the room. Dorje slept soundly throughout.

By morning the dogs had vanished and the view from the steps made up for all the trauma of the previous night. Ahead of the monastery, at the end of the Rongbuk valley, lay the massive wall of the north face of Everest, rising up nearly 4,000 metres higher than where I was standing. I looked in awe. A plume of snow was blowing off the peak, held high in the air like the spray of a breaking wave with an offshore wind. There was nothing around us. Just the little monastery, ice, rock, absolute desolation and this massive grey wall.

Dorje took me further down the trail to the start of the glacial moraine and the location of Everest Base Camp. It was far cleaner than I had expected. A team of Americans, calling themselves 'Mountain Madness' had been to Base Camp the previous season with the noble aim to clean it of the tons of rubbish left over the years by environmentally unfriendly mountaineering groups. They had done an excellent job – all I could find was a small piece of a disposable razor.

The wind howled around me as I walked across to an area where slabs of stone had been set upright. The rocks bore inscriptions to those who have never returned. Wherever I looked, my eyes were taken up to the great mountain. Bleak and unforgiving. The taker of lives. You had to be crazy even to think about it.

Dorje beckoned me. It was time to move on. We waved to the monks at Rongbuk as we passed them on our way back. For the first time I noticed the ruins of many other small buildings. The Red Guards had even carried their dynamite this far.

Unfortunately, the Red Guards had finished their dynamiting by the time the Shigatse Hotel was built. It was one step higher than the Xegar Hotel but that is about all that can be said in its favour. I could see why an American tour leader had returned to Lhasa, describing the Shigatse Hotel as 'vomititious'.

After stopping off at Gyantse to see the amazing Kumbum, built in the shape of a Mandala, we moved on to Lhasa, via lake Yamdrok and the Kamba La. Yamdrok is known as the 'turquoise lake' and is a sacred place for Tibetans. It is also an important wintering spot for migrating waterfowl. On just the tiny portion of the lake which can be seen from the road, a thousand Red-crested Pochard and hundreds of Pintail and Bar-headed Geese stop over in winter.

Younghusband, who had led the British troops into Tibet in 1904, described lake Yamdrok as, 'One of the most beautiful lakes I have ever seen . . . in colour it varied from every shade of violet and turquoise blue and green.'

The description is still true today. The depth and range of colours are remarkable. In the winter the lake is predominantly turquoise as the water absorbs light from the high altitude sky. In summer, the colour changes with the passing of clouds, from moody black to purple and deep sea greens. The view of the lake has remained unchanged from the time when the Capuchin missionaries walked along its shores, the Tartars swept through, the Indian pundits counted their paces, the British expedition carried their trade treaty to sign and the Red Guards marched past with their rucksacks of dynamite.

Unchanged that is until now. For today a great and terrible scheme is afoot by the Chinese. The beauty of lake Yamdrok is being shattered by the construction of a Chinese concrete monstrosity by the lake-side and the excavation of a mighty tunnel out of the lake to the Tsangpo river (down on the other side of the Kamba La). This is an appalling solution to the electricity needs of expanding Tibet. A hydro-electric plant that will drain the Turquoise Lake. Communism and the Environment were never good friends. Unfortunately, the new capitalist China is even worse. We bounced down the hairpin bends on the Lhasa side of the Kamba La and descended into the Tsangpo valley. We were in sight of home and Dorje increased speed, knowing that he would soon be back with his family. Covered in dust from the four day journey and without sight of a bathroom since standing in the cold puddle of the Zhangmu Hotel – I breathed a sigh of relief when Dorje swung the Landcruiser into the forecourt of the Holiday Inn Lhasa. It was the very height of luxury.

But all was not well at the hotel. To start off with, we had no guests. Secondly, my mountain bike, my pride and joy, which I had left chained to the security guards' hut had been stolen. Thirdly, the dreaded visit from the Holiday Inn Worldwide Inspector was about to take place. And fourthly, we were all under house arrest.

11

High Season Approaches

We spent our time preparing for the inspector's visit which all seemed rather futile. We dressed up two staff as doormen and trained them to look as though they had been standing by the door all day, for when he arrived. Everything received a coat of new paint. This is a very convenient way of cleaning, especially in the kitchens where all sorts of apparitions were disguised with a fresh coat of white emulsion. Holiday Inn inspectors are used to this trick and take it for granted, as the Queen does, that everywhere they go there is the smell of fresh paint.

We even hired a special carpet to cover the cold marble floor of the lobby. It was a stunning Tibetan carpet – a pale blue background with flower designs around the border and the eight auspicious Tibetan symbols in a line down the centre. But it was more than just a beautiful carpet – it was the Dalai Lama's carpet. We had borrowed it from the Norbulingka, the Summer Palace of the Dalai Lamas, where it had decorated the floor of the fourteenth Dalai Lama's private cinema. I had some reservations about walking on it. I was not worthy. Alright, the Dalai Lama wasn't home, he was in exile in India, but does that mean we can just borrow his carpets when we want to? I was doubtful and was very pleased when His Holiness's carpet was returned to the Norbulingka.

We were all very pleased when the inspector was returned to where he had come from. He was a small unassuming man without a sense of humour. He wasn't impressed with the Dalai

Lama's carpet, as he did not know who the Dalai Lama was. Despite our Herculean efforts, he wasn't impressed with the hotel either. He was careful to praise the management and staff but pointed out that certain criteria simply did not meet the regulations laid down by Holiday Inn.

'The car-port is not wide enough for two cars to open their doors side by side.'

'What do you mean, *car-port*, nobody can drive here?' Barba asked, restraining his anger.

The inspector continued; 'The telephone cords – the length of wire from the receiver to the set – are not the stipulated length.'

'So what?'

'There is no special menu for children.'

'We don't have any children here.'

'There are no ice machines in the corridors.'

'You want ice in this weather?'

Barba was on the edge of a massive attack and we calmed him down by suggesting that perhaps Holiday Inn would close the hotel. He went off grinning and rubbing his hands together as the inspector finished the report.

In America, Holiday Inns are allowed a waiver if, for any insurmountable reason, they cannot comply with all the expectations laid down in the Holiday Inn Operations Manual. The most they are allowed is one waiver. Holiday Inn Lhasa was granted 27 and still permitted to carry on trading. Several conditions were specified for improvement. The most important one concerned the thickness of the doors. Apparently, none of the 500 doors in the hotel were the correct thickness in millimetres, according to the inspector's bible, the Operations Manual. This alteration alone would cost in excess of $200,000 – a difficult demand on the owners considering the hotel had no guests.

Barba waved his hands. 'Who cares about Holiday Inn's stupid doors? I am going to make this a hotel to be proud of. What do we need here that would really make a difference?'

We all tried for the right answer;

'A change from yak meat?'

'A laundry service that works?'

'Heating?'

'Guests?'

Barba shook his head. 'No, no, no. Gentleman, and Conny, what we need is an outdoor swimming pool!'

As Barba worked day and night to persuade Party A to part with vast sums of money to invest in a swimming pool, Conny and I spent our time trying to convince tour operators not to cancel their Tibet programmes.

The Chinese soon relaxed their grip and allowed us to venture out of the hotel again but Tibet remained closed to tourists. There were several checkpoints between the hotel and the Jokhang and soldiers stood to attention in little sentry boxes at every street running off from the Barkhor. Soldiers wearing headphones and with radio sets strapped to their backs stood by the sentry boxes, ready to call for backup in case a dangerous unarmed monk or nun came past. Sorties of nine soldiers at a time, laden down with AK47's, led by an officer carrying a revolver marched around the Barkhor every so often – usually in the wrong direction.

Once every couple of days a great cavalcade of motorbikes with side-cars would pass along the roads, with soldiers carrying mounted weapons hanging out of the side. An armoured personnel carrier stood on guard by the empty rickshaw stand at the front of the Barkhor square. It was an obvious and rather crude way of saying, 'Don't mess with us because we've got lots of very big guns.'

To remind everyone of the military strength and 'unity with the Motherland,' several large billboards displayed comradely paintings of Brother and Sister Tibetans carrying Chinese arms.

Smaller pictures on the billboards proudly showed nuclear fallout clouds. No one could speak out against it.

Despite the modernisation within China and the new economic prosperity, freedom of speech is still a luxury not afforded by the Chinese or Tibetans. Neither the student in Tianamen Square, nor the Tibetan in the Barkhor is permitted to say what he or she likes. Socialism rules with an iron fist and a new wave of inmates filled Trapchi prison, guilty only of thinking aloud; 'Free Tibet.'

Watching army patrols and knowing that, as a foreigner, I was being watched by them, was not my idea of fun. I avoided the Barkhor on my trips out of the hotel and instead went on day hikes into the hills and marshes around the Lhasa valley.

After being nursed back to health by Conny, I planned to take her for a romantic picnic to a spot looking over the marshes by Drepung monastery. We walked up through the tree-lined fields beneath Drepung and along the base of the foothills to a quiet corner sheltered by a large granite boulder. We spread out a table cloth and unpacked our picnic of luxuries unknown in Lhasa. Generous tour leaders who knew of our limited diet would bring us life-saving supplies: chocolate from Switzerland, Buffalo cheese from Kathmandu, bottles of French wine with corks. It was the perfect setting. Tame snipe and bar-tailed godwits were feeding in the meadow in front of us. Beyond the field, vast tracts of reeds swayed in the gentle breeze. The golden roofs of the Potala Palace shimmered in the distance. If there was going to be time for romance, it was to be now.

Just as I leant closer to Conny, two Chinese soldiers appeared from around the boulder. I leapt to my feet. The soldiers jumped back, just as startled to find us as we were to see them. To my great relief they were not carrying AK47's, but curiously they were each clutching a blond Barbie doll. After the initial shock of finding us there, they smiled and waved to us as they walked off down the pathway, hand in hand with their Barbie dolls dangling by their side.

I thought we were alone again when a group of Tibetans suddenly came running down the hill waving frantically at us. Either these were exceptionally friendly Tibetans or something was wrong. They crouched down behind boulders and motioned for us to do the same. An almighty explosion tore through the peaceful Sunday morning. The birds in the meadow took flight, their shrill alarm calls filling the air. A shower of granite splinters rained down around us. How was I to know that the romantic picnic spot was beneath one of the main quarries of Lhasa? We packed up and left.

We walked through to the eastern end of the marshes, just behind the Potala, where we came across the ruins of an old Tibetan house. Even in ruins, the house was majestic. The walls still stretched three stories high, with black trapezoid frames around the outside of the empty windows. The roof and most of the interior walls had caved-in and now filled what was once the ground floor. Some timbers still remained – their blue and red paint faded after decades of exposure to the elements. The plaster on the inside of the walls had kept some of their original red, blue, green and gold colours.

A second house, much smaller but in a perfect state of repair, stood ten metres away with the Chinese flag flying over it. Tatters of Chinese newspapers which had been plastered over the walls of the second floor ruins, blew in the wind. I stood on tip-toe on the rubble to see the date on one of the pages. '9.7.1972'.

As I read the date out to Conny a group of small children arrived. They had come from the other side of a new drainage ditch, 15 metres wide and three metres deep which the Chinese had sliced through the former courtyard of the house. They were the usual group of inquisitive and friendly little children that track you down wherever you are. They smiled at us and played on the rubble, picking up stones with the remains of colourful frescos and hurling them into the drainage ditch. It was a sad sight. Between the *tashi delai's*, I thought I heard one say 'Lhalu.'

Could this be true? Was this the house where Younghusband had stayed in 1904? Where the best *chang* in Lhasa had been brewed? One of the five wonders of Lhasa? Where the serf parties had burnt the slave debts in the courtyard?

Yes. 'Di Lhalu rey,' the little boys replied to my question. 'This is Lhalu.' They should have used the past tense for there was not much of any use now.

Conny and I returned to the hotel. It had not been the best of days – my hopeful romantic picnic had been spoiled by Tibetan dynamiters, the marshes were being threatened by a 'progress' drainage ditch and we had found one of the historical treasures of Lhasa in ruins.

It had also been a bad day for Nancy and Bob. They were fired. Party A made an official complaint about their methods and they were asked to leave. Nancy's supply of Mr Smiley stickers had been used up and it was time to move on. As a farewell gift they left us with the results of the latest multiple choice English test, which had been used to recruit our crack team of Receptionists and Cashiers. The top candidates had filled in the blanks with the following underlined words:

'I can't find your folio. Would you please wait a moment while I <u>miscellaneous</u>?'

'<u>Bill</u> means the price is very high.'

'Can I use my <u>complaining</u> to pay for this?'

'<u>Expensive</u> is another word for angry.'

'You should always smile when talking to guests, never <u>window panel</u>.'

'Goodbye. Have a <u>department concerned</u>.'

Fortunately, our new top English speaking team was in place just in time. No sooner had the test results come through than the Chinese announced the news that they would allow tourists to return to Tibet. There was just one hitch. Tourists could only come in groups of 15 persons or more and had to be accompanied by a guide at all times on a pre-arranged tour package. This suited the Chinese government perfectly. They do not care about economics, only about politics. In this way they could say that Tibet was open but at the same time fix the rules so that no one would come. This is why boycotts of China do not work. They have no effect whatsoever on the government – they only hurt the people. This is an important point that many Westerners do not understand. The government is only concerned with national security and being seen to be politically correct. But with a boycott, the rickshaw driver and the Khampa ladies at the Barkhor, the Tibetan staff at the hotels, the Tibetan guides, the Tibetan drivers, the Tibetan suppliers of drinks and food, the Tibetan herdsman selling yak meat – they and their families all suffer.

With the rules from Beijing and an understandable but misguided wish to boycott China and Tibet, the odds were stacked up against us again. It looked as though we would be stuck with an empty hotel for some time. The only people allowed to organise package tours to Tibet were the Lhasa travel agents and we knew what a disaster these companies were. We asked for meeting with Ape Renchen, head of the Tibet Tourist Bureau and Mao Ru Bai, the Vice Governor of Tibet, to argue that the hotel should also be allowed to operate tour groups. Very surprisingly, they agreed. We were the only hotel in China permitted to become a tour operator. Our prices would have to meet with official approval and we would be issued with certain guidelines for carrying out the tours but otherwise we would be free to operate programmes as we saw fit.

At last there was light at the end of the tunnel and we set to work immediately on planning tours throughout Tibet. It was an exciting challenge. The costs were calculated for transport, accommodation, meals, entrance fees and guide services. The hotel had a large fleet of Landcruisers and Japanese Hino buses so most of this money would be coming straight into the profit centres of the hotel. On top of these costs a modest 10% profit margin was included. What could go wrong?

Everything. We had not anticipated the mind-numbing bureaucracy from Beijing and exactly what it means to have state controlled prices. We were told in no uncertain terms that this was completely the wrong way to make a tour costing and we were thoroughly reprimanded for our sheer ignorance and incompetence in our way of 'fabricating' the charges. No prices could be calculated logically but all had to be made according to the documents from Beijing. We were proudly given a set of these documents complete with the large red greasy rubber stamps on the most important pages and we were shown how to make a real tour cost. Using inexplicable calculation methods, the authorities in Beijing had obtained a predetermined price for what they considered to be essential items of a tour package; 'the comprehensive fee, service fee, handling fee, receiving fee, organising fee, promotion fee, visa fee' and my favourite, 'the unforeseen circumstances fee.'

No one was sure exactly what this fee was for but they all knew that we had to charge it. It was only ten dollars but when all these little fees had been added to the accommodation and transport costs, guests could be paying up to $300 per day.

Every so often, new regulations would come out, with extra fees which had to be charged. Consequently, the prices quoted and already confirmed to tour operators in the West would have to be increased. We could not operate in this way – if we had sent out a price we would honour it – so I built in an extra margin on the tour costs to cover any price rises. I named it the, 'Comprehensive, Receiving And Promotion' fee whose initials spelt exactly what I thought of the regulations. This 'CRAP' fee had to go to the government to receive official permission, and the 'CRAP' papers were duly returned to me with the greasy red stamp of government approval.

Once Western tour operators knew that we were organising the tours ourselves, the sales boomed. All efforts at the hotel went into preparations for the high season. Barba had workmen brought up from Chengdu to work through the night excavating his swimming pool. We looked at the food and beverage outlets to see what changes were necessary. First, the Coffee Shop. The Communists who had set up the tourism master-plan for Tibet had used the same logic inside the hotels as they had when they named the hotel in Lhasa the 'Lhasa Hotel' and the hotel in Shigatse the 'Shigatse Hotel.' Hence the coffee shop was called imaginatively, the 'Coffee Shop.'

After much deliberation the Coffee Shop was re-christened: the 'Hard Yak Cafe'. It had been a difficult choice and YacDonalds had come a close second. The Giant Yak Burger could have been renamed the Big Yak – but the Hard Yak Cafe won the day. The name change was an instant success with the first tourists who came in and Barba commissioned T-shirts with the slogan 'Hard Yak Cafe – Lhasa' in the style of another cafe with a fairly similar name. These sold even faster than Giant Yak Burgers.

The Picnic Corner also needed revamping. The Chinese spam was out of stock and we were only left with some seriously out of date and rather soft 'fruity nut bars.' We threw them out and changed the shop into a tavern, calling it the 'Tintin Bar', after Herge's cartoon character and his book *Tintin in Tibet*. Our hotel artist painted an incredibly good Tintin as a mural on the back wall and the bar was decorated with pages from the book.

Unfortunately the bar did not survive long. Unlike Mr Herge who wrote all his books without leaving his armchair in Belgium, Mrs Herge is an avid traveller. Her voyages took her to the Holiday Inn Lhasa – where she was somewhat surprised to find the Tintin Bar. Apparently the Herge Foundation is very strict on use of the 'Tintin' name and will not allow it to be associated with cigarettes or alcohol. Tut, tut. The Tintin Bar was closed down.

Somehow, the stock of 'Tintin in Tibet' T-shirts which Barba had commissioned, managed to reappear and we could not fill the lobby shop with them fast enough.

The T-shirts were brought in from Kathmandu under very difficult conditions. First there were problems with foreign exchange – we were not allowed to spend any of the dollars earned outside China so we had to barter the T-shirts for hotel rooms from tour operators based in Kathmandu. It was all very complicated. Then there was the physical problem, as each box of T-shirts had to be carried by porters over the landslides at the border and then face a four day ride through the dust.

For the rest of the supplies we relied on China. Mr Han was sent off on a purchasing trip to look for foodstuffs and essential equipment such as new woks for the kitchen. His reports were read out daily in the Morning Meeting.

Unfortunately, it was Mr Pong who read them out. Heather translated as we ducked; 'Today Mr Han has arrived in Beijing. He has looked for food like you asked and has found fresh fish. He will send samples to Lhasa. He has sent melons from Chengdu.'

The supplies from Chengdu faced an even worse journey than the T-shirts arriving from Kathmandu. We employed a fleet of truck drivers to ply the 20 day return trip. Ten days down to Chengdu and ten days back again. Some of the lorries never returned and at least one driver lost his life on the treacherous roads.

The trucks were occasionally stopped en route and goods confiscated or drivers imprisoned. When the trucks did arrive in Lhasa, their contents often had to be thrown away. Chef went to inspect Mr Han's melon trucks as they pulled into the hotel courtyard. Water dripped out of the back of the trucks and when he opened the doors a great fruit cocktail sloshed out onto the concrete. The melons had been loaded without any packaging and had been turned into melon puree during the journey.

Mr Han had also sent up trucks containing the bottled water supply for the summer. This was an excellent sales item. In the welcome talk we gave to each group, Conny and I would emphasise the medical advice that you should drink at least three litres of water per day to combat altitude sickness. While we drank the hotel tap water, which was perfectly safe, most guests and especially super sensitive Americans, insisted on drinking bottled water. This was a beautiful arrangement for the hotel, which sold horrendously overpriced bottles of water in vast quantities to each new batch of tourists.

One of the reasons for the high price was to cover the losses incurred in bringing the water to Lhasa. Mr Han's first convoy of trucks carrying bottled water spent one of the nights on the way at the top of a mountain pass. The temperature dropped below zero and one by one the bottles shattered as the water froze.

We learnt our lesson from this experience and gave instructions that liquid supplies could only be brought over the passes by day. This safeguard still did not help all our supplies. One in three cans of Indian Tonic Water exploded as they were brought up to higher altitudes. Coca-Cola cans seemed to last longer but would pop in the store room months after arriving in Lhasa, oozing out in a black treacly pool across the floor.

We did occasionally try flying in supplies with CAAC from Chengdu but this was even worse. Cases of fresh foodstuffs would be forgotten about for days on the Chengdu runway and then delivered to us when the food was rotten.

But we did not accept defeat. It was our job to make the hotel function as best as we could despite the circumstances. Our problems were not to be passed on the guests. For a VIP banquet we gave CAAC one last chance. Mr Han had found a 'very good' supplier of frozen prawns in Chengdu and he arranged with CAAC that the frozen consignment must be sent up to Lhasa without delay.

For once, everything went like clockwork and Chef went down to the airport to collect the blocks of ice. He took them back to the hotel and defrosted them in the sinks. As the ice melted our high hopes began to fade. In each block of ice there was just one prawn. One miserable, lonely, crustacean. The 'prawn salad' on the menu became literally 'a prawn' and 'salad.' The cost per prawn worked out at $12 apiece.

Mr Han was useless and yet the local management insisted that his work was excellent. The daily news bulletin in the Morning Meeting became farcical; 'Mr Han reports that there are no woks in Beijing.'

'No woks in Beijing!?' screamed Barba. For once Party B could turn the screws on Party A. Barba signalled for Mr Liu, our Party B accountant, to make clear our knowledge of a fiddle concerning the delivery of yaks. Mr Liu read out the charges.

'We have an invoice for three yaks. Also an invoice from the trailer driver for the transport of three yaks but according to our records, only two yaks arrived at the hotel.'

Party A immediately found the explanation. Heather translated. 'Yes, there had been three yaks. But one of the yaks jumped out when the driver went over one of the passes and he couldn't catch it again.'

'What was it, a homing yak?' asked Bonetti.

We knew they were up to something but catching them out was very difficult. There was a very great temptation for the local staff in positions of authority to cook the books. Their wages were pitifully low and yet vast sums of money, the equivalent of many lifetimes salary passed through their hands every day. But if ever there was a deterrent against large scale corruption, the Chinese had one.

Tashi told me one morning that a Chinese girl at the Lhasa branch of CAAC had been caught fiddling. When work units booked flights, for example for 20 employees to travel down to Chengdu, she would write out 20 tickets but put the money for only two of them in the till. The rest she put in her pocket. She had carried out this system for a staggering four years without being caught. The girl was known as the 'Queen of Lhasa' and was a regular at the Holiday Inn disco, had a motor bike, limitless money and a range of handbags which would rival Imelda Marcos's shoe collection. No one had questioned how this lowly CAAC employee should have all this money or why the CAAC office in Lhasa made such a drastic loss each year.

I laughed when Tashi told me the story. 'What a joke,' I said. 'How can CAAC have let it happen?'

There was no reply.

'Well,' I continued, 'I hope the CAAC auditor loses his job. And what will the girl get? A few years in Trapchi? Four years? Five?'

No one in the office laughed. They normally had such bright faces, so ready to smile and joke but they looked back at me with cold expressions.

'No, Mr Alec.'

Tashi clenched his fist, holding two fingers out in the shape of a gun, put his hand up to his head and pulled an imaginary trigger. I could not believe it. The poor girl's artifacts were put on display in a museum building beneath the Potala Palace. Queues formed outside to see the exhibition of her motorbike, her handbags, her expensive clothes. She was paraded around Lhasa in the back of a truck and a week later she was executed. Her family was sent the bill for the bullet.

While Mr Han trod on dangerously thin ice in Beijing, we continued with preparations in Lhasa. Charlie sent his lawn mowing team out into the grounds. They had no lawn-mower – just a pair of shears. Six of them crawled across the lawn on hands and knees, clipping the turf as they went. It took so long that by the time they had completed a circuit of the grounds it was time to start again. Bonetti opened up eight food and beverage outlets. Harry converted two of the Economy Rooms in to a massage suite and we supplemented the Western health care offered by Dr Grubby, by opening a Tibetan Medicine clinic.

The clinic was run by a Dr Ga Ma Qun Pei, who had been the private physician of the Panchen Lama. On first consideration this was not such a good advertisement, as the

Panchen Lama had just died, or passed on to his next incarnation, but Dr Ga Ma was an excellent physician. He decorated the room with *thangkas* from the Tibetan Medical Hospital and brought in dozens of packets of little brown pills. He came to the hotel every evening with his interpreter and they waited patiently in the clinic, sitting on Tibetan mattresses drinking tea. Dr Ga Ma had been trained in the Medical College which stood on Chagpori, the hill opposite the Potala Palace. Fortunately he had graduated in 1950, a few years before the college was blown off the hill by Chinese troops.

He was a quiet man but you could see that he had many stories within and he exuded an aura of wisdom. He diagnosed his patients by reading their pulse. First the left wrist for two minutes and then the right wrist. He would then nod slowly and speak in Tibetan to his interpreter. While Dr Ga Ma was short and stocky, his interpreter, an equally gentle man, was tall and skinny. He had been one of the children sent for schooling in India before the Chinese 'peacefully liberated' Tibet. In the new Tibet he had not been able to practice his English and it had become rather rusty. A lengthy diagnosis in Tibetan from Dr Ga Ma, was often translated as a smile and 'you have a cold,' or 'you are okay.'

Although I liked Dr Ga Ma and his translator enormously, I have always been sceptical of anything that cannot be explained by strict scientific principals. Yes, Dr Ga Ma has had a medical education as long as it takes a doctor to graduate in the West, and yes, he did seem to be a very special man but apart from telling that someone is alive – how can reading the pulse possibly give any idea of someone's medical condition? It was not until I accompanied a French couple to the clinic that my views changed. The French spoke no English, so I was to translate for them. First Dr Ga Ma to the interpreter in Tibetan, then the interpreter in English to me and I would translate into French for the guests. It sounded like Chinese whispers and I was very doubtful about the outcome.

Dr Ga Ma read the pulse of the French lady. He nodded. Through the various translations I apologised and told the French lady she had a problem with her kidneys. Amazingly, she did. She was receiving treatment every week in France.

The husband's turn was even more startling. The interpreter mulled over the doctor's words and said to me; 'Dr Ga Ma says he has a problem with his spleen.' I had to look up 'spleen' in a French dictionary. 'Ma rate! Mais comment il le sait?!' exclaimed the Frenchman. It turned out that his spleen had been removed following a motorbike accident twelve years previously.

Never again did I doubt the word of Dr Ga Ma. He was so honest and refreshingly unaware of commercialism. He could have sold all the Tibetan medicine he could make but if anyone asked for pills the interpreter would say for him, 'Well, Dr Ga Ma says you can buy some of these if you want but they may not be necessary.'

I tried his pills once when I had a stomach ache. Apparently they were mixtures of wild herbs and minerals but they tasted as bitter as boiled Shanghai coffee and looked suspiciously like mouse droppings. Dr Ga Ma became increasingly busy and had to step up the production of mouse droppings as the high season approached.

One of the first groups to arrive was an expeditionary force of the English upper class, or the English 'upper-strata clique' to give them the correct Communist Chinglish title. They were stopping off in Lhasa as one of the stages on the Jules Verne London to Saigon rally. We sold more champagne in the two days they stayed than in the rest of the year put together. They were paying $20,000 each for the trip, so a bottle of champagne at $120 was quite a bargain. Although most of the cars were four wheel drive Range Rover types, there was also a beautiful 1950s Daimler – without doubt the first and only Daimler to run in the streets of Lhasa. After the Morning Meeting, I found the owner of the Daimler in the Hard Yak Cafe trying to order toast and marmalade. Each time he asked, Zhang Li replied, 'Yes' and smiled. She then went about her business clearing tables. She had no clue what he was talking about. Breakfast consisted of yak yogurt, doughnuts, cake, egg, hairy pork fat and fried spam. What was 'marmalade?'

I rescued him from this near disaster and enquired how the trip from London had been.

'Until now the last decent hotel we had was in Moscow. The rest has been simply dreadful.'

It also appeared that the food had been 'simply dreadful.'

'Fortunately we had a Fortnum and Masons' hamper in the back of the car and we have survived on potted quail for the last three days.' He bit into his toast and strawberry jam which had now arrived. 'But mind you,' he continued, 'one can dine at the Ritz any night of the week. When can one experience this?'

Lhasa was certainly an experience that many people will never forget. A group of Japanese tourists arrived in the lobby, shaking and white. Harry was placing bets for a record breaking drop factor – but their fears were not from the altitude. Their tour leader explained to us what had happened. As they had crossed the bridge over the Tsangpo on the way to Lhasa from the airport, Chinese troops had suddenly dived in front of them from all directions. Soldiers in full combat gear crawled along the pavements with AK47's outstretched. Commandos scaled the sides of the bridge on rope ladders and charged along the road. The Japanese had found themselves caught in the middle of a practise assault on the bridge by the PLA.

We had no warning of the mock attack on the bridge but we were informed of another army manoeuvre which would effect tourists. We were told that the overland route would be closed for several days. We could not know the exact days as this was a secret. Any tourists who had paid thousands of dollars for their trip of a lifetime would just have to wait until the road was open again. But how long this would be was also a top secret. We pushed Party A and the owners of the hotel, the Tibet Tourism Bureau, to use their *guanxi* to the full extent. A compromise was reached. Tourists could take the overland route but only at night and as long as they promised not to look out of the windows. So much for 'top secret' – everyone knew there was an arms delivery going on between China and Nepal.

Occasionally the military were actually helpful to us and it was due to the Chinese government that occupancy soared above 20 percent for the first time in the year, when they booked both presidential villas and an entire wing of the hotel. Unfortunately it was the same wing that the expatriates lived in and we were all kicked out for a week. It was on the happy occasion of the fortieth anniversary of the 'peaceful liberation' of Tibet and the signing of the famous 17 Point Agreement. This was the paper signed by old Ngapoh Ape Renchen, which the Communists wave around as their right of ownership of Tibet.

The whole of Lhasa was tidied up for the celebrations. A ten metre high statue of two golden yaks was built at a new roundabout on the way to the Potala. A six lane tankway was built for no particular reason from the Unknown Road Builders' Monument by the Kyi Chu up to the hotel. Rows of street lights were put up all over town and hideous railings enclosed the open land by the Norbulingka. Other wild parts of Lhasa were also subjected to this unnecessary urbanisation as the Chinese made another unwanted attempt to drag Lhasa into the twentieth century – socialist style. Propaganda booklets, written in English, poured into the hotel from Beijing. The booklets had subtle titles such as *Why Tibet is an Integral Part of China*. They are crammed with 'indisputable facts' including explanations of how the Dalai Lama did not flee from Lhasa in 1959 being chased by nasty Communists, but was actually abducted and forced into exile by Tibetan 'upper-strata splittists'. Amazing. All this time we thought he was on the run from the Communists but actually he is being held prisoner by splittists. This is an 'indisputable fact' published by the New Star Press of Beijing, so it must be true. Reading the booklets is as painful as reading the anti-Chinese articles published by the Tibetans in exile. We did eventually find a good use for the booklets – they do not burn as fiercely as yak dung, but the smell doesn't stick to your clothing.

There was also a serious attempt by the Chinese to clean the streets of the thousands of stray dogs which roam around Lhasa. The Tibetans were horrified. It is well known that not only are all forms of life sacred but the dogs around monasteries are the reincarnations of naughty monks. Sue, from Save the Children Fund, heard the best suggestion to the dog problem from the Tibetan mayor of Lhasa. He asked the Chinese to catch all the male dogs and put them in one pen and all the female dogs and put them in another pen. They could be looked after until they had all died of old age, there would be no more stray dogs on the streets and everyone would live happily ever after.

The Chinese were not so sentimental. Poison was laid along the streets and shooting parties patrolled at dawn. Dorje saved the favourite of the hotel's pack of dogs by giving her a lift down to the airport. She was a beautiful Lassie look-alike and was taken regular food supplies by both the Tibetan and Chinese hotel staff. We heard many other stories of Tibetans hiding dogs and no one ate in the Chinese restaurants for weeks.

Strolling around the grounds of the hotel, while dead dogs were carted off out of the back entrance, were some of the elite leaders of China. Soldiers stood to attention as Li Tie Yin, the all powerful State Councillor from Beijing, checked in to one of the Presidential villas. We had also been home to Zhang She Min on a state visit, popping up from the motherland to see how the Tibetan Comrades were getting on.

The hotel was crawling with Chinese VIP's and heavily laden soldiers. I tried to take a group of Germans into our newly opened Himalayan Restaurant, but found the door blocked by two armed guards. I was furious. They had taken over half the hotel but they could not just ban us from feeding our Western guests. I found Jig Me and told him that Party A could not let them push us around like this. An official appeared and after a long discussion in Chinese, barked an order at the two soldiers. Their jaws dropped, they saluted and sped off down the corridor clutching their automatic weapons. Jig Me chuckled as he whispered to me what had happened. The soldiers had been told to stand in front of the red door and not let anyone in. They had seen the red door to the Himalayan Restaurant and taken up their positions. But this was the wrong red door – they should have been standing in front of the door where Li Tie Yin was dining.

On 23 May, the phone rang all day long with Western journalists looking for action. But there was none. The 'peaceful liberation' celebrations were passing peacefully. A few undercover journalists had sneaked into Tibet under the guise of being 'teachers' on holiday. They probed us with questions. 'There were gun shots this morning. Do you how many Tibetans have been killed?'

These people were as annoying as the New Star Press of Beijing and would not leave us alone. A Frenchman from *Le Monde* who had been going around giving his business card to every Tibetan he met accosted me in the lobby one evening.

'I 'ave been stopped by ze police! I 'ave to leave tomorrow. It is all because of you. You are a *Communist spy*!'

At the same time as the accusation of being a Communist spy, I found my mail was being censored by the Chinese. I received a letter from home which had been steamed open and re-sealed. I would never have known if they had not forgotten to rub out the pencilled-in words. Neatly written above my father's news about the beans growing well in Jersey was a Chinese translation. They gave up half way through, realising that news on the variety of vegetables growing in Jersey was not a threat to Chinese national security. Or could it have been in code?

It was a relief when the Chinese and the journalists checked out and we could go back to our own rooms again. Barba was back in a happy mood and invited any female guests of his 'target market' to his private dining table. He homed in on a Baroness who fell immediately for his powerful, seductive charm.

Conny was away on a sales trip. Chef, Harry and Bonetti came to my room with a bag of Tsing Tao beer cans. We had given up on Lasa Beer after hearing a report from two visiting American diplomats from the embassy in Beijing. They had been given the customary 'progress' tour of Lhasa by the Foreign Affairs Office, which had included a trip to the Lasa Beer factory. They did not know that it had just been built by our Romanian comrades, but thought that the factory dated from the 1950s. Very little of the machinery was working and the Romanian bottle washing machine was permanently out of order. They found groups of Tibetan ladies, sitting outside around large brown puddles, washing the bottles by hand. Tibetan hygiene standards leave much to be desired at the best of times and when you have 5,000 bottles to clean and a pool of muddy water, it is easy to see why each bottle of Lasa Beer has its own distinctive flavour.

We sat in my room holding empty Tsing Tao beer cans. We had seen the in-house videos dozens of times. The hotel had originally possessed 47 video tapes but the Chinese had confiscated all but four of them. Among those never returned were several *Fawlty Towers* videos which we had been using for training. Also ruled out, presumably for being too subversive, was the *Sound of Music*. Was the sight of nuns dancing away to freedom over mountain passes too dangerous?

The remaining four films had gone around so many times that they were now becoming unrecognisable. *Death on the Nile* looked like it had been filmed during a snow storm and the *Thirty Nine Steps* was now missing the final three minutes.

We looked around for something to do.

'I have an idea!' Bonetti called out. 'Harry, you still have fireworks left over from Chinese New Year don't you?'

'Sure,' Harry replied, 'I have a whole bag in my room.'

'Okay, let's give Barba a surprise – he's gonna love it!'

'No, no, no.'

It was Chef who spoke.

'I am not doing anyzing like zat.'

But it was not too difficult to persuade Chef, and with military precision, we crept out of a ground floor corridor window and lined up the fireworks in front of Barba's window. We strung firecrackers in the trees, planted a row of 'golden rain' beneath his window-ledge and stepped back either side of the opening. Bonetti stood against the starlight and gave us the countdown for ignition. He brought his arm down in silence – three, two, one. Harry lit the blue touch paper of the cones beneath the window, Bonetti turned to light the strings of firecrackers and Chef and I primed Chinese Bangers, fat as cans of soup. When Bonetti and Harry were clear and the first of the Golden Rain sent a shower of sparks skywards, we lit the bangers and lobbed them in front of the window.

Thunderclaps echoed between the hotel and the concrete walls of the staff quarters. Flashes of light streaked out across the night sky. The trees shook with the explosions of the firecrackers. We scrambled for cover, dived back in through the corridor window and disappeared, undetected, back to our rooms.

There was no reaction from Barba during breakfast and the Morning Meeting passed smoothly. At the end of the meeting, Barba said calmly, 'Bonetti, Alec, Harry, stay here.'

We exchanged glances nervously and looked up at Chef who was leaving with the rest of expats and the local deputies. He gave us a thumbs up sign from through the door, turned on his heels and sped away down the stairs.

'Let me tell you the story of how I, as a junior officer, went to Taiwan with my General.'

Barba started in a low and calm tone.

'When we arrived at the brothel, the girls could not tell us apart – we looked about the same size. We joked a bit and in the end we swopped uniforms around and I pretended to be the General.'

We relaxed, Barba was telling us one of his surplus testosterone stories.

'When we got back to base, even though I knew I shouldn't, I told my friends all about it. The General got to hear about this and called me into his office. He said, "I used to consider you as one of my finest officers. But now you have spurned by trust. I now consider you to be the lowest scum possible."'

Barba leant forwards slightly and started to shake. He was a fully wound spring that was about to snap. He was Mount Vesuvius on the eve before Pompeii was buried. A few moments passed as the vibrations became stronger. He lost control and shouted at the top of his voice,

'And that gentlemen is how I feel about you! I was in the middle of one of my numbers! *You are all fired! Get out of here!*'

12

Overbooked

The first of the summer rains fell against the window pane of Bonetti's office. He busied himself by the small electric stove, making three espresso coffees. We watched the drops of water forming paths through the winter dust on the window. We were not in a mood to talk – being fired was a depressing start to the day. It was Bonetti who broke the silence.

'He liked it. I can tell.' Bonetti held his hands out with his palms uppermost and shrugged his shoulders. 'Trust me,' he said. We didn't trust him.

'We've just been fired for your stupid idea and you ask us to trust you!' Harry was upset.

Chef came into the office sniggering. 'Harry, next you time you have some firevorks left over, you can stuff zem up Bonetti's arsh!'

The day passed quietly, with no more news from Barba. We carried on working, the occupancy had grown to over 50 percent and we could not just sit around waiting for an official letter.

The next morning Barba called Bonetti over to his breakfast table. He was giving him the gory details of his night with the Baroness. I was spared this part but was summoned to hear the conclusion, '. . . and then fireworks! Alec, this will be your punishment. From now on we shall start a new programme for ladies travelling alone on the Roof of the World. Those under thirty, let's say they are your market, you will have to look after them. The more mature ones, my market, I shall look after. You shall invite them to my suite, where they will have a private dinner served by Bonetti in a tuxedo, a musical serenade and finally a firework display arranged by Harry! What do you say? Send off a press release immediately!'

The 'Ladies Travelling Alone on the Roof of the World' programme was a great success and Bonetti had been proved right. The special programme coincided with a loosening of the rules from Beijing. Each group travelling to Tibet still had to be accompanied by a guide and charged exorbitant fees, but the minimum number of travellers in a 'group' was reduced to just one person.

Occupancy soared as the rules were relaxed and the summer season kicked off. It was what we had all been waiting for. Harry read out the figures in the Morning Meeting, 'Last night sixty four percent. Today sixty eight percent. Tomorrow seventy three percent.'

All the sales work and the preparations were paying off. The local travel agents kept bringing in their reservations to Harry. Although the guests may have booked their trip to Tibet a year in advance, and the tour operator in the West booked many months in advance with the local agency, the Lhasa agents invariably walked up to the Front Desk with the reservation the day before the group's arrival. Sometimes the group even arrived before the reservation. It made forecasting very difficult and in the middle of August the inevitable happened.

Harry counted up the reservations which had come in during the day. 'Wow, we are going to be ninety percent tonight,' he told me in the afternoon.

At 7 pm he was still in his office. I called in to see him on my way to the Hard Yak Cafe. His face was red and his usual relaxed expression was replaced by a deep frown. He stared at the lap top PC into which he was loading the figures. 'I have checked and double checked. There is nothing wrong with the programme,' he said. He picked up a pile of papers with Chinese writing, red chops and group codes and waved them at me. 'I still have these to add. I am already over one hundred percent!'

I counted through the papers with him. 108 percent. 110 percent.

'I have checked everything!' he stammered.

We counted up the last papers. He stared at the spreadsheet on his PC and whispered in disbelief, 'On Thursday we are going to be one hundred and twenty percent.'

An emergency meeting was called for and the hotel was switched into overdrive. All time off was cancelled. Mr Han was sent purchasing in the local markets. Chef brought the kitchens up to full power, running them like a military machine. There were no more empty corridors, no empty seats in restaurants – we now had to cater for over 3,000 covers per day. Derek worked with his engineers through the night to make every available piece of machinery in order. There could be no breakdowns now, no rooms out of order. Party A called in extra staff, bringing the number up to 800 employees. Camp beds were laid out in the meeting rooms. The Presidential Villas were cleared out ready for use. The massage rooms were converted back to bedrooms. Dr Ga Ma was sent home and a blanket stretched over his couch. Despite the strong smell of his mouse dropping medicine we managed to sell the room at full price as a 'unique Tibetan experience.'

Still it was not enough. The local agents kept on piling up reservations on the Reception counter. We could have refused them but the consequences for tourism in Tibet would have been severe. Tour operators would have dropped us from their brochures, unhappy guests would sue their travel agents and tell their friends about their Tibetan nightmare. In desperation, we asked the Tibet Tourism Bureau to take over the government guest house which was 100 metres down the road. The entire building was requisitioned and Derek's team spent a day trying to fix the broken plumbing, power, fixtures and fittings. Our Housekeeping Department tried in vain to shampoo the crushed egg shell out of the carpets and remove the brown stains from the bathroom tiles. We ran out of camp beds in the meeting rooms and used the government guest house for the guides and drivers who accompanied the groups. Each day was a battle – the main battlefield being the Holiday Inn lobby.

National guides refused to be separated from their groups. Guests who had paid hundreds of dollars for single supplements refused to share rooms. Guests who had booked with their travel agent a year previously, refused to believe that the first we knew about them was when they walked through the front door. Crossing the lobby was becoming increasingly hazardous. A suit was an obvious target – it became impossible to get through without being bombarded with question after question from irate guests. Barba avoided them by stepping through the windows across the back corridors of the hotel. Somehow, Chef was never approached by the angry guests but instead attracted the stupid ones. They would see him dressed in his blue chequered trousers, chefs' jacket and hat and ask, 'Do you work here?'

'No. I am at a Chefs' convention,' he would reply and the guests wouldn't bother him again.

I was a glutton for punishment and headed through the lobby to reach the Hard Yak Cafe and my room. A guest handed me a torn rag which he pointed out had been a perfectly good sock when he had given it to the Housekeeping Department.

'So the other one is okay then?' I asked him. 'And you expect a *full* refund?'

The Bank of China ran out of small bank notes, so we had no change to give guests. The post office ran out of stamps and resorted to selling philatelic sets. These were very beautiful stamps, but they were in such small denominations that once you had stuck the required 18 stamps, each 5 centimetres by 4 centimetres, on the back of a postcard, there was no room to write the address, let alone a message.

In the middle of the chaos, I had a call from the town of Shigatse. There was no direct line and the call had been passed via the Beijing operator. It was an English tour operator and through the crackles I could just make out her distraught voice.

'Is that Mr Alec? I was told to contact you. One of our group has died. Peacefully. In her sleep. Heart attack. There is no telex here. No fax. No phone to the outside world. The group has gone on to Kathmandu. None of the drivers will touch the body. Can you pass a message on to my travel agency in England?'

I placed the call to London and passed on the sad news. As Lhasa was the only point of communication, I became the messenger between the tour guide stuck in Shigatse, the British Embassy in Beijing and the travel agency and insurance company in London.

I broke the news to Barba.

'One of our guests has died.'

'Oh no. Where?'

'In Shigatse.'

'Thank God for that! Alec, there is nothing worse than a stiff in the hotel.'

The insurance company called with the news that the relatives wanted a cremation and would come out to Tibet to witness it. I asked Tashi for the number of the Shigatse Hotel so that I could place the call with our hotel operator, who in turn would call the Beijing operator, who would relay the call to Shigatse.

'I don't know the Shigatse Hotel telephone number Mr Alec.'

'Well just call up the operator and ask her to look up the number.'

He picked the receiver up, dialled 2222 for our operator and asked her. She didn't know either. One of our staff had a bright idea; 'Mr Alec, you could call the Shigatse Hotel and ask them for their number – they must know.'

It was a painful process but we eventually managed to find the number and place the call. The connection was weak and I had to shout, 'The relatives want to come out to see the body. They want a cremation.'

There was silence down the other end of the phone. Then I heard the faint voice back. 'Listen, there is no fridge here. You can smell the body from the lobby – there is no time for family visits.'

I placed a call back to the insurance company. The call came through as I was crossing the lobby. I fought away a guest who was complaining about the toilet paper being too stiff. He wanted his money back and was going to write to Holiday Inn head office.

'If you will excuse me, I shall have to attend to your stiff toilet paper in a while,' I said politely to him.

The receptionist passed me the receiver across the counter. It was another bad connection and I had to shout, *'You can smell the body in the lobby. We strongly recommend cremation on the spot!'*

I looked around me. The crowd in the Holiday Inn lobby had gone silent. The man with the stiff toilet paper was running away down the corridor. 'Not here. Not here.' I called out to the stunned guests. 'But if you go to Shigatse tonight, don't ask for room 238.'

'No,' the voice came back down the line, 'the family insists that the deceased's son comes out to attend the proceedings.'

The local travel agency involved had managed to find a truck driver willing to transport the body back to Lhasa. It had taken several cartons of cigarettes and promises of Johnnie Walker Black Label. The tour leader had sat in the passenger seat of the truck as the driver raced through the night back to Lhasa.

They arrived early in the morning and went straight to the hospital. The doctors refused to take the body – there was no point – and in despair the driver came to the hotel and demanded that the body be stored in the hotel's walk-in refrigerator.

Chef would have had a heart attack – going in to take out the spam for breakfast and finding Mrs Simkins laid out on the floor. We declined their request. We had enough trouble from live guests.

There are no morgues in Tibet as bodies are not stored as they are in the West. Under the Tibetan system of sky burials, where the corpses are taken out at dawn and fed to friendly vultures, morgues are a waste of time. After much persuasion, the hospital admitted that they had a freezer but they would only keep the body for a few days. There was not long to wait, as the Chinese had cut through the normal red tape and allowed a permit to be issued immediately to the son, who was already on his way to Lhasa. He would be arriving the following morning and the local travel agency had arranged a cremation for the same day.

I had a stiff drink with the tour leader. It had been a harrowing experience for her – stuck in Shigatse with a body and then a ten hour Tibetan truck drive through the night with Mrs Simkins bouncing around in the back. But the worst was yet to come. What kind of cremation did the relatives expect? A few kind words from the vicar in a little village church? Organ music, a coffin on the conveyor belt and the parting of velvet drapes?

The son arrived, somewhat dazed – knocked out from altitude and emotions. The tour leader and I accompanied him in the hotel Landcruiser, and we pulled out of the courtyard at the head of a long cavalcade of cars towards the hills near Drepung monastery. We stopped for a while by the side of the road and when a lorry overtook us we started off again.

The tour leader suddenly started to strike up stupid conversation with the son. 'Look a tree!' she said pointing out of the window. 'What glorious weather today. Look! A cloud in the sky over there!' I knew we had to make polite conversation to keep his mind busy but this was ridiculous. Then I saw what she had seen – the lorry in front of us was loaded with a loose pile of firewood and on top of the wood was something wrapped in a white sheet, bouncing up and down as we sped over the bumps. Mrs Simkins!

'Look!' I said to the son, 'There is a yak over there and if you look behind us you can see some more trees.'

We turned off the main road and along a narrow dust track up the foothills to the east of Drepung. The track became progressively steeper and at the sharpest gradient, by a vertical drop into a quarry, the lorry in front of us spluttered to a halt. The wood for the funeral pyre and Mrs Simkins shot back towards us and the body balanced on the lorry's tailboard above our windscreen. Fortunately they could start the engine again and the body swung back onto the lorry-side of the tailboard. We carried up another few metres and arrived at the base of small mound which was to be the cremation site.

We waited by the car while the preparations were carried out. There were dozens of people about, many in uniform, including a Chinaman who seemed to be the official photographer of the event, who zoomed in on all of us with a video camera. We were called up when everything was ready and the son was able to pay his last respects. The tour leader had cut a bouquet of flowers from the hotel greenhouse. A monk sat cross-legged by the pile of wood, reading aloud prayers from the Tibetan book of the dead.

A very cheerful Tibetan then arrived wearing overalls spotted with brown flecks. The Chinese travel agent motioned for us to go back to the car.

'No. No. You don't understand,' said the son. 'I have come all this way just to be here for this moment.'

The Chinaman became anxious. 'You really must go now. Please!' He looked at me. 'Please go now!'

My mind clicked into action. Of course there are no cremations in Tibet as we know them in the West! I suggested that we could go down to the car and return when the fire was going. Reluctantly the son agreed with me. As I hurried him down the slope, we could hear the sound of steel against steel – the Tibetan was sharpening his knives. I glanced around and caught the glint of sunlight on the sharpened edge of his rusty sky burial daggers. 'Just some preparations they have to make before they can start,' I said quietly.

'Look out there! Some trees,' the tour leader pointed out to the valley, continuing our inane conversation from the car. The minutes seemed like hours. At long last we heard the crackle of the fire and saw smoke rising from the hill above us. We returned up the path to the cremation site. A Chinese policeman was urinating over the track from on top of the mound and we waited for him to finish before we could pass. They were pleased that everything was going so well and had already started on the beers.

The funeral pyre was in a spectacular setting – with the view of the surrounding hills, the town of Lhasa far below and the Potala Palace framed at the bottom of the valley. It is going to happen to all of us one day and as I watched the flames lick the sky I thought that there can be no better ending than this. To pass away peacefully in the night and then go up in smoke with the Potala in the background and a Tibetan monk chanting prayers for your soul. It was a moving experience for all of us.

Our profound thoughts were interrupted by the Tibetan in the splattered overalls who approached the fire carrying a bucket. He flung the contents on to the fire and a gigantic fireball engulfed the sky. The son and I dived for cover, but the monk who was sitting cross-legged could not get out of the way quick enough and had his eyebrows singed. The Tibetan came up to us with his empty petrol bucket, grinning from ear to ear. His gold tooth flashed at us in the sunlight and he gave us the thumbs up sign as if to say, 'It's a good one!'

We shared a gritty bottle of Lasa Beer and returned to the hotel in a daze. It had been quite a day for all of us and I was not in the mood to face the pack of guests who were shouting in the lobby. They had been down to the airport two days in a row and had returned again to the hotel, having been refused boarding passes for the aircraft. Some of them were at the CAAC office, staging a sit-in – the first demonstration by foreigners in Tibet. Our Holiday Inn tour groups had also been victims of the over-booking and we were doing our best with cartons of cigarettes and invitations to dinner to try and get them seats. CAAC were in a bit of a sticky situation. Their plane to Kathmandu had 123 seats and they had sold 420 tickets.

That evening I had a call from Mrs Simkins' son. He had been given a black metal box to take the ashes in back to England but there was a problem. They rattled. He was right, he couldn't go back with his mother rattling under the seat. I suppose a few twigs and a bucket of petrol does not match the fierce heat of a Western crematorium.

'Do you have a cloth to wrap them in? And a piece of string?' he asked. I promised I would find some. I managed to persuade Charlie to open up the Housekeeping store and I found an old bath mat and a piece of telephone wire. This would have to do.

I returned to room 3101 to give them to the son. He thanked me for them and said, 'There's just one more thing. Do you think you could wrap them up for me?'

He did have a point. To me they were just pieces of bone but I could understand his feelings.

'Of course.'

He went off into the bathroom. I spread out the bath mat on the luggage stand in the room, opened up the metal box and tipped out the bones. I had expected there to be a small pile of ash and a few larger pieces but no, the box had been full. Splinters and bone fragments went everywhere – rolling off the luggage stand on to the carpet and across the floor.

'Just a minute!' I called out, frantically picking up pieces and stuffing them into the rolled up mat. 'Just a minute! Nearly ready!'

Happy that I had collected everything I gave him the all clear. Just as I was leaving I saw one more piece – right down by the bedside, precisely where he would step with his bare feet when he got into bed. I started the same ridiculous conversation that the tour leader had struck up in the car. 'Oh lovely weather today wasn't it? Look! Have you seen that picture over there?'

As he turned, I dived for the floor, scooped up the fragment and put it in my pocket. After bidding him farewell and wishing him a safe trip home I emptied my pocket into the rose bed of the Holiday Inn Lhasa. Whether in heaven, nirvana or back as a reincarnation, I hope that Mrs Simkins approves.

Ever since, I was known by the expats as 'Alec the Undertaker.' Fortunately, I never had to deal with any more cases. The only other fatality that year had taken place in the no-man's land between the borders at Zhangmu. A Frenchman had died on the slope. The rest of the group travelling with him just thought he wasn't feeling very well and carried him up the three hour hike to the Chinese customs post. The Chinese pointed out that he was dead and refused to accept him. The group had to carry him down to the Nepalese customs again who also refused to accept the body. 'He was definitely alive when he left here. The Chinese must deal with it.'

I never did find out the end of the story – perhaps he is still there.

The closest we came to a fatality in the hotel was not through natural causes or altitude sickness but as a result of 'Karaoke Night.'

A Hong Kong film crew came up to Lhasa to make a karate film in Tibet. Although the reservation of 30 rooms for two months had been very tempting, we had calculated that we would need these rooms for higher paying tourists, as indeed was the case. So the film crew stayed at the Tibet Hotel next door to us. Each night they came to the Holiday Inn to drink in the bars, the disco or their favourite – the Karaoke.

Karaokes have been a phenomenal success in Asia. They are bars where *you* become the entertainment. You choose a song from a juke box but only the music is played – you have to sing the words. You are presented with a microphone and a giant video screen shows you the lyrics. A little dot passes over the words to show you which syllable you should be on. You have to pay for making an exhibition of yourself with each song. The Holiday Inn Lhasa Karaoke had a rather slow system. You had to give your choice of song to the waitress and wait for her to come back and call out the song name when it was your turn.

On the Saturday evening of the infamous 'Karaoke Night' the bar was packed. It was the karate film crew's last night in Tibet and they were out celebrating in force. Chef had also chosen this night to throw a party for his cooks as a celebration for coping with no leave and preparing 3,000 covers a day.

The Karaoke room was crowded – too crowded. Burly Chinese and Tibetan chefs squeezed into the sofas, while the Kung Fu stars perched on each others' laps on the chairs around the drinks tables. The waiting time for songs lengthened. A waitress called out the name of a popular Chinese song and one of our chefs jumped up to take the microphone. The same song had also been ordered by the film crew and one of the karate stars leapt to the stage to grab the microphone from the chef. It was all that was needed to ignite the powder keg. Chairs and sofas were hurled across the bar and a real-life scene from a karate movie was re-enacted in the Karaoke.

The waitresses ran for cover. The security guards ran for help and the Tibetan and Chinese chefs fought a pitched battle against the Kung Fu movie stars across the hotel grounds. They fought them all the way to the perimeter fence, with only 12 casualties. Seven were kept in hospital and most of the chefs were absent from work the following day. Chef had 3,000 covers to serve and an empty kitchen.

It was not only the staff who were missing. We were also suffering from a terrible lack of supplies. In order to become more self-sufficient, the previous General Manager had started a farm in Lhasa. But this had fallen into neglect and had been closed down after the problem with rabbit stew. The menu had been prepared, the dishes on the buffet table were ready, the pots in the kitchen on the boil – but as the farmer was a Buddhist – he had released all the rabbits into the wild on the previous day.

'No rabbits.' Tu Dian laughed.

Chef was not in such a funny mood. Overbooked, without rooms, chefs or food – and yet the tourists kept pouring in. Our own tour group sales, even with their obligatory 'unforeseen circumstances' fees and the new 'CRAP' fees were still selling like hot yak dung patties. We had been particularly successful with small, personalised groups and we had organised a very special tour for the Shoton Festival in August.

Most of the activity for the Shoton Festival takes place in the grounds of the Norbulingka – the Summer Palace of the Dalai Lamas, next to the hotel. Thousands of Tibetans cram in to watch performances of Tibetan opera. The crowds love them, especially the comic routines, but if you are a foreigner and not fluent in Tibetan, it is difficult to last longer than ten minutes. The music consists of alternately slow and fast clashes of cymbals and drums and is accompanied by high pitched and very rapid shouting from the men and a group of dancing girls singing through their noses. No doubt that, as with yak butter tea, there are some Westerners who can appreciate Tibetan opera, but it leaves me begging for the silence of the mountains.

The highlight of the Shoton Festival is the unveiling of a giant thangka at Drepung monastery and this was to be the central part of our tour. It is an amazing event, with thousands of Tibetans covering the hill-side at Drepung monastery to see an applique banner, the size of a football pitch, unrolled down the monastery's thangka wall. It only takes place at dawn – on the thirtieth day of the sixth month of the Tibetan calendar. On this occasion it would be on 21 August, and our special tour group of just four people would be arriving on 19 August.

On 17 August we were told that the date had changed and it would now be on 19 August . Our guests, who were on their way from America and Europe to see the thangka, were going to be disappointed. Conny sent out telexes with the bad news.

On 18 August we were told that the date for the thangka ceremony had changed again and it would now be on 20 August. Conny sent out telexes with the good news.

On 19 August it was confirmed that the ceremony would definitely be on 20 August, but that it had been decided that foreigners would not be allowed to attend. We gave up sending telexes. We decided never to organise a tour around a festival again. I had heard of a worse scenario, when a group of Western lawyers had travelled for weeks to see a horse-racing festival in eastern Tibet – only to find when they arrived that the Tibetans had decided to hold the festival a week earlier and that everyone had packed up and gone home.

On 19 August, late afternoon, Jig Me appeared triumphantly from a meeting with the Public Security Bureau. He had arranged a permit for the foreign staff of the Holiday Inn to attend the thangka ceremony – our four guests suddenly became enrolled as new staff and we were back in business.

We met up at 6:30am, well before dawn, in the hotel lobby. It had rained heavily in the night and a steady drizzle continued as we jumped across puddles in the forecourt to board our minibus. The road to Drepung was packed with Tibetans trudging through the rain. Over 30,000 would be present at the great event. There were several checkpoints on the way and we were expecting to be turned back at any moment. We stopped in the traffic jam beneath Drepung and Jig Me looked anxiously at the confusion outside. If anything happened, he would be held responsible for our conduct and our safety.

Hundreds of trucks, buses and Landcruisers lined the route up the hill to Drepung. It was pitch dark and pouring with rain when we reached a muddy car-park and left the minibus, setting off up the steep, winding path around Drepung. Jig Me called out; 'We must stay together. Everybody keep in a line.'

At this stage he disappeared into the darkness, swept upwards in the moving crowd. Our group fragmented, stumbling through streams and carried on upwards by the laughing, soaked Tibetans. I managed to latch on to Miss Houghton – an 81 year old from California – the keenest member of our group. Despite having no time to acclimatise, Miss Houghton was determined to see the thangka. But the altitude, the hill climb, the crowds and the smell of yak butter proved too much and I took her to rest in a small outhouse of the monastery.

I carried on up the slope and bumped into Jig Me with a guest from Austria. He was easy to recognise – he had a plastic bag on his head. 'I alvays go viz my plastik bag!' he called out to me. I left him as soon as I could – he was completely crackers – and climbed up to find a good vantage point amongst the Tibetans. Daylight came but the rain was still falling and the Tibetans told me that nothing would happen until the rain stopped. I thought I had better go and pass the news on to Miss Houghton, as two hours had now passed since I left her in the dark outhouse. I hurried past the mad Austrian who was still telling Jig Me about the use of plastic bags, and started searching the monastery for Miss Houghton. In the dark, one Tibetan building had looked very much like another and it took some time before I found the right one. When I did, I found her sitting happily on the steps exactly as I had left her.

She was not at all worried by the delay. On the contrary, the small outhouse had been used by pilgrims as a hostel for the night and she had been made very welcome by the innkeeper and offered yak butter tea and tsampa for breakfast. She had been greeted by every one of the thousands of pilgrims who were carrying on up the path next to the inn. I had to drag her away as she was enjoying it so much. I pointed out that she only had to move around the corner to find a perfect view of the thangka wall.

Another hour and a half passed before the rain stopped and the ceremony could begin. Prayers were said by the head Shengo of Drepung, who sat in splendid red robes, at the base of the slope. Masked dancers spun around on a small flattened area in front of the Shengo and piles of incense were lit on the hillside. A line of monks came from the monastery carrying the rolled up thangka. Ropes were thrown down from the monks at the top of the wall, attached to the uppermost edge of the thangka which was then hoisted to the top. A thin white covering was then drawn off from above and the multi-coloured silk patterns of Buddhas was unveiled. It was an awesome moment. From above the thangka, two Tibetan horns held high on a dragon yoke, blasted eerie sounds across the valley. Cymbals clashed. The smell of burning juniper and incense hung in the air. *Khatas*, the white offering scarves, cascaded forwards down the hill-side, thrown by the devout Tibetans. Wherever a khata dropped to the ground, it was picked up and thrown a few yards closer until it was finally thrown onto the thangka itself. The same process as toilet rolls being thrown onto the pitch at a football match but somewhat more meaningful.

For Miss Houghton, it had been an experience unrivalled in her 81 years. A trip to Tibet is not just a holiday it is an 'experience' – something which stays with you forever. Goldie Hawn had found just this experience when she watched the full moon-rise over the roof of the Jokhang temple and had wished aloud, 'Oh, if only Kurt could be here.'

Not all the experiences are good ones. Harrison Ford experienced the food in the Himalayan restaurant and spent the following day running much faster than is advisable at high altitude.

For some the 'experience' was greater than they had anticipated. A group of wealthy Americans dropped in to the hotel on a stopover from their world tour. There were nearly a hundred of them on the trip and each had paid a staggering $34,000 for the 37 day journey. It made the English car rally look like a cheap package holiday. They had been whisked around the wonders of the world in their own private jet – all accept for Lhasa where they had to catch the rotten cabbage smelling CAAC up from Kathmandu. They were a big success with our staff who could not believe that people like this really existed. They minced painfully across the lobby, faces stretched taught after the third or fourth lift and fingers weighed down with gold bullion and large chunks of stone.

They were in such a state of shock that they were quite easy guests to look after. We put a new menu item on for them – iced tea – but had to take it off again when we found that the waitresses served it as a cup of steaming tea with an ice cube floating in the middle. Their only major complaint was the lack of 'bathroom tissue' in the toilets opposite the Hard Yak Cafe. This was certainly a problem. No matter how often Charlie checked the toilets – the toilet paper was always missing. In peak season we were losing 23 rolls a day. Was it due to the Giant Yak Burgers served just across the corridor, the Himalayan Restaurant next door, or was someone walking off with them? We thought of placing a security guard on the door to frisk guests coming out but decided against it. There could have been another explanation. At the same time that Charlie reported the missing toilet rolls in the Morning Meeting, Harry passed around the VIP list. This was usually a very dull piece of paper – a few diplomats, occasionally a film star, important tour operators and the like. But on the morning of the highest toilet roll loss, the VIP list included the name of an official from the South Korean Embassy in Beijing – a Mr Li Kee Bum.

It was not only the toilet rolls that went missing. Although the finger of blame was never pointed at Mr Li Kee Bum, the teaspoons suffered a similar fate. They disappeared. So too did the salt and pepper pots. Not only did this add to the expense of running the hotel, but it was impossible to buy replacements in Tibet. But we were not too concerned about the comments on the lack of teaspoons, or that this news appeared in the *New York Times* and on the front page of the *International Herald Tribune* – it was the end of the season and we could relax once more.

We had survived. The summer profits had made up for the losses of the winter and occupancy was down again to manageable levels. Barba had opened his swimming pool and took a dip every morning in the near freezing water. This seemed to have a calming effect on him. He had nearly finished his studies and although he had not been fired he was happy that he had given Holiday Inn a good run for their money. The expats had worked together as never before – *Paris Match* even labelled the team as, 'l'equipe de choc.' They typed out their CV's, eagerly looking for their next assignments.

I had extended my contract three times and sat through five National Day speeches when I too typed out my CV. I felt privileged to have lived through such a time of change in Lhasa. It was just a pity that I didn't like many of the changes – the spreading urbanisation, the new concrete architecture, the threat to the Lhasa marshes and lake Yamdrok. Martial Law had been and gone. The Tibetan General Manager of the Tibet Hotel had escaped to the West with all the hotel's money. Jacob had been caught pimping in the new Lhasa night clubs. Renchen who had won the prestigious 'Guide of the Year' award had been arrested for being just a bit too informative about the situation in Tibet. He was charged with 'stealing state secrets' – a crime which carries the death penalty. Yes, it was definitely time to leave.

Fortunately, there had been some positive events. The new *Kharmapa* was crowned. Renchen was released after intervention from Amnesty International and other pressure groups and, as the Vice-Governor, Mao Ru Bai, pointed out when I left: 'Foreign managers find many things in Tibet but Mr Alec is the luckiest because he has found Miss Conny.'

And I had been stupid enough to think that we had kept that a secret. I should have listened to the words of the Holiday Inn Vice President in Hong Kong – they really do know when you break wind.

As the season came to an end, Harry announced the latest figures in the Morning Meeting: 'Last night fifty eight percent. Today fifty seven percent. Tomorrow fifty two percent.'

We were caught off guard by a lengthy speech by Mr Pong – there is only so long you can hold your breath when you live two and a half miles above sea-level – and waited for the translation from Heather.

'Mr Pong says the live seafood arrives today.'

'Seafood?' Barba exclaimed. 'The nearest sea is a thousand kilometres away over the Himalayas, what do we want seafood for?' Heather translated.

'You ordered it.' Was the reply from Mr Pong.

It appeared that 'seafood' was the translation for 'fish' which Mr Han had ordered on his purchasing trip in the spring. Now we understood why we had received a shipment of broken shards of glass from CAAC which was marked 'aquarium.'

'*Live* seafood?' Barba queried. 'Where do you propose we put it?'

Heather translated the simple answer, 'We can use the swimming pool.'

Barba held on to the table and started to shake. Jig Me quickly suggested the fountain in the forecourt would be a better solution and adjourned the meeting.

At 11am a truck pulled in to the courtyard and emptied the tanks of water, which it had brought up over the mountains from Chengdu, into the fountain. A security guard was posted to them and a constant stream of onlookers turned up to see these curious animals alive in Lhasa. There were crabs and crayfish, eels, catfish and five little terrapins. They seemed to be freshwater fish, not 'seafood' but they were not very happy and started to die off rather soon. The only animals which were surviving well were the terrapins but these were quickly dispatched and put aside for a Chinese banquet.

Shortly after the delivery of the fish, a second lorry arrived with two unmarked barrels. They were unloaded at the back doors of the kitchen. Chef lifted the cover off one of the barrels and leapt half a metre off the ground.

'*Snakes*!' he shouted. 'Vat are zese snakes doing in my kitchen!'

One hundred and fifty kilos of live snakes slithered around in the two barrels. They had been delivered as part of Mr Han's 'seafood selection'.

'I vant zem locked up,' Chef called out to his staff, 'and I shall ask just vat the hell zey vant me to do viz zem!'

There were plenty of places to lock away the snakes. Unlike most hotel kitchens, which are architects' afterthoughts, the kitchens of the Holiday Inn Lhasa are the size of a grand ballroom. Row upon row of white-tiled work areas stretch out past garde-mangers, side chambers, walk-in refrigerators, walk-in deepfreezes, dry stores, the butchery, the pastry section and the chefs' offices. Three of the 80 kitchen staff do nothing more than sweep the dirt from one end of the kitchen to the other and then sweep it back again, washing it out along the slop channel.

The chefs chose one of the white-tiled side chambers to lock away the two barrels. The snakes would never be able to get out and even if the impossible happened, the room was locked.

Chef Wang Xi Li stretched a long yawn as he gazed out of the pastry kitchen window at the night sky. The only clouds Wang Xi Li could see were the mists of the Milky Way. But the sound that had aroused him from his sleep was not from outside. Something was in the kitchen with him. It was not one of the managers, they would not be making rounds of the kitchen at 3:30 am. It certainly would not be one of the security guards, they would be sound asleep in the Galleria above the lobby where any night prowling managers would not find them.

It must just have been one of the rats he thought as he dozed back to sleep. Twenty minutes later he leapt from his position, slouched over the croissant rolling counter, as out of the corner of his eye he had caught sight of a one and a half metre long serpent disappearing down the drainage system. It was the first of the seven discovered escapees from the barrels. Another was found in the pastry kitchen, three in the main kitchen area behind the woks and two coiled above the chamber door on the electricity line, along which they had made their escape. There were signs that others had escaped down the slop channel than runs under a grill down the centre of each chamber in the kitchen. Perhaps there are some, still out there, in the sewers or growing fat in the air-conditioning slithering after Himalayan Hamsters.

Chef decided that it was time to dispatch the reptiles out of their miserable existence and put them in the freezer with the terrapins. No one would help him. His Tibetan chefs refused due to their Buddhist beliefs and the Chinese chefs all found reasons why they too could not help – either due to their religion or as a result of their Karaoke Night injuries.

He resorted to the traditional gentle methods of persuasion used by chefs. And after a short discussion involving many expletives, the mentioning of genitalia and simple sign language, he managed to persuade his Chinese Sous Chef to help him with the work. But after the Sous Chef's Tibetan wife found out, Chef was left on his own to finish the job.

The next day in the Morning Meeting Chef announced that he wanted no more live animals coming into the hotel.

'It is totally unacceptable. I run a kitchen not an abattoir.' Heather translated.

'Ah,' said Mr Pong, 'so what are you going to do with the two hundred pigeons that arrive today?'